New Perspectives in Policy & Politics
Edited by Sarah Ayres and Matt Flinders

HOW DOES COLLABORATIVE GOVERNANCE SCALE?

Edited by Chris Ansell and Jacob Torfing

First published in Great Britain in 2018 by

Policy Press
University of Bristol
1-9 Old Park Hill
Bristol
BS2 8BB
UK
t: +44 (0)117 954 5940
pp-info@bristol.ac.uk
www.policypress.co.uk

North America office:
Policy Press
c/o The University of Chicago Press
1427 East 60th Street
Chicago, IL 60637, USA
t: +1 773 702 7700
f: +1 773 702 9756
sales@press.uchicago.edu
www.press.uchicago.edu

Policy & Politics is a leading international journal in the field of public and social policy, published by Policy Press. Spanning the boundaries between theory and practice and linking macro-scale debates with micro-scale issues, it seeks to analyse new trends and advance knowledge by publishing research at the forefront of academic debates. It is published four times a year, and is ranked on the Thomson Reuters Social Science Citation Index. Please visit the website for more information: http://policypress.co.uk/journals/policy-and-politics

British Library Cataloguing in Publication Data
A catalogue record for this book is available from the British Library

Library of Congress Cataloging-in-Publication Data
A catalog record for this book has been requested

ISBN 978-1-4473-4055-3 hardcover
ISBN 978-1-4473-4057-7 ePub
ISBN 978-1-4473-4058-4 Mobi
ISBN 978-1-4473-4056-0 epdf

Cover design by Policy Press
Front cover image: kindly supplied by Asif Akbar
Printed and bound in Great Britain by CPI Group (UK) Ltd, Croydon, CR0 4YY
Policy Press uses environmentally responsible print partners

Contents

—

Notes on contributors

Chris Ansell is Professor of Political Science at the University of California, Berkeley. He has published extensively on governance, organisation theory, network analysis and regulation and is the author of *Pragmatist democracy: Evolutionary learning as public philosophy* (Oxford University Press, 2011).

Esther Conrad is a postdoctoral fellow at Stanford Law School's Gould Center for Conflict Resolution. Her PhD dissertation at UC Berkeley focused on collective learning in the context of regional-scale collaborative governance within California's Integrated Regional Water Management process.

Bodil Damgaard is Associate Professor and Deputy Head of the Department of Social Science and Business at Roskilde University. Her research focuses on governance and network management in the field of employment policy.

Lisa Dellmuth is Associate Professor of International Relations at the Stockholm School of Economics and the Department of Political Science at Stockholm University. Her research focuses on transnational actors in global governance with an emphasis on global environmental governance.

Torbjörn Einarsson is a researcher in the Center for Civil Society Studies at the Stockholm School of Economics. His research examines the societal significance of civil society organisations and governance in complex multi-level associations such as confederations and federations.

Ben Farr–Wharton is a lecturer in the UTS Business School, University of Technology Sydney, Australia. His research examines the factors that influence the relationships between employees and their managers in public and health care sector contexts, and the impact this has on work outcomes.

Robyn Keast is a professor in the School of Business and Tourism, Southern Cross University, Australia. She researches networked arrangements and collaborative practice and currently focuses on understanding micro-processes and longevity factors shaping design and investment decisions in collaborative research networks.

Charles Kirschbaum is Assistant Professor and Dean of the Professional Masters in Business Administration program at Brazil's Institute of

Education and Research (Insper). His research focuses on organisational sociology and investigates the intersection between markets, networks and institutional fields.

Christopher Koliba is Professor in the Community Development and Applied Economics Department at the University of Vermont and Director of UVM's MPA program. His research interests include environmental governance, governance networks, community resilience, network performance and accountability.

Eliza W.Y. Lee is professor in the Department of Politics and Public Administration and Director of the Centre for Civil Society and Governance, The University of Hong Kong. She is the lead author of *Public Policymaking in Hong Kong: Civic engagement and state-society relations in a semi-democracy* (London: Routledge, 2013).

Jack Meek is Professor of Public Administration at the College of Business and Public Management at the University of La Verne. His research focuses on metropolitan governance including the emergence of administrative connections and relationships in local government, regional collaboration and partnerships, policy networks and citizen engagement.

Achim Oberg is Assistant Professor in the Department of Management at the Vienna University of Economics and Business. He is a specialist in social network analysis and his research investigates organisational networks and network governance.

Juan Manuel Restrepo is a PhD candidate in Politics and Public Administration at the University of Hong Kong and co-founder and co-director of Low Carbon City, a citizen-led global platform building collective solutions to tackle climate change in cities. His research interests lie in the areas of collective governance, scaling-up social innovation, and urban sustainability.

Kerstin Sahlin is Professor of Public Management in the Department of Business Studies at Uppsala University, Sweden. Professor Sahlin has published widely in the fields of organisational institutionalism, public sector reforms, transnational regulation, the global expansion of management ideas, and the development of global standards and regulations.

Anna Schulz is a graduate research assistant in the Community Development and Applied Economics Department at the University of Vermont. Her research focuses on how transportation governance networks assess resilience, primarily as it relates to flooding. She is currently collecting and analysing data on how New England states prioritise and fund bridge projects.

Eva Sørensen is Professor in the Department of Social Sciences and Business and Deputy Director of the Roskilde School of Governance. Her research has focused on the democratic anchorage of network governance and she is currently writing a book on political leadership.

Jacob Torfing is a Professor in Politics and Institutions, Department of Social Sciences and Business, Roskilde University, Denmark. He is the founder and director of the Roskilde School of Governance. His research expertise includes network governance, public innovation, policy reform, institutional theory, and discourse analysis.

Peter Triantafillou is Professor in the Department of Social Science and Business, Roskilde University, Denmark. His research investigates the exercise of power and the production of knowledge within public policy and management, with a focus on performance management, evidence-based policymaking, and the role of the state.

Filip Wijkström is Associate Professor in the Department of Management and Organization at Stockholm School of Economics and the Director of the Stockholm Center for Civil Society Studies. His research focuses on the role and position of civil society and its many modes of organising, with particular attention to civil society's role in governance.

Asim Zia is Associate Professor of Public Policy and Decision Analysis in the Department of Community Development and Applied Economics, with a secondary appointment in the Department of Computer Science, at the University of Vermont, USA. His research interests include computational policy analysis, governance networks, social ecological systems, coupled natural and human systems, and sustainable development.

CHAPTER ONE

How does collaborative governance scale?

Chris Ansell and Jacob Torfing

Introduction

Although hierarchies and markets continue to play a crucial role in regulating society and the economy and delivering public and private services, collaborative forms of governance are proliferating, fuelled by institutional complexity and political fragmentation and driven by the recognition that no single actor has the knowledge or resources to solve complex societal problems (Kooiman, 1993; 2003). A growing number of studies analyse how collaboration provides learning-based mechanisms for solving ill-defined and hard-to-solve problems and for constructively managing differences (Gray, 1989; Roberts, 2000). Scholars have found that collaborative governance can be difficult to trigger and sustain as it rests on a number of contingent conditions (Ansell and Gash, 2008) and they have probed how collaborative forms of governance are managed and institutionalised (Koppenjan and Klijn, 2004; Torfing et al, 2012). However, a fundamental issue has largely been overlooked: the scale and scaling of collaborative forms of governance.

There are numerous studies of collaborative governance at the local, subnational, national, supranational and global scales (Marcussen and Torfing, 2007) and a growing body of literature examines how governance at different levels or scales combine in complex and tangled ways to produce elaborate systems of multi-level governance (Hooghe and Marks, 2003; Bache and Flinders, 2004). However, few studies have investigated scale itself as an important variable or explicitly dealt with the phenomenon of *scaling*, the dynamic processes through which collaborative forms of governance move from one scale to another. The scaling of governance networks and other forms of collaborative problem-solving is crucial because the failure to scale can become a major cause of policy failure.

In this special issue, we take up this important task of investigating the scalar dimensions of collaborative governance and explore the challenges of operating at a single scale, across scales or at multiple scales and of moving between scales. This introductory chapter sets out a general framework for thinking about the scale of governance and for conceptualising dynamic processes of scaling. These general ideas also provide a basis for examining the challenges of collaborating across scales or at multiple scales. This introduction is followed by eight chapters that explore the issues of scale and scaling in a wide range of empirical settings: European employment policy (Sørensen, Triantafillou and Damgaard), California water governance (Conrad), regional transportation planning in the US (Zia, Koliba, Meek and Schultz), global public health governance (Ansell), transnational university governance (Sahlin, Wijkström, Dellmuth, Einarsson and Oberg), creative workers in Australia (Farr-Wharton and Keast), child welfare in a Brazilian state (Kirschbaum), and humanitarian relief in Hong Kong (Lee and Restrepo). Each of these cases raises specific issues about scale and scaling. Taken together, they present an important opportunity for more general theorising about this important topic.

Our first task is to clarify some of the basic concepts that we will use. We use the term *governance* to refer to collective attempts to steer society and the economy in accordance with common goals and norms subject to continuous negotiation (Torfing et al, 2012). *Interactive governance* is a subset of the broader field of governance that highlights the interaction between a plethora of public and private actors as the vehicle for initiating, designing and implementing policies and regulations. Interactive governance can take many specific forms, including corporatism, public–private partnerships, deliberative forums. However, we refer to these forms in general as *network governance*, which signals that the collective attempts to steer society and the economy are conducted by a plural and distributed group of stakeholders whose mode of interaction is neither hierarchical nor merely contractual. We use the term *collaborative governance* – or simply, *collaboration* – to indicate a specific mode of interaction that is deliberative, multilateral, consensus-seeking, and oriented toward joint production of results and solutions (Ansell and Gash, 2008). While the terms *governance, interactive governance, network governance* and *collaborative governance* often appear to be interchangeable, they have different scope and meaning.

We examine the term *scale* in more detail in the next section, but basically it refers to the extent or resolution of some phenomenon. It is therefore a very general concept and has many different dimensions (temporal, spatial and functional). Our goal in this special issue is to examine how interactive and networked forms of governance in general, and collaborative governance in particular, relate to the concept of scale and its several dimensions. Originally, we were primarily interested in whether scale affects the potential for collaboration. Is collaboration on a large scale possible or is it primarily an intimate small-scale mode of governance? However, as we have become immersed in the issue, our focus has expanded. We have increasingly come to think that there are two additional issues related to scale that represent fundamental governance challenges. The first is the issue of understanding the tensions inherent in governing *across scales* or at *multiple scales*. The second is the dynamic process of *scaling* collaboration in order to adapt to different or changing problems and demands.

Understanding cross- and multi-scale collaboration and the dynamics of collaborative scaling are critical for realising both the potential and the limits of collaborative governance. The goal of this special issue is to develop theoretical insight into these issues. The next section briefly reviews the contributions of the disciplines of geography and environmental governance to our conceptions of scale and scaling and then proceeds to elaborate a framework that can specifically apply to interactive, network, and collaborative governance. While this framework is abstract, it provides a useful orientation to the scalar dimensions of interactive governance. In the third section, this basic framework is further elaborated in order to illuminate the cross-scale and multi-scale tensions that arise in interactive governance and to discuss the more dynamic properties of scaling (as opposed to the more static conception of scale). In the fourth section, we then use this framework to introduce the eight empirical chapters.

Scale and scaling

What is scale? Various literatures point to different types of scales. Geographical or spatial scale is probably the basic referent type and the easiest to conceive. It refers to the extent of geographical space. Temporal scale is also commonly distinguished and refers to the time frame in question (for example, short term or long term). Other types of scale might include jurisdictional or institutional, functional or operational, quantitative, or analytical. Gibson, Ostrom and Ahn (2000) argue that the two basic dimensions of scale are 'extent' (magnitude of a dimension) and 'resolution' (precision of measurement). They also describe 'level' as a 'region along a measurement dimension' of scale – for example, a micro-, meso-, or macro-level phenomena (2000, 219). Based on this distinction between scale and level, Cash et al (2006) have distinguished between 'cross-scale' and 'cross-level' dynamics.[1] This distinction between scale and level arguably adds precision to the discussion, but we will not follow it here because we find that it is counter-intuitive when dealing with the dynamic concept of scaling.

The greatest attention to the issue of scale comes from the discipline of geography, which has vigorously debated the 'politics of scale' (Marston, 2000; Brenner, 2001; Smith, 2008). A core thrust of this literature is to challenge 'naturalised' conceptions of scale that interpret scale as a fixed hierarchical order (for example, local, subnational regional, national, supranational regional, global).[2] This literature has focused on the transformations of politics and the economy that arise from the 'rescaling' of the state and the market. Smith (2008) describes 'scale-bending' as the reorganisation of spatial scale in a way that contorts our more naturalised hierarchical sense of spatial scale. This literature tends to emphasise how networks transgress fixed geographical scales – for example, allowing cities to operate at a more global scale (Leitner, 2004; Bulkeley, 2005).

Studies of environmental governance have also been very attentive to the issue of scale in recent years. This literature tends to note that environmental management strategies often fit poorly with the scale of environmental problems, a problem dubbed 'scale mismatch' (Cummings et al, 2006). At the heart of this literature is the idea that complex environmental problems can only be addressed by organising governance at the right scale or level, or more realistically, at multiple scales and levels (Buizer et al, 2011). Since fixed political jurisdictions are often poorly matched to the scale of problems, this literature has searched for alternative institutional strategies of scale-matching. Networks are understood to be one possible solution to this scale mismatch problem (Juhola and Westerhoff, 2011).

Beyond the literatures on geography and environmental governance, the general literature on governance rarely uses the concept of scale (for an important exception, see Yasuda, 2013). There is, of course, an extensive literature on 'multi-level governance', but this literature does not directly address the idea of scale. Nevertheless, it is implicit in much of the governance literature that network governance and collaborative governance are often used when calls for action are not being met by existing institutional jurisdictions, or at least unilaterally by a single jurisdiction (such claims are similar to the point about scale mismatch). Clearly, we find governance networks operating at very different scales of activity – from networks within a single organisation to networks traversing the globe. We often talk about networks and collaboration, however, as if they were scale-free. But is the task of coordinating a network within a single organisation equivalent to networking at the global level? Is collaborating with 10 stakeholders the same as collaborating with 100? Is collaboration among distant cities the same as collaboration among neighbouring cities? We suspect not, but have little beyond our intuitions to guide us.

If we are going to address the issue of scale, we need an understanding of scale that is specific to interactive governance. To make progress on this issue, we identify three different dimensions of scale in networks and in collaboration related to membership, interaction and strategic horizon. *Membership* refers to the partners or stakeholders who participate in the network or collaboration. Each member may have a scale (be small or large) and the membership as a whole may have a scale (few or many members). *Interaction* refers to the scale at which members interact – for example, locally, nationally, or globally. *Strategic horizon* refers to the scope of applicability and the scale of production that result from this interaction. For example, does the public–private partnership plan to mass produce a new vaccine so that it can be delivered world-wide? Or will they produce a limited batch for a local group? Table 1 combines these three dimensions of scale with three dimensions of scale drawn from the discussion of geography and environmental governance to produce a nuanced framework for analysing the scale of governance networks and collaborative governance.

Generally, the expectation is that as scale increases, so will the challenges of interactive governance. Transaction costs, heterogeneity and trust-based social learning are at the heart of these scale challenges. It can be costly to bring a large number of stakeholders together. Moreover, a large number of stakeholders typically represent a greater diversity of opinion and interest, requiring more complex negotiation. Larger numbers and greater diversity may also discourage quality deliberation, undermining the trust-based learning that is the basis of successful interactive governance. Different

Table 1: Scale dimensions of network and collaborative governance

Scale dimensions	Temporal (t) or quantitative (q) scale	Geographic (g) or jurisdictional (j) scale	Functional scale (f)
Membership (M)	Duration of membership (episodic; permanent) (Mt); Number of stakeholders (Mq)	Spatial (Mg) or jurisdictional scale (Mj) of individual stakeholders (eg, local versus global NGOs).	Level of commitment and demands placed on members as condition of membership (Mf)
Interaction (I)	Frequency, duration and simultaneity of interaction (It)	Localised or geographically dispersed (proximity) (Ig); within or across jurisdiction border (eg, trans-boundary) (Ij)	Intensity of interaction required for successful production (eg, resources spent; extent of Mobilization) (If)
Strategic horizon (S)	Time horizon and time span of goals, projects, and results (short-term versus long-term) (St)	Geographic scale (Sg) or number or size of jurisdictions (Sj) encompassed by strategy	Extent and resolution of strategic target or output (eg, individuals or nations? eg, mass or customised production?) (Sf)

dimensions of scale may also interact to make interactive governance more challenging. Geographical distance may also increase transactions costs, cultural heterogeneity, and the challenge of social learning. If a large group of geographically dispersed members must be brought together, it is reasonable to expect that interactive governance will become more challenging. However, Table 1 also suggests the possibility for more positive interactions. The challenge of large numbers or geographical dispersion can be partially offset by scaling up representation. In traditional corporatism, for example, peak associations represent many individual unions or firms at a national scale, transforming the challenge of numbers and geographical dispersion into negotiation between a few national associations located in the capital city. Thus, while the general expectation is that larger scale will complicate interactive governance, the scale of representation may simplify the problem. Clearly, the relationship between scale and collaboration is a complex one.

Some governance networks are fairly simple in terms of scale because there is no variation of scale across the three dimensions. For instance, the governance network for crime prevention in Oakland has local members (membership scale) who meet in local arenas (interaction scale) in order to find local solutions to local problems (strategic horizon scale). In a scalar sense, complexity increases when interactive governance must combine different scales across these dimensions. Global city networks to address urban climate change mitigation offer a good example. The network members are metropolitan cities, but they interact globally, for the purpose of achieving local solutions. Even more complex networks will combine multiple scales on a single dimension. Members may be organised at local, national or transnational scale and also interact at multiple scales and have multiple strategic horizons. While combining multiple scales is not necessarily problematic, doing so may produce organisational, institutional, and social learning challenges under some conditions.

Cross- and multi-scale challenges and the issue of scaling

Building on the analytical framework set out in Table 1, we can suggest a number of conditions that generate challenges or tensions for networks or collectives operating across scales or at multiple scales.

Cross–scale interactive governance often creates situations where networks or collaboratives have to operate simultaneously at different scales. Or it might create the need to shift interactive governance to different scales. A global public health network may have to shift from long-term strategic planning to rapid response as a new disease outbreak occurs and then back to long-term strategic planning once that situation is under control. This point leads us to a more dynamic understanding of scale as 'scaling'. To match the scale of a problem, interactive governance often needs to alter the scale of its membership, arena of interaction, or strategic horizon to correspond to a specific temporal, spatial or functional scale.

Scaling can be upward to a higher scale (for example, more or larger members, more expansive geography, or longer-term planning horizons) or downward to a lower scale (fewer or smaller members, more localised interaction, or shorter planning horizons). At least two different factors may affect scaling. On the one hand, a problem can be either spreading or shrinking (or localising). This dynamic creates a need to actively adapt the scale of the network to the scale of a problem. On the other hand, the task focus of a governance network might be shifting. For instance, it might shift between policy design and policy implementation (it can go both ways). Often, for policy design, you want to scale up to the higher scales. But when it becomes time to implement the policy, there will be incentives to scale down. Building on our earlier discussion of cross-scale interactive governance, we note that scaling is not a matter of a whole network simply scaling up or down. The network may scale up on some dimensions but not others. While many of these dimensions may be interrelated in practice, an important lesson of this analysis is that some dimensions can be 'scaling up' while others are 'scaling down.' In Table 3, we offer some tentative explanations for why networks might scale up or down on a particular dimension.

Empirical studies of scaling

The chapters in this book address various aspects of scale and interactive governance. In this final section of our introduction to the special issue, we briefly describe how each of them refers to scale to describe patterns of interactive governance. Building on the framework elaborated in Tables 1, 2, and 3, we find that the chapters appeal to multiple dimensions of scale, though geographical or jurisdictional scale of interaction are perhaps the most commonly mentioned. Our survey of these chapters also reinforces the idea that the most important issue for interactive governance is not whether networks or collaboratives can scale (more or less, the chapters suggest that they can), which was the issue that originally motivated this inquiry. Rather, the key issue seems to be the tensions inherent in cross-scale interactive governance. In addition to introducing each chapter, we try to call out common themes that emerge across the chapters. The main theme seems to be the importance of intermediary institutions for brokering and smoothing the tensions inherent in cross-scale interactive governance.

The Sørensen, Triantafillou, and Damgaard chapter builds on the idea of a continuum of interactive forms of governance as described by Keast, Brown and Mandell (2007). They distinguish three forms of interaction: cooperation, coordination and collaboration. *Cooperation* refers to paying attention to the goals of others and to exchanging knowledge and ideas. *Coordination* seeks to avoid conflicts and duplication (negative coordination), and to create synergies (positive coordination). Finally, *collaboration* implies on-going and institutionalised forms of interaction that provide for negotiation of conflicting interests, the establishment of shared strategies and goals, and the joint implementation and funding of these strategies and goals. As this framework suggests, coordination requires more intensive interaction than cooperation, and collaboration requires more intensive interaction than coordination. The key dimensions here are temporality (for example, collaboration is on-going as opposed to episodic interaction) and jointness (collaboration requires a deeper integration of the goals and strategies of participating stakeholders).

This is a useful analytical framework and it is worthwhile discussing very briefly how it maps on to our own elaboration of the dimensions of scale, as set out in Table 1. First, for Sørensen, Triantafillou and Damgaard the basic meaning of 'scaling up' is jurisdictional (primarily **Ij** and **Sj**). But they also ask whether jurisdictional scaling leads to collaboration, which can itself be understood in terms of scaling – that is, the temporal and functional demands placed on member-states and their interaction (**Mf**, **It**, and **If**). Their key finding with respect to the horizontal interaction among member-states is summarised below:

> the description of the processes behind formulating and monitoring the core EU employment policies…suggests extensive *cooperation* at the EU level between a number of relevant actors. Also the consultation and negotiation processes indicate *coordination* that may reduce conflicts and to enhance synergies… The processes do not, however, amount to *collaboration* as the involved actors (at this stage) are not themselves committed to implement the goals and policies formulated and even less committed to provide resources to meet these goals (Sørensen, Triantafillou and Damgaard, this volume).

They characterise the weakness of member-state commitment as a cross-scale tension between strongly institutionalised member-state employment policies and (multi-jurisdictional) European policies and institutions (see Table 2). Although this is a familiar finding in EU studies, their chapter also suggests that scaling might be a developmental process. Cross-scale

–

interaction may develop from more limited cooperation into more extensive collaboration over time.

Table 2: Challenging conditions of cross-scale governance

Scale dimensions	Temporal or quantitative scale	Geographic or jurisdictional scale	Functional scale
Membership	Some activities require a subset of members; others require all members	Organisations at different geographical or jurisdictional scales involved	Fluctuating or widely different commitments and demands placed on members
Interaction	Frequent interaction required over long-term	Both localised or uni-jurisdictional and geographically dispersed or multi-jurisdictional action	Intensity of interaction varies across time, place, or subgroups of members
Strategic horizon	Short-term 'rapid response' and long-term strategic planning both required	Compound strategies involving focused planning for specific places or jurisdictions along with general multi-locational or jurisdictional planning	Shifting extent and resolution of strategic targets or output (coarse-grained and fine-grained resolution; narrow and wide extent)

Sørensen, Triantafillou and Damgaard refer to both the horizontal and the vertical dimensions of scaling, a theme further developed and explored by Conrad's chapter in this special issue. Her chapter investigates the state-wide meta-governance of local water governance regions in California and focuses on the development of successful regional learning (along cognitive, strategic, and institutional dimensions) through collaboration. She argues that to understand the scaling up of collaboration from a local to a state-wide scale (**Sj**), it is critical to understand how network managers mediate the relationship between horizontal collaboration and learning within regions and the vertical (hierarchical) authority of state government. She contrasts how one region (Region A) developed deeper learning than a second region (Region B) and attributes the differences to the role and capacity of the lead agency:

A trusted lead agency appears to have enabled [learning] in Region A in three ways. First, Lead A set the stage for learning by helping to establish a vision for regional water management that accommodated state rules as well as regional interests. Second, Lead A's administrative capacities enabled it to turn the rule-heavy grant proposal process into an opportunity for practical, problem-oriented engagement among participants. Third, Lead A's stable and trusted presence provided the environment needed to allow the development of informal rules and norms that are crucial to institutional learning in a collaborative setting (Conrad, this volume).

Her analysis suggests that cross-scale governance tensions can be mitigated by intermediary institutions – in this case, the lead agencies of local networks – that promote horizontal collaboration and mediate vertical (hierarchical) demands.

Table 3: Examples of reasons for 'scaling up' and 'scaling down'

Scale dimensions	Scaling up	Scaling down
Membership	*Quantitative*: to mobilise greater support, capacity, expertise, legitimacy or revenue *Geographic/jurisdictional*: to enable wider geographical or jurisdictional representation; *Functional*: to intensify production	*Quantitative*: to bring together the key players for a certain project; *Geographic/jurisdictional*: to engage actors with more context-specific or localised authority, knowledge, capacity, or resources; *Functional*: to avoid overburdening members
Interaction	*Temporal*: to speed up a project or to extend operations; *Geographical/jurisdictional*: to enhance policy learning, innovation or diffusion through wider exchange; *Functional*: to ramp up projects	*Temporal*: to slow down a project or to bring forward a project deadline *Geographical/jurisdictional*: To ensure coordination or service delivery on a more localised scale; *Functional*: to bring projects to a close
Strategic Horizon	*Temporal*: to engage in longer-term planning; *Geographical/jurisdictional*: to deal with geographically dispersed or trans-boundary problems; *Functional*: to pursue economies of scale by developing joint strategies	*Temporal*: to produce just-in-time products; *Geographical/jurisdictional*: to deal with more localised problems *Functional*: to engage in greater customisation

Zia, Koliba, Meek, and Schultz (this volume) examine the scale of collaboration of metropolitan planning organisations (MPOs) in the US, which are regional planning bodies established by the Federal government for transportation planning. Like the regional lead organisations in the case discussed by Conrad (this volume), MPOs are intermediary organisations between national, state and local scales. Based on a survey of these bodies by the General Accounting Office, they measure the scale and intensity of collaboration of these intermediary bodies with external stakeholders. For the purposes of their analysis, scale of collaboration refers to the number of stakeholders (**Mq**) who participate on these bodies and intensity refers to the level of formal involvement and representation (**If**). Both can be described as scale dimensions in the terms set out in Table 1.

The main goal of the Zia et al chapter is to examine the relationship between the scale and intensity of collaboration and each MPO's 'performance management gap' (the gap between survey respondents' view of how useful a range of indicators are for evaluating MPO performance and their perception of how important each indicator actually is to the MPO). Their statistical analysis finds that while the larger scale of collaboration (more stakeholder representatives) has a variable effect on the performance gap (for example, it depends on which stakeholders are included and which performance indicator is in question), more intensive collaboration with stakeholders leads more uniformly to a smaller performance management gap. They conclude that '[a] theoretical implication of this empirical research is that cross-cutting polycentric governance networks, such as MPOs, can potentially minimise performance management gaps by improving the strength of their ties with external stakeholders and partners across the vertical scales (ranging from local governments to federal government) and horizontal scales (ranging from public sector agencies to private sector firms and advocacy groups)' (Zia et al, this volume).

The chapter by Sahlin, Wijkström, Dellmuth, Einarsson and Oberg (this volume) directly investigates intermediary organisations in transnational university governance, which refers to the complex organisational field that has developed at the global level in higher education. From their perspective, intermediary organisations are organisations that 'circulate, edit, and mediate ideas' about university governance (Sahlin et al, this volume). Intermediary organisations function as 'arenas' for other interests, but they also form links with each other, which makes them 'critical drivers' in the scaling up of university governance to the transnational level. These organisations have considerable influence in higher education policy formulation. Scaling up refers here to the movement upward from national universities to more intensive transnational interaction among the institutions associated with higher education. In our terms, scaling up refers to the expansion of the geographical scale of interaction (**Ig**), and secondarily to the expansion of the geographical scale of strategic horizons (**Sg**).

Sahlin et al's chapter explores the number and global interaction of these intermediary organisations using a web-crawling technique. Through this process, they identify 451 intermediary organisations involved in transnational university governance. They find that most of these organisations are non-governmental, not-for-profit, membership organisations. Mapping the networks of these organisations, they find that they compose a 'milky way' of organisations, with a core of 243 organisations. They detect several distinct 'clusters' within this larger core, such as a Brussels-based EU cluster. Sahlin et al argue that intermediaries operate as boundary spanners across sectors (public, private, non-profit) and have dense relationships with one another. Building on our discussion of the previous chapters, the Sahlin et al chapter both reinforces the importance of understanding intermediaries in the scaling process and also adds the dimension of understanding the (horizontal) linkages between intermediaries. The Conrad and Zia et al chapters both focus on the importance of the intermediary role between scales. The Sahlin et al chapter adds horizontal networks among intermediaries – a dimension either missing or unexamined in the previous two chapters. It is these horizontal networks (creating a distinctive organisational field of intermediaries) that shape the influence that intermediaries have over university governance.

In their contribution to this special issue, Farr–Wharton and Keast (this volume) focus on the scaling up of collaboration among Australian workers in creative industries. These workers are subject to precarious labour conditions that can lead to their exploitation. While prior research has focused on the local networks of creative workers, this chapter specifically focuses on their non-local network ties, which may offer local access to regional, national, or international resources and opportunities. As in the Sahlin et al chapter (this volume), scaling up refers here primarily to the expansion of the geographical scale of interaction (**Ig**) and secondarily to the expansion of the geographical scale of strategic horizons (**Sg**). The authors hypothesise that '"scaled-up" networks will positively correlate with actors' *network size*, local embeddedness (*clustering*), *structural hole* and the *time* that they have spent within a network' (Farr–Wharton and Keast, this volume). In other words, they hypothesise that creative workers are more likely to establish non-local networks when their networks are larger, when they are embedded in local clusters, when their networks bridge across different creative sectors, and when they have been involved in networking for a longer period of time.

Based on a survey of 271 creative workers in Australia, the authors find that non-local networks (for example, scaled-up networks) are particularly correlated with whether a worker's networks bridge across creative sectors (for example, their position in bridging structural holes). The size of a worker's networks and their involvement in local network clusters also has a positive influence on scaling up. They also find that non-local networks have a small effect on reducing the precariousness of labour conditions. From these findings, the authors draw the tentative conclusion that policies of promoting local economic development of creative industries need to be careful not to undermine the development of non-local scaled-up networks. The findings of this study can be broadly compared with the findings on intermediaries in transnational university governance. In that chapter, the suggestion is that the scaling up of networking among educational intermediaries gave them influence over transnational university governance. The parallel finding here is that non-local (scaled-up) networks among creative workers enable them to avoid precarious labour conditions. In each case, the scaling up of networking mobilises resources and support that build capacity.

The chapter by Ansell on global public health governance compares three different global public health partnerships – UNAIDS, the Stop TB Partnership, and the Roll-Back Malaria Partnership. Each of these partnerships operates on a global scale to provide funding, advocacy and leadership to the international efforts to eradicate the major global diseases of AIDS, tuberculosis and malaria. In order to be effective, these partnerships must mobilise collaboration among UN agencies, donors and the global public health community at the international level. However, to be effective, these partnerships must also create collaboration at multiple scales. They must scale up to a global scale to coordinate international efforts, but they must also scale down to the national and the local level to deliver health care. Thus, they often face many of the cross-scale challenges noted in Table 2.

The three public health partnerships have each been successful in scaling up collaboration among stakeholders to achieve global collaboration on these specific diseases. In terms of Table 2, this scaling up is primarily a matter of increasing the interaction among multiple (national) jurisdictions (**Ij**) who are geographically spread across the globe (**Ig**). However, it has also entailed creating, refining, and mobilising support for a global strategy (for example, strategic horizon) to prevent, slow, or treat these diseases, which in turn has the effect of expanding the functional scale of commitment of members and stakeholders to a coordinated global effort.

Arguably, then, these global health partnerships 'scale up' on many of the dimensions described in Table 1. Ironically, these global partnerships all confront challenges when they try to 'scale down' to the national level for the relatively straightforward reason that national level public health efforts are largely independent and sovereign. Global efforts can provide knowledge, resources and facilitation, but they always operate as quite constrained 'meta-governors' of national efforts. The chapter finds that the secretariats of these partnerships play a key focusing and bridging role in achieving successful horizontal and vertical multi-level collaboration. This is similar to the point made in the chapter by Conrad about lead organisations as intermediaries between levels.

The chapter by Lee and Restrepo investigates the scale properties of a Hong Kong-based international humanitarian organisation named *Crossroads*. Starting from a one-off effort to provide aid to flood victims in China in 1995, this organisation has grown to include over 9,000 volunteers (**Mq**), representing 71 nationalities (**Mg** and **Mj**), and contributing well over 100,000 hours of work time. This NGO offers a good illustration of how scaling up actually means expanding along multiple, interdependent dimensions at the same time. As donors learned of the early successes of this organisation, *Crossroads* began to receive many different types of donations from many different donors (an increase in functional scale; **If**). It became a 'hub' between donating companies and humanitarian needs and began to add new services to support its emerging intermediary role in a dense external network of in-kind donations and services. The organisation has developed eight operating divisions, managed by permanent staff, and guided by a steering committee. It has developed a distribution network that covers over 100 countries (**Ig** and **Ij**) that has served over half a million people (**If**).

The authors explore the institutional mechanisms that have allowed this humanitarian organisation to successfully scale up. These mechanisms include formal capacity building (more warehouses, more staff, and so on). However, the authors also note the importance of what they call 'indirect scaling', which relies on the clever leveraging of personal networks, a conscious choice to rely on informal governance, and a reliance on in-kind donations. This informal mode of 'indirect scaling' is possible, they argue, because *Crossroads* is embedded in the networks of a global city, Hong Kong. This argument adds a new and important dimension to the theme of intermediary institutions that has emerged from the comparison of the chapters in this book. While *Crossroads* does operate as a critical broker or intermediary in a web of relations (as does the Lead Organisations described by Conrad's chapter or the secretariats described by Ansell's chapter), Lee and Restrepo are arguing that this brokerage role is enhanced by the fact that *Crossroads* is located at a crossroad – the global city of Hong Kong with its dense and far-flung networks. This argument complements the findings of Sahlin et al, on the 'Milky Way' of intermediaries in transnational educational governance. In that chapter, it was the global networks among intermediary organisations that enhanced their roles as arbiters of global educational ideas.

The chapter by Kirschbaum examines how rescaling is used in response to the failure of network governance. In the early 2000s, the southern Brazilian state of Rio Grande do Sul created a programme to integrate educational, health and social services for disadvantaged children and their families. The programme was known as Better Early Childhood (*Primeira Infância Melhor*) or PIM. Local committees were created to implement the programme under the guidance of state government. The programme grew quickly, but quality suffered and the state eventually took over the administration of the programmes. In terms of Table 1, this was a scaling up of interaction (in this case, control) to a higher jurisdictional level (**Ij**). Kirschbaum analyses this rescaling effort through the lens of the sociological concept of control and discipline developed by Harrison White. This framework of analysis identifies at least three different 'disciplines' of control, which are referred to here as 'interface communication', 'mediating inclusiveness', and 'purifying selection.' The first – interface communication – is essentially about quality control across interfaces (for example, a supply chain). The second discipline – mediating inclusiveness – refers to the degree of inclusion of stakeholders and is similar to what the Zia et al (this volume) chapter called the 'scale of collaboration'. Finally, the third discipline – purifying selection – refers to the sifting of evidence or access according to some criteria of purity. As Kirschbaum notes, these control disciplines are often in tension in network governance.

As in the global health partnerships described by Ansell (this volume) or the relationship between regional water governance networks and the state of California described by Conrad (this volume), this organisation had a vertical (meta-governance) relationship that was somewhat problematic. A key institution of state oversight was the Technical State Group (TSG) and its functional equivalent at the local level was the Technical Municipal Groups (TMG). Prior to rescaling, the TMGs had a dual accountability to the TSG and to the local agencies that it coordinated (and in particular, to the secretary of the department who sponsored the PIM – in essence, the lead agency). In the larger municipalities, there were tensions among stakeholders and a tendency to demand more autonomy from the state. As the state became concerned about quality, however, it made the TMGs more directly accountable to the TSG, weakening the TMGs relationship with the local lead agency. It did this by accentuating a 'purifying' and quality control discipline over the local programmes. This change, however, exacerbated local tensions among stakeholders and reduced local commitments to the programme. The result might be described (to extend our comparative theme) as a politicisation of the intermediaries (the TMGs), who were pulled between the competing disciplines of stakeholder inclusiveness and quality programming. To compare this outcome with the findings of the Conrad chapter, an intermediary may be a mechanism of adjudicating tensions between scales and different stakeholder goals, or it may itself become an arena of contestation.

Conclusion: what have we learned and where do we go next?

Scale is an important but largely overlooked issue in network and collaborative governance. Our own exploration of this topic began with a concern about whether network and collaborative governance can be scaled up. Many examples of network and collaborative governance, we noted, are local in scale and we wondered whether this signified the limited applicability of these models. Does the intensity of interaction, trust and deliberation required by networking and collaboration limit them to the local level? Certainly, informal networks and sustained face-to-face communication facilitate collaboration and geographic distance and large-scale efforts can increase transaction costs and render intimate communication challenging.

A quick survey of the literature on networking and collaboration, however, turns up many examples of network and collaborative governance on a global scale, a finding supported by several of the chapters in this special edition. The chapters by Ansell on global public health governance, Sahlin et al on transnational university governance, and Lee and Restrepo on an international humanitarian organisation all suggest modes of network and collaborative governance operating on an extended scale. We suspect that the predominance of the local is more of a reflection on the problem-driven nature of local governance, with its active mobilisation of many stakeholders and jurisdictions, than a reflection of insurmountable barriers to large-scale networking and collaboration.

Of course, any judgement about the possibilities of network and collaborative depends on the standards we use to gauge networking and collaboration. The chapter by Sørensen, Triantafillou and Damgaard, for instance, finds that EU member-states have achieved relatively limited forms of cooperation and coordination on employment policy, but not deeper forms of collaboration. Yet at the same time, Kirschbaum finds concerns about local network governance of child welfare in Brazil, and Conrad finds significant variation in collaborative learning in local watershed organisations in California. Network and collaborative governance may simply be challenging at any scale. These chapters do sensitise us, however, to the tensions that arise between scales of governance and to the challenges of shifting from one scale of governance to another.

The goal of this book is to open up a dialogue about the relevance of scale and scaling. To further this goal, we have introduced a framework to describe the scale and scaling of interactive governance. While the literatures of geography and environmental governance have advanced our appreciation for scale, they do not really analyse how scale affects governance per se. The environmental governance literature, for example, focuses on the scale of environmental problems and the problems that arise when governance does not operate at the same scale. While building on this prior work, we introduce scale dimensions specific to interactive governance – membership, interaction and strategic horizon. As a descriptive framework for analysing governance scale, Table 1 clarifies the multi-dimensional character of scale. An important insight from this framework is that interactive governance may combine multiple scales.

While quite preliminary, our conceptual analysis does provide a vocabulary to engage in more systemic investigations. This book suggests that future research would benefit from further exploration of the co-variation of different scaling dimensions. It would also be useful to directly investigate the specific challenges that arise from the magnitude of operations or geographic distance between members. Do new communication technologies, for example, enable trust-building and deliberation when stakeholders cannot easily avail themselves of face-to-face communication? And perhaps what is more important, what are the specific competencies and capacities that interactive governance needs to shift scale or to manage across or at multiple scales? What kind of leadership, for example, is required to scale interactive governance up or down? Such issues are likely to become even more prominent in the years to come.

Notes

[1] They also distinguish 'cross-scale' from 'multi-scale' and 'cross-level' from 'multi-level', using the term 'cross' to indicate interaction across scales or levels, and the term 'multi' to refer to the existence of different scales or levels without necessarily implying interaction.

[2] The debate is sometimes referred to as a 'realist' versus a 'constructivist' approach (Buizer et al, 2011).

References

Ansell, C, Gash, A, 2008, Collaborative governance in theory and practice, *Journal of Public Administration Research and Theory* 18, 4, 543–71

Bache, I, Flinders, M, 2004, *Multi-level governance*, Oxford: Oxford University Press

Brenner, N, 2001, The limits to scale? Methodological reflections on scalar structuration, *Progress in Human Geography* 25, 4, 591–614

Buizer, M, Arts, B, Kok, K, 2011, Governance, scale and the environment: the importance of recognizing knowledge claims in transdisciplinary arenas, *Ecology and Society* 16, 1, www.ecologyandsociety.org/vol16/iss1/art38

Bulkeley, H, 2005, Reconfiguring environmental governance: towards a politics of scales and networks, *Political Geography* 24, 8, 875–902

Cash, DW, Adger, WN, Berkes, F, Garden, P, Lebel, L, Olsson, P, Young, O, 2006, Scale and cross-scale dynamics: Governance and information in a multilevel world, *Ecology and Society* 11, 2, 8

Cumming, GS, Cumming, DH, Redman, CL, 2006, Scale mismatches in social-ecological systems: Causes, consequences, and solutions, *Ecology and Society* 11, 1, 14

Gibson, CC, Ostrom, E, Ahn, TK, 2000, The concept of scale and the human dimensions of global change: A survey, *Ecological Economics* 32, 2, 217–39

Gray, B, 1989, *Collaborating: Finding common ground for multiparty problems*, San Francisco, CA: Jossey-Bass Inc

Hooghe, L, Marks G, 2003, Unraveling the central state, but how? Types of multi-level governance, *American Political Science Review* 97, 2, 233–43

Juhola, S, Westerhoff, L, 2011, Challenges of adaptation to climate change across multiple scales: A case study of network governance in two European countries, *Environmental Science and Policy* 14, 3, 239–47

Keast, R, Brown, K, Mandell, M, 2007, Getting the right mix: Unpacking integration meanings and strategies, *International Public Management Journal* 10, 1, 9–33

Kooiman, J (ed), 1993, *Modern governance: new government-society interactions*, New York: Sage

Kooiman, J (ed), 2003, *Governing as governance*, New York: Sage

Koppenjan, JFM, Klijn, EH, 2004, *Managing uncertainties in networks: a network approach to problem solving and decision making*, Abingdon: Psychology Press

Leitner, H, 2004, The politics of scale and networks of spatial connectivity: Transnational interurban networks and the rescaling of political governance in Europe, in Sheppard, E, McMaster, RB (eds), *Scale and geographic inquiry: Nature, society, and method*, pp 236–55, New York: Wiley

Marcussen, M, Torfing J (eds), 2007, *Democratic network governance in Europe*, Basingstoke: Macmillan

Marston, SA, 2000, The social construction of scale, *Progress in Human Geography* 24, 2, 219–42

Roberts, N, 2000, Wicked problems and network approaches to resolution, *International public management review* 1, 1, 1–19

Smith, N, 2008, Scale bending and the fate of the national, in Sheppard, E, McMaster, RB (eds), *Scale and geographic inquiry: Nature, society, and method*, pp 192-207, New York: Wiley

Torfing, J, Peters, BG, Pierre, J, Sørensen E, 2012, *Interactive governance: Advancing the paradigm*, Oxford: Oxford University Press

Yasuda, J, 2013, *The scale problem: Food safety, scale politics, and coherence deficits in China*, PhD dissertation, Berkeley, CA: University of California, Berkeley

CHAPTER TWO

Governing EU employment policy: does collaborative governance scale up?

Eva Sørensen, Peter Triantafillou and Bodil Damgaard

Introduction

What role does collaborative governance play in transnational governance processes? With few exceptions (Bohman, 2005; Slaughter, 2002; de la Porte and Natali, 2009) the bulk of the collaborative governance literature focuses on local governance (Gray, 1989; Hirst, 1994; Fung and Wright, 2003; Ansell and Gash, 2008). However, an increasing amount of research on multi-level governance in the European Union (EU) suggests that collaborative governance takes place at all levels of governance in the EU as well as between the levels (Bache and Flinders, 2004; Benz and Papadopoulos, 2006). Despite some variation between policy areas, a wide range of public and private stakeholders interact in governance processes that lead to the formulation and implementation of EU policies both at the EU level and between the EU and the member states (Münch, 2010, 3).

The interactive character of the policy process is illustrated by the many policy arenas in which the EU Commission, other EU institutions, member state representatives and stakeholder organisations meet. A prominent example is the extensive web of policy committees and the procedures associated with the 'Open Method of Coordination' (OMC) (Ansell, 2000; Pollack, 2003; Esmark, 2011) that play a key role in EU employment policy as well as in other policy areas where the EU does not have authoritative powers. Although the interactive character of the policy processes of these policy areas is well documented, we know little about the collaborative quality of these interactions.

This chapter aims to assess the collaborative quality of the interactive policy processes in the area of EU employment policy. Employment policy is particularly relevant in this context because the policy ambitions are high and because specific institutional arrangements have been put in place to promote interactive governance. Rising levels of unemployment in many parts of the EU in the wake of the financial crisis in 2008 have pushed employment further towards the top of the policy agenda in the EU, and lacking formal powers, the EU seeks to govern by means of interactive forms of governance, for example, the OMC that accommodates interaction between the EU, member state representatives and the social partners (Lange and Alexiadou, 2007; Borrás and Ejrnæs, 2011; de la Porte and Pochet 2012).

To clarify the extent to which collaborative governance scales up in the EU, we first develop an analytical framework for studying interactive governance. This framework is then applied in an analysis of the collaborative quality of the processes that lead to the formulation and implementation of EU's joint employment policy strategy supporting the 2020 ambition of smart, sustainable and inclusive growth. We focus on two sites of interactions: horizontal interactions between actors at the EU level and vertical interactions between the EU Commission and the member states. As the chapter is interested in the extent to which interactive processes scale up, we focus only on interactive processes at the international and the transnational levels, not at the domestic level (Esmark et al, 2011). The chapter concludes with a discussion of the new insights about the conditions and prospects for collaborative governance to scale up.

Collaborative governance: qualities and preconditions

Over the last 30 years, there has been a heated debate among governance researchers on the concept of *collaborative governance*. Key questions have been what collaboration really is, under what conditions it is likely to occur and how collaboration can influence the governance of society. In her seminal book *Collaborating* (1989), Barbara Gray helped clarify the first question by arguing that collaboration is not a matter of reaching consensus, but rather constructive management of differences in ways that make shared action possible. In other words, the crux of collaboration is the ability to act together in the pursuit of goals that are defined through collaboration. Collaboration involves not only deliberation but also hard negotiation and bargaining among actors with different and more or less conflicting interests. Collaboration is a result of the strategic willingness of the involved actors to find the common ground needed to achieve what they cannot achieve individually. In governance, collaboration is valuable to the extent that it contributes to creating a shared understanding, ownership and commitment among the relevant and affected public and private actors who are involved in formulating and implementing governance objectives.

The definition of collaborative governance as the constructive management of differences in an attempt to promote shared governance objectives suggests that *not all forms of interactive governance are collaborative*. While some forms of interaction imply a strong commitment to shared governance goals, other forms imply lower levels of shared purpose and commitment (Kooiman, 1993; Klijn and Koppenjan, 2004; Dente et al, 2005). Governance researchers have made several efforts to formulate a typology of interactive forms of governance that takes differing levels of shared commitment and integration between the involved actors into account. David Marsh and Rod Rhodes (1992) have developed a typology of different forms of collaboration, and Fritz Scharpf (1996) draws a distinction between negative coordination, defined as mutual adjustments within a group of autonomous actors, and positive coordination, that is, formulation and implementation of negotiated governance objectives. As Robyn Keast, Kerry Brown and Myrna Mandell (2007) point out, however, it is valuable to place interactive forms of governance on a continuum. Based on their terminology, we propose a continuum of interactive forms of governance running from cooperation to coordination to collaboration, progressively adding to the demands of the concepts. *Cooperation* points to less demanding interactions that involve exchange of ideas, knowledge and know-how; *coordination* is more demanding and consists of mutual adjustments to reduce unintended consequences and create synergies; while *collaboration* involves long-term and institutionalised forms of interactions in which actors are committed to negotiate diverging interests and develop shared governance goals, implement such goals in practice, and possibly share resources to meet these goals. Collaboration is thus the most demanding form of interaction.

In our case of EU employment policy, we regard interactions as collaboration if they involve deliberation, negotiation or bargaining in the pursuit of shared objectives. We categorise them as cooperation if they mainly involve the exchange of ideas and knowledge, and define them as coordination if they mainly involve accommodation of mutual adjustments. Although cooperation and coordination are valuable contributions to governance, only collaboration leads the actors to join forces.

Collaboration is the most demanding of the three forms of interaction as efforts to join forces among autonomous actors are constantly in danger of being undermined by centrifugal forces. Collaboration is conditioned by two factors. First, existing literature agrees that *interdependence* between involved actors is conducive to collaboration (Kooiman, 1993; Kickert et al, 1997; Sørensen and Torfing, 2007). When engaged in cooperation and coordination, the actors can continue to pursue their own goals and interests, but moving into collaboration the actors must refrain from pursuing all their aspirations, and even sometimes give up something to gain something else. In the end, the likeliness of such a move depends on the outcome of the individual actors' assessments of what they may gain from joining forces with other actors as opposed to losses and potential gains if they pursue their interest by non-collaborative means. It should be noted that asymmetries in power are not a hindrance to collaboration. If the parties share a sense of interdependency collaboration is possible.

Second, recent studies indicate *that leadership and management* of collaborative governance is important for its success or failure. A substantial literature on collaborative leadership and management argues that the success or failure of collaboration processes depends on how these processes are organised and conducted (Agranoff and McGuire, 2003; Ansell and Gash, 2008). Governance research follows suit by introducing the term metagovernance defined as tools of governance designed to govern more or less autonomous actors (Kooiman, 1993; 2003; Jessop, 1998, 2002). These tools can be divided into hands-off and hands-on metagovernance (Sørensen and Torfing, 2009). Hands-off metagovernance is exercised through storytelling, political framing, incentives steering and institutional design, while hands-on metagovernance takes the form of process facilitation and participation in interactive governance processes.

From a metagovernance perspective, the degree to which interactive governance leads to cooperation, coordination or collaboration depends on how it is metagoverned. The interrelatedness between forms of metagovernance and levels of interaction is described in Table 1.

Table 1 stipulates that if metagovernance is designed to promote cooperation and coordination, interactions will rarely result in collaboration. If we assume that the EU Commission is the metagovernor of EU's employment policy, an analysis of the collaborative quality of the interactive forms of governance in this policy area must include a study of how the EU Commission metagoverns the interactions. *We hypothesise*

Table 1: Metagovernance strategies

	Hands-off metagovernance	Hands-on metagovernance
Cooperation	Provision of opportunities for exchange of ideas, knowledge and know-how between relevant actors	Accommodation of communication that promotes the diffusion of ideas, knowledge and know-how
Coordination	Collection of relevant data and stage initiatives that encourage the actors to adjust their actions to those of others in order to avoid externalities and promote synergies	Supporting mutual adjustments by pointing out how, where and when the individual actors can benefit from taking the actions of others into account
Collaboration	Storylines that promote strong feelings of interdependency and institutions that condition the formulation of shared objectives	Helping actors to overcome conflicts and stalemates that prevent collaboration

that collaboration is more likely if the EU Commission metagoverns the OMC in ways that create a sense of interdependency between member states and stakeholders, promote institutional conditions that encourage the formulation and implementation of shared objectives, and help the involved actors to overcome conflicts, stalemates and other barriers to collaboration. The stories told by the EU Commission promote collaboration to the extent that the stories define a problem that can only be solved through collaboration between the member states and the stakeholders. The extent to which the incentives built into the OMC promote collaboration depends on (1) whether or not the incentives reward actors who work together, and (2) whether or not the interactive governance arenas are designed to support collaborative endeavours. Third, collaboration is promoted if the EU Commission assists in overcoming conflicts and other barriers through direct, engaged facilitation of and participation in the interactive governance processes.

In the following, we first account for the institutional set-up and procedural characteristics of EU employment policies from 1998 to 2014 with focus on developments in the institutionalisation and pursuit of vertical and horizontal forms of interactive governance. We conduct two separate analyses of interactions in the policy processes and the EU Commission's efforts to metagovern them: one analysis centres on horizontal interactions and the other on vertical interactions. Both analyses draw on EU policy documents from the period 2000 to 2014, the bulk of which were issued by the EU Commission and located through its publication database (European Commission, 2015). These data are supplemented with interviews conducted between 2003 and 2007 with top civil servants in the departments of employment and social partners in Denmark, England and France, and with officials from Employment Committee (EMCO) the EU Commission, and key European social partners (Borrás and Lynggaard, 2011, 329–30).

Interactive governance in EU employment policy

This section outlines the main elements and reforms of EU's employment policy in order to identify the key arenas and procedures for promoting interactive governance. We argue that the OMC constitutes the key structure of interactive governance in EU employment policymaking and that it essentially contains two dimensions of interaction: a horizontal and a vertical.

As illustrated in Figure 1, the EU's employment policy is a relatively recent but rapidly developing phenomenon. It is only in the mid-1990s that steps are taken to partially encroach on national sovereignty in the area of employment. With the Amsterdam Treaty in 1998, the member states decided to launch a joint European Employment Strategy (EES). At the horizontal level, the EES entails political treaty negotiations, social dialogue (member states, labour unions, employers and various NGOs exchange new ideas on how to boost employment and to assist states in implementation), intergovernmental dialogue (focusing on the development of annual employment guidelines), and peer reviews (member states meet to discuss concrete elements of their national employment policies in order to disseminate best practice). At the vertical level, we find dialogues between the Commission and EMCO on the one hand, and the member states on the other that centre on formulating strategies and guidelines in the EES. Based on these guidelines, the member states must report on their policy performance and future actions through annual National Action Plans with obligatory involvement by social partners (since 2005 part of the National Reform Programme). These instruments and processes constitute the instrumental framework available to the EU Commission. Through forms of metagovernance influencing and guiding the self-governing member states operating within this framework, the EU Commission may pursue its employment policy ambitions.

The interactive processes revolving around the EES are at least partially influenced by the substantive employment goals and strategies favoured by dominant actors and discourses in the EU. Since the early 1990s, the employment strategy has focused on increasing and upgrading the supply of labour (Trubek and Mosher, 2001; Jacobsson, 2004a). More recently, this focus has been expanded under the heading of social investments to ease and facilitate individuals' attachment to the labour market, for example, via childcare facilities, job search assistance and education (European Commission, 2013). The Growth and Stability Pact (introduced in 1997 and refined since then) and, more recently, the introduction of the 'European Semester', 'Six pack', 'Two pack', and 'Fiscal Compact' all aim at strengthening budgetary fiscal discipline and not at regulating the demand for labour (see de la Porte and Heins, 2015). As these instruments focus more on fiscal policy than on enhancing employment (or reducing unemployment), they are not analysed in this chapter.

In 2010 Europe replaced the unsuccessful Lisbon Strategy. While its goals are more modest than those of its predecessor, Europe 2020 contains stricter mechanisms of surveillance and coordination of member state policies in order to promote economic growth and employment, i.e. the European Semester. The National Reform Programmes, the national spin-off of the EES, are now integrated in an annual cycle of monitoring and reporting on national measures contributing to the realisation of Europe 2020. Finally, the EU has introduced ad hoc measures to alleviate

Figure 1: Timeline of main developments in European Union employment policy and its governing regime

some of the social effects of the post–2008 crisis and boost employment. This includes the Euro-Plus Pact, the Social Investment Package, an Employment Package, and the Youth Guarantee. The Euro Plus Pact was established in 2011 to ensure that member states undertake reforms to secure fiscal balance and improve their competitiveness by way of regular and extensive monitoring and comparison of member state progress on key performance indicators (Gabrisch and Staehr, 2014).

In brief, the majority of the policy measures adopted by the EU to address unemployment focus on macroeconomic stability rather than on employment per se, particularly following the 2008 financial crisis. Moreover, not all policies targeting employment hinge on interactive processes, but rely rather on monitoring and comparative assessments (benchmarking) whereby low-performing countries are encouraged to recognise themselves as such and to undertake reforms. These qualifications notwithstanding, we do find EU employment policy instruments in which interactive processes seem to play a substantial role at both the horizontal and vertical levels. These are analysed further below.

Horizontal interactions at the EU level

This section examines in three steps the horizontal interactions related to the development of EU employment policy. Focus is on the interaction between the member states, EU institutions and the social partners in order to determine if we are witnessing cooperation, coordination or collaboration according to our conceptualisation of these terms. First, we examine the processes of interaction established in the chapter on employment in the Treaty on the Functioning of the European Union. Second, we examine how recent developments expressed in treaties and recently adopted ad hoc pacts affect the quality of interactions between the involved actors. Third, we look at the intergovernmental interactions involved in peer review processes under the mutual learning programme.

Treaties and intergovernmental processes

At the most general level, involvement of member states, specific EU institutions and social partners in the processes surrounding EU employment policies is established in the Treaty on the Functioning of the European Union (TFEU) article 145–50. These articles stipulate that the EU *must* have an employment policy in relation to which the member states must develop a coordinated strategy, that the employment policy must be consistent with the broad guidelines of the economic policies, and that the sovereignty of the member states must be respected.

Finally a number of procedural tenets are specified which are of particular interest for assessing the scope of interaction between various actors. The Council and the Commission must annually produce a joint report on the employment situation in the Union upon which the European Council (that is, the ministers of employment) is to issue conclusions. Based on these conclusions, the Council draws up employment guidelines – the most substantial manifestations of the European Employment Strategy – and the member states commit to pursuing these guidelines in their national policies. Formally, the Commission can do little to influence the guidelines without the consent of the Council, but in practice the Commission seems to play a substantial role in the sense that it sets the agenda by proposing joint guidelines, provides expert knowledge justifying which guidelines are reasonable and which are not, and structures negotiations between the different member state positions (Borrás and Lynggaard, 2011). More generally, the Commission is important for promoting intense member state interactions around the guidelines by providing a narrative couched in terms not of national self-interests, but of a joint European destiny and a joint EU vision on how to enhance job creation most effectively in the EU at large. While policy documents as well as our interviews with top civil servants from the departments of employment in Denmark, England and France suggest a certain convergence of the understanding of the problem of (un)employment and how it should be addressed, important differences remain between the member states' actual policy approaches. By exercising hands-on metagovernance, the Commission is trying to tackle these differences and further a shared understanding through interactions approximating actual collaboration.

Outside the intergovernmental negotiations in the Council, a set of more low-key but still essential processes are taking place in EMCO. The EMCO, legitimised in the TFEU (article 150), consists of two permanent representatives from each member state (usually high level civil servants from the national ministry of employment) and two from the Commission. The EMCO is in charge of monitoring employment policies and their implementation both nationally and at the EU level and issues opinions when asked to do so by the Council or the Commission or on its own initiative. The EMCO writes up the final draft of the proposal of the employment guidelines before they are handed over to the Council for adoption. Moreover, the EMCO is the forum where the dialogue with the social partners takes place and as such it functions as an important gateway between the EU institutions and the social partners. Again, the Commission plays an important facilitating role as secretariat for the EMCO (compare TFEU article 240). By implication, the Commission provides analyses and expertise, structures the agenda, mediates between potentially diverging national interests (which tend to be less pronounced in the EMCO among ministerial civil servants than among the ministers in the high-profiled Council) and moves the process ahead by organising meetings, enforcing deadlines for reports and so on.

The processes involved in formulating the EU employment guidelines and monitoring their implementation as stated in TFEU suggest extensive *cooperation* at the EU level among a number of relevant actors. Also the consultation and negotiation processes indicate *coordination* that may reduce conflicts and enhance synergies. It adds weight to the processes that the member states participate both through their permanent representatives in EMCO and ultimately through the Council. We will even suggest that *collaboration* takes place during Council negotiations and EMCO activities in the sense that we find a certain willingness to formulate joint goals and guidelines and to embark on national initiatives to these. This conclusion comes with the crucial qualifier that the EU employment policy at this level does not specify *how* – by what means or by which specific member state policies – these goals and guidelines are to be met. Here the interests remain quite diverse.

Social dialogue

The limited scope of the social partners' involvement in the employment policy is another reason why the interactions at the EU level do not at present scale up to collaborative governance. While the processes prescribed in the TFEU *on paper* suggest coordination, statements by the social partners indicate that *in practice* the EMCO has not paid sufficient attention to the goals of others and as such the processes do not even meet our requirements for cooperation. In 2013, the four main social partners at the EU level – BUSINESSEUROPE, UEAPME, CEEP and ETUC (along with the liaison committee Eurocadres/CEC) – issued a joint declaration stating that 'it is important to ensure that when social partners are invited to address the EMCO…the agenda allows for a real discussion with them' (BUSINESSEUROPE et al, 2013). This collective outcry suggests that the social partners do not feel heard and taken seriously in the processes. Moreover, the fact that the employment guidelines have not been changed the least since 2010 suggests that the processes behind the formulation of the EES are ritual dances rather than actual policy making.

Finally, many social partners on the labour side have felt increasingly alienated because of the quite narrow focus on macro-economic stability in the many reform packages adopted over the last decade. The integration of the EES in the Broad Economic Policy Guidelines (BEPG) in 2005 effectively subordinated employment policy objectives to macro-economic priorities. This submission has repercussions for the processes behind the EES and for the quality of collaborative arrangements. Also, the social partners were hardly involved at all in the introduction in 2010 of the European Semester – the streamlining of the economic policy planning in the EU (see European Commission, 2014). A European Semester starts with the publication of an Annual Growth Survey (AGS), which outlines the main economic (and employment) policy priorities of the EU. As established in the TFEU article 148, the social partners are invited to comment on the AGS, but their efforts are in vain as their comments are not attached to the AGS when this is sent to the Council, which decides on priorities, policy recommendations and guidelines (BUSINESSEUROPE et al, 2013, 3). Likewise, the intensified monitoring of the labour market and the subsequent work to develop labour market performance indicators has taken place without the involvement or consultation of the social partners (BUSINESSEUROPE et al, 2013, 3). The *de facto* downgrading of EU employment policy ambitions is also seen in the adoption between 2011 and 2013 of the 'Six Pack', the Fiscal Compact and the 'Two Pack' – three treaties that entail still more nuanced, detailed and possibly semi-automatically sanctioned economic, financial and budgetary policies and as such illuminate the lack of ways to impose and sanction employment policy ambitions.

Even the Commission's enthusiastic embrace of the flexicurity approach back in 2007 seems to have confined itself to suggestions and recommendations. Initiatives that would commit social partners or member states have been avoided. While these developments (and lack of same) in themselves do not alter the quality of the interaction between multiple stakeholders regarding employment policy at the EU level, they do appear to turn both attention and commitment away from the employment agenda. Thus, even if the processes behind formulating the EU employment policies do entail a number of interactive processes that may qualify as *coordination*, a number of developments in the surroundings of the employment policy field suggest that the quality of the coordination is challenged. In sum, we assess the processes to be stronger than mere cooperation though not elaborate or strong enough to qualify as collaboration.

The peer reviews

It has been argued that 'soft' processes inducing reflection and learning may be as efficient in changing the conduct of an actor, including a nation state, as regulative laws backed by possible 'hard' sanctions (Teubner, 1983; Jacobsson, 2004b; Trubek and Trubek, 2005). Most likely in recognition of these arguments and in the absence of hard law alternatives, the EU, propelled by the Commission, has developed a Mutual Learning Programme as part of the OMC in employment as well as in other policy areas in which the Union has no legal sanctions at its disposal. The Mutual Learning Programme in the employment field consists of peer reviews, thematic events, learning exchanges, dissemination of good practice and a database on labour market practices (see http://ec.europa.eu/social/main.jsp?catId=1072&langId=en). Each instrument induces interaction between participating member states and to varying degrees with experts, EU institutions, social partners and other relevant actors. However, the primary activities consist of exchanging knowledge and ideas and may not even lead to recognition of the goals of others (as required to be considered cooperation). As participation is voluntary (and for peer reviews and learning exchanges requires an invitation) the instruments in the Mutual Learning Programme are weak even among the 'soft' instruments.

Despite this limitation, the mutual learning sessions may under some circumstances spur a sense of common understanding, shared purpose and perhaps ultimately even increasing commitment to joint employment approaches. First, the peer review offers a forum for member states to present and promote selected features of their national employment policy (as when Denmark hosted a peer review on flexicurity in November 2014) and as such functions as a channel for sharing of good practices and for policy upload. Though peer reviews do tend to be showcases of successful national practices with the effect of reinforcing existing national policies, the peer reviews have on some occasions made some member states question and ultimately even change parts of their existing employment policy approach. This was the case when France in 2000 hosted a peer review on its work sharing programme (35-hour work week) introduced in 1997. During the review, harsh criticisms of the programme were voiced and soon after France abandoned the programme and returned to a 39-hour work week (Triantafillou, 2011). Another feature that seems to be increasingly valued is the possibility of focusing on very technical matters as when the Czech Republic hosted a peer review on the use of counterfactual impact evaluation in October 2014. This and a series of subsequent peer reviews indicate the consolidation of a common understanding of the importance of systematically assessing the (cost) efficiency of the public employment services (the PES to PES dialogue, see http://ec.europa.eu/social/main.jsp?catId=964&langId=en).

The peer reviews then do hold some potential and even some concrete cases of interaction characterised by a common understanding, a sense of shared purpose and a certain level of commitment to joint employment approaches. However, this trend of cognitive and normative convergence

---

has been counterbalanced by the member states' domestic interests, that is, concerns about the national constituencies, which makes it difficult to make unpopular reforms that erode existing social rights and benefits. Moreover, while the peer reviews in some cases have contributed to disseminating good practices and ideas from one member state to another, the reviews entail no efforts to avoid conflicts or to create synergies between member states, which are required to be considered coordination. Moreover, the list of reviews made available by the Commission shows that the social partners only participate on rare occasions, and it is therefore questionable if the conditions of cooperative interaction is fulfilled even with this instrument (see http://ec.europa.eu/social/main.jsp?langId=en &catId=1070&furtherNews=yes&limit=no). In brief, while the Mutual Learning Programme and particularly the peer reviews hold a large potential to promote collaborative forms of interaction, they rarely manage to go beyond *cooperation*.

In conclusion, we find that the horizontal interactions around the EU employment policy display sustained elements of both *cooperation* (the peer reviews) and *coordination* (the social dialogue). We also find occasional signs of actual collaboration in the intergovernmental processes around the treaty formation and in the peer reviews. Thus, we do find incidents of common understandings and articulations of shared purpose. However, when push comes to shove and the implementation of joint employment strategies runs counter to existing member state policies, the commitment to change is weak. So even if we do find important indications of converging cognitive and normative horizons on the employment challenge among member state policy elites and even some of the social partners, concerns about national constituencies and the next national election often outweigh the commitment to a joint EU employment approach.

Vertical interactions between the Commission and the member states

This section examines interactions on the vertical dimension in EU employment policy making. We focus on the interactions between the Commission (including EMCO) and the member states as these are the dominant players. The vertical relations centre on two proceedings, one related to defining future employment policy goals and strategies and one related to the assessment of and commenting on past member state performance.

Setting future employment political goals

How does one – anyone – make 27 independent countries with their own domestic interests, ideas and agendas endorse a united approach to employment policy having only 'soft' tools at one's disposal? The notion that the EU enjoys a united approach to employment policies should not be exaggerated as national interests are too strong. Yet the EU does have a common employment strategy and every year produces common employment guidelines that all member states have committed to work to implement.

A first objection would be that the wordings of the employment guidelines (reproduced in Box 1) are so general that no one can object to them. However, as Jacobsson (2004b) points out, behind these seemingly toothless wordings lie the acceptance of a joint language (a 'Eurodiscourse', compare Jacobsson (2004a)) focusing on increasing employment rather than reducing unemployment. This again has implications for how the area is and can be monitored as statistics describing labour market participation are vastly different from statistics describing unemployment. Jacobsson identifies three 'discursive regulatory mechanisms' – joint language, common classification and indicators, and the building of a common knowledge base – and identifies the Commission as the prime user of these mechanisms or, in our terminology, a metagovernor. Borrás and Lynggaard (2011) have also identified the Commission as a metagovernor in the employment policy arena.

Box 1 EU employment guidelines 2014

- Increase labour market participation of women and men, reducing structural unemployment and promoting job quality
- Develop a skilled workforce responding to labour market needs and promote lifelong learning
- Improve the quality and performance of education and training systems at all levels and increase participation in tertiary or equivalent education
- Promote social inclusion and combat poverty

What enables the Commission to take on the role as metagovernor in the employment field is – apart from bureaucratic and administrative strength, which is matched by no other potential metagovernor in the field – the opening provided first in the Amsterdam Treaty and now in TFEU that allows the Commission on its own initiative to take steps to enhance cooperation between different actors to work towards implementation of the employment strategy. Much of the work under the Mutual Learning Programme discussed above may be considered the basis for disseminating the Commission's ideas about employment policy; an example is the Commission's embracement – and reinterpretation – of the flexicurity concept (Klindt, 2011). So far most member states have been more enthusiastic about flexibility than about security (Klindt, 2011). Yet, attention to securing individuals economically when they pass from one job to another (and hence facilitate flexibility) is seen for instance in the Social Investment Package.

The Commission's capacity as a metagovernor is documented by Borrás and Lynggaard (2011), who find that it clearly outweighs the role of EMCO in the employment field. Nonetheless, the position as metagovernor does not imply that the Commission is in a position to decide upon the substance of the employment policy. Member states have clear and conflicting interests that limit the Commission's influence and its role as metagovernor. However, the Commission has largely succeeded in 'setting the scene' via its discursive mechanisms and in facilitating and hence influencing the regular meetings in which the member states, EMCO and the Commission discuss future employment policy objectives and ambitions.

What type of interaction does this leave us with? The subtle discursive influence does not as such involve interaction, but the Commission's work in this field, although disputed, undoubtedly creates dialogues that over time help construct a common goal, maybe reduce barriers and create synergies. In that sense, we are witnessing *coordination*. However, since the actors do not commit directly to implementing the strategies or to funding their implementation, we cannot call it collaboration. And again, the social partners are rather absent in the processes.

Assessing and discussing member state performance

The European Employment Strategy entails institutionalised and regular assessment and commenting on member state performance. Member states are committed to produce an annual report on the principal measures taken to implement its employment policy in the light of the guidelines (TFEU article 148.3). The Council is required to monitor implementation of the employment policies based on the incoming reports and EMCO's views. If recommended by the Commission, the Council may make recommendations to the member states (TFEU article 148.5). Again, the Commission plays a key role in assessing and commenting on member states' performance and policies; a role that has become all the more central as new treaties on economic, fiscal and budgetary discipline (see above) give the Commission competences to comment and recommend and even sanction in these new areas and thus further the coordination of its intervention towards member states.

As seen above, commenting on past performance takes place in peer review settings and in other Mutual Learning Programme initiatives. To the extent that an institution at the EU level directs itself to a national audience, this falls under vertical interaction. The Learning Exchanges, the Disseminations of Good Practices and the Database of Labour Market Practices are in this category, but they are hardly interactive in their set-up.

What is more important, the Commission is conducting bilateral dialogues with all member states based on their National Reform Programmes (NRP). This dialogue may – and most often will – end in country-specific recommendations formally issued by the Council, but in practice developed by the Commission. In fact, the process of developing the precise country-specific recommendations is interesting and minutely described by Copeland and ter Haar (2013). Contrary to the common understanding that the Commission issues the country-specific recommendations principally by measuring the performance of a given member state against the employment guidelines, Copeland and ter Haar document that each member state engages in intense negotiations about the number and substance of the recommendations. The recommendations are, as the authors put it, 'politically negotiated' (2013, 31).

At first glance, the procedures for developing country-specific recommendations seem to meet our requirements for collaborative governance. The processes are firmly institutionalised forms of interactions in which the actors are committed to negotiate diverging interests and to develop shared governance goals. Moreover, the member states have committed to implement the shared goals and to provide the necessary funding. These appear to be elements of common understanding, shared purpose and even a level of national commitment, but for several reasons it would be problematic to regard this as outright collaboration. First, member states tend to 'cherry pick' (Copeland and ter Haar, 2013, 29) those goals and instruments propagated by EES that are most in line with their existing policies. Thus, the so-called development of 'shared governance goals' in practice amounts to the Commission and a single member state bilaterally agreeing on implementing one (or a few) policy goal(s). It by no means implies that all 27 member states agree on the same goals and measures. Again, like in the case of the horizontal interactions, concerns about domestic reactions seem to overrule the convergence of understandings and the sense of shared purpose developed among the top national employment policymakers in Europe. Moreover, the absence of the social partners in these processes seriously questions the collaborative dimension of this particular form of interaction.

In sum, the assessment and discussion of the member states' employment performance and the processes leading to country-specific recommendations entail a high degree of vertical interactions between the Commission, the EMCO and the member states. Despite their intensity and regularity, the bilateral scope of these governance interactions makes it hard to regard them as collaborative. Rather, the vertical interactive processes seem to amount to *coordination* in the sense that the actors pay attention to the goals of others, seek to promote limited mutual adjustment of policy goals and measures, and to a limited extent provide synergies.

Conclusion

This chapter has assessed the interactive processes that have been part of the EU's employment policy since the late 1990s. As this policy involves a variety of instruments and has changed considerably in the studied period, any straightforward assessment is difficult. With these qualifications in mind, the EU's employment policy only displays very few instances of genuine collaboration in the sense of long-term and firmly institutionalised forms of interactions in which actors are committed to negotiate diverging interests and develop shared governance goals, implement such goals in practice, and possibly share resources to meet these goals. Such instances of collaboration are found in the horizontal Council negotiations on Treaties and the employment guidelines, in the work of EMCO, and in a few incidents during the peer reviews, but not really anywhere else. The policy documents we analysed and the interviews we conducted suggest a certain sense of common understanding and shared purpose among policymakers and top civil servants in the employment services. However, commitment to actual implementation of policy reforms seems to depend to a large extent on concerns about the possible reaction of national constituencies. The French abandonment of the 35 hours work week, which suggests a certain commitment to a common European understanding of how best to solve the employment problem, seems to remain an exception to the rule that national interests prevail. Thus, the collaborative quality of the interactions seems to decline the closer we get to policy implementation and launch of actual reforms.

By implication, our study shows that even if interdependence may be conducive and perhaps even a requirement for collaboration, it is not sufficient. Interestingly, EU policymakers – in Brussels and in the member state capitals – and many economic experts repeatedly stress that coordinated efforts in the EU are necessary to tackle employment effectively. That these are not just empty words is proven by our study, which demonstrates many instances of cooperation and coordination in the making and implementation of employment policies. Moreover, the persistent high levels of unemployment and low economic growth rates in the EU after 2008 could have provided a window of opportunity for a change in policy style towards more genuinely collaborative styles of policymaking. However, our data material suggests that the member states are reluctant to take the joint employment policy a step further and engage in genuine collaboration.

One likely reason is that the member states do not want to give up their sovereignty and independence in this policy area. Another key explanation is the way the process has been metagoverned. While the EU Commission has designed the OMC to promote collaboration in the EU Council and the EMCO, interactions in the implementation phase are designed to promote cooperation and coordination rather than collaboration. Hence, peer review processes, reporting arrangements and consultations focus on the individual member states' performance rather than on promoting and encouraging the member states to work together in a shared effort to implement the policy guidelines. Chances are that a restructuring of the metagovernance strategy that forms the backbone of the OMC will enhance the collaborative quality of the implementation efforts in EU's employment policy. Relevant metagovernance tools could be story lines calling for bilateral collaborations, funding schemes that strengthen interdependencies and encourage collaborations, guidelines that measure the degree to which member states work together, and workshops and events that inspire and facilitate such collaboration. In other words, collaborative governance does scale up. Its actual scope is among other things conditioned by the way it is metagoverned.

References

Agranoff, RI, McGuire, M, 2003, *Collaborative public management: New strategies for local government*, Washington, DC: Georgetown University Press

Ansell, C, 2000, The networked polity: Regional development in Western Europe, *Governance: An International Journal of Policy and Administration* 13, 3, 303–30

Ansell, C, Gash, A, 2008, Collaborative governance in theory and practice, *Journal of Public Administration Research and Theory* 18, 4, 543–71

Bache, I, Flinders, M, 2004, 'Themes and Issues in Multi-Level Governance', in I Bache, M Flinders (eds) *Multilevel governance*, pp 1–11, Oxford: Oxford University Press

Benz, A, Papadopoulos, I (eds), 2006, *Governance and democracy: Comparing national, European and international experiences*, London: Routledge

Bohman, J, 2005, From demos to demoi: Democracy across borders, *Ratio Juris* 18, 3, 293–314

Borrás, S, Ejrnæs, A, 2011, The legitimacy of new modes of governance in the EU: Studying national stakeholders' support, *European Union Politics* 12, 1, 107–26

Borrás, S, Lynggaard, K, 2011, Europa Kommissionen som metaguvernør af EU's beskæftigelsespolitik, in B Damgaard, E Sørensen (eds) *Styr på beskæftigelsespolitikken*, København: DJØF forlaget

BUSINESSEUROPE, UEAPME, CEEP, ETUC (and the liaison committee EUROCADRES/CEC), 2013, *Joint declaration: Social partner involvement in European economic governance*, www.etuc.org/declaration-european-social-partners

Copeland, P, ter Haar, B, 2013, A toothless bite? The effectiveness of the European Employment Strategy as a governance tool, *Journal of European Social Policy* 23, 1, 21–36

de la Porte, C, Heins, E, 2015, A new era of European Integration? Governance of labour market and social policy since the sovereign debt crisis, *Comparative European Politics* 13, 8–28

de la Porte, C, Natali, D, 2009, Participation through the Lisbon Strategy: Comparing the European Employment Strategy and pensions OMC, *Transfer* 15, 1, 71–92

de la Porte, C, Pochet, P, 2012, Why and how (still) study the Open Method of Co-ordination (OMC)?, *Journal of European Social Policy* 22, 3, 336–49

Dente, B, Bobbio, L, Spada, A, 2005, Government or governance of urban innovation?, *disP- The Planning Review* 41, 162, 41–52

Esmark, A, 2011, Europeanisation of employment polity: Changing partnership inclusion in Denmark, Great Britain and France, in P Triantafillou, J Torfing (eds) *Interactive policy making, metagovernance and democracy*, pp 75–95, Colchester: ECPR Press

Esmark, A, Poulsen, B, Sørensen, E, 2011, Institutionelle effekter af EES og OMC på den ministerielle coordination og inddragelse af eksterne parter, in B Damgaard, E Sørensen (eds) *Styr på beskæftigelsespolitikken*, København: DJØF forlaget

European Commission, 2013, *Towards social investments for growth and cohesion*, Commission Communication, COM(2013) 83 final, 20 February

European Commission, 2014, *The EU's economic governance explained*, Memo/13/979

European Commission, 2015, *European Union: Publications*, URL: http://europa.eu/publications/index_en.htm

Fung, A, Wright, EO (eds), 2003, *Deepening democracy: Institutional innovations*, London: Verso

Gabrisch, H, Staehr, K, 2014, The Euro Plus Pact cost competitiveness and external capital flows in the EU countries, *Working Paper Series* 1650/March 2014, Frankfurt: European Central Bank

Gray, B, 1989, *Collaborating: Finding common ground for multiparty problems*, San Francisco, CA: Jossey-Bass

Hirst, P, 1994, *Associative democracy: New forms of economic and social governance*, Cambridge: Polity Press

Jacobsson, K, 2004a, A European politics for employability: The political discourse on employability of the EU and the OECD, in C Garsten, K Jacobsson (eds) *Learning to be employable: New agendas on work, responsibility and learning in a globalizing world*, Houndmills, Basingstoke: Palgrave Macmillan

Jacobsson, K, 2004b, Soft regulation and the subtle transformation of states: The case of EU employment policy, *Journal of European Social Policy* 14, 4, 355–70

Jessop, B, 1998, The rise of governance and the risk of failure: The case of economic development, *International Social Science Journal* 50, 155, 29–46

Jessop, B, 2002, *The future of the capitalist state*, Cambridge: Polity Press

Keast, R, Brown, K, Mandel, M, 2007, Getting the right mix: Unpacking integration meanings and strategies. *International Public Management Journal* 10, 1, 9–33

Kickert, WJM, Klijn, E-H, Koppenjan, JFM (eds), 1997, *Managing complex networks: Strategies for the public sector,* London: Sage

Klindt, MP, 2011, From rhetorical action to policy learning: Understanding the European Commission's elaboration of the flexicurity concept, *Journal of Common Market Studies* 49, 5, 971–94

Klijn, E-H, Koppenjan, JFM, 2004, *Managing uncertainties in networks,* London: Routledge

Kooiman, J (ed), 1993, *Modern governance: New government–society interactions,* London: Sage

Kooiman, J, 2003, *Governing as governance*, London: Sage

Lange, B, Alexiadou, A, 2007, New forms of European Union governance in the education sector? A preliminary analysis of the open method of coordination, *European Educational Research Journal* 6, 4, 321–35

Marsh, D, Rhodes, R (eds), 1992, *Policy networks in British government*, Oxford: Oxford University Press

Münch, R, 2010, *European governmentality: The liberal drift of multilevel governance*, London: Routledge

Pollack, MA, 2003, Control mechanism or deliberative democracy, *Comparative Political Studies* 36, 1–2, 125–55

Scharpf, F, 1996, Negative and positive integration of the Political Economy of European Welfare States, in Marks, G, Scharpf, FW, Schmitter, PC, Streeck, W (eds) *Governance in the European Union*, 15–39, London: Sage

Slaughter, A-M, 2002, Global government networks, global information agencies, and disaggregated democracy, *Michigan Journal of International Law* 24, 1041–75

Sørensen, E, Torfing, J (eds), 2007, *Theories of democratic network governance*, Basingstoke: Palgrave MacMillan

Sørensen, E, Torfing, J, 2009, Making governance networks effective and democratic through metagovernance, *Public Administration* 87, 2, 234–58

Teubner, G, 1983, Substantive and reflexive elements in modern law, *Law and Society Review* 17, 2, 239–86

Triantafillou, P, 2011, Konsekvenser af EU's metastyring af beskæftigelsespolitikken i Danmark, Frankrig og Storbritannien, in B Damgaard, E Sørensen (eds) *Styr på beskæftigelsespolitikken*, København: DJØF forlaget

Trubek, D, Mosher, J, 2001, New Governance, EU Employment Policy and the European Social Model, *Jean Monnet Working Paper 6/01*, http://falcon.arts.cornell.edu/dg78/govt431/documents/trubek.doc

Trubek, D, Trubek, L, 2005, Hard and soft law in the construction of social Europe: The role of the open method of co-ordination, *European Law Journal* 11, 3, 343–64

Bridging the hierarchical and collaborative divide: the role of network managers in scaling up a network approach to water governance in California

Esther Conrad

Introduction

Network governance is an increasingly common approach to managing complex problems, including in the context of water and environmental management (Kettl, 2006; Sabatier et al, 2005). One of the most important reasons for this is that networks offer greater capacity to support learning and innovative solutions than do hierarchical approaches (Newig et al, 2010; Innes and Booher, 2010). In understanding how networks function to promote learning, researchers have paid considerable attention to the role of network managers in structuring dialogue and exchange of knowledge among network participants so as to build a shared understanding of problems (Koppenjan and Klijn, 2004; Weber and Khademian, 2008). However, only limited research has been conducted on how network management is affected by the larger institutional context. Hierarchy continues to play an important role in governance arrangements today, and top-down, formal requirements imposed upon networks can constrain informal dynamics that are so crucial for learning (Currie and Suhomlinova, 2006; Lejano and Ingram, 2009).

Network managers may play an important role in facilitating the interface between hierarchy and collaboration. In this chapter, I compare how network managers have supported learning in two water planning networks that are part of a statewide programme in California to promote regional-scale collaboration among water stakeholders. I find that within a centralised network structure, network managers can help establish conditions for learning while also complying with state requirements. I identify three specific ways in which a trusted, central entity can support learning in the context of hierarchy: 1) brokering across state interests and the needs of stakeholders in the region; 2) developing processes that transform external requirements into learning opportunities; and 3) supporting the development of informal dynamics in addition to ensuring stability through rule compliance.

Understanding these dynamics is important for building better knowledge of how collaborative governance operates at multiple scales. Collaboration at a watershed scale is now common as a way to generate more integrated, holistic water management strategies (Gerlak, 2008). However, water systems are often interconnected at larger scales, where hierarchical public agencies continue to play a central role. In order to 'scale up' collaborative governance in such settings, we need to better understand how collaboration interfaces with hierarchy, allowing for vertical as well as horizontal coordination (Newig and Fritsch, 2009; Cash et al, 2006).

I begin by reviewing research on learning in networks, the role of network managers, and their interface with the external environment. The next section provides background on the Integrated Regional Water Management programme in California. I then discuss the study's methods, and provide an overview of two regional planning networks selected as case studies. The subsequent sections present findings regarding learning in the two regions and the role of network managers in bridging collaborative and hierarchical modes to support learning. The conclusion discusses these findings and implications for future research.

Theoretical framework

Networks and learning

Network governance involves relatively enduring, self-regulated relationships between state and non-state actors to address policy problems that cannot be managed by a single entity (Sorensen and Torfing, 2009; Agranoff, 2006). Networks are well suited for managing complex problems because of their capacity to promote learning (Newig et al, 2010; Innes and Booher, 2010). This is particularly true in the context of environmental management, which requires drawing upon multiple forms of knowledge to build a shared understanding of problems, and the capacity to continue learning over time (Folke et al, 2005).

While learning in collaborative settings has been variously defined (see Heikkila and Gerlak, 2012; Reed et al, 2010), most definitions incorporate three key elements, described here as they are laid out by Koppenjan and Klijn (2004) and Torfing et al (2012). *Cognitive learning* refers to an improved understanding of a problem, its causes, and solutions. *Strategic learning* involves developing a greater understanding of each other's interests and mutual dependencies. Finally, *institutional learning* relates to the development of rules, norms and practices that increase the predictability of interactions and build trust. Torfing et al (2012) frame the combination of cognitive, strategic and institutional learning as an indicator of network effectiveness, with the potential result of creating 'favorable conditions for future cooperation' (p 172). This definition of learning is adopted here because it treats learning as an outcome separate from policy change, which may be influenced by other factors (Reed et al, 2010). This makes it possible to distinguish between two networks that each change their behaviour in response to externally imposed requirements, but generate different types or degrees of learning among stakeholders.

The role of network management

Network management refers to activities intended to 'steer' interactions between participants to enable the coordination of goals and interests (Klijn et al, 2010). Koppenjan and Klijn (2004) discuss ways in which network managers help structure dialogue between stakeholders so as to uncover mutual dependencies and re-frame problems, thereby promoting cognitive and strategic learning. To accomplish this, network managers require skills such as relationship building, conflict resolution, leadership and vision-setting (Williams, 2002; Weber and Khademian, 2008).

A framework provided by Provan and Kenis (2008) suggests that network governance arrangements vary in their capacity to support network management activities. They hypothesise that small, relatively homogenous networks with high degrees of trust may require only limited investment in network management. In these cases, a 'shared' governance arrangement, in which the tasks of sustaining the network are shared among participants, may be effective. As the number of actors involved or the diversity of their goals increases, networks require a greater capacity for coordination. Provan and Kenis argue that this demands greater centralisation, achieved through one of two additional governance modes. In a 'lead agency' mode, one network member is designated to carry out coordination tasks, and in a 'network administrative organisation' (NAO), a new entity is created or hired to perform this role. In both modes, a central entity performs routine management and decision-making, although multiple members may still be involved in governing the network. The 'lead' and 'NAO' modes are distinguished by whether the central entity is a member of the network or an external actor (Provan and Kenis, 2008, 235–6).

Additional research supports the perspective that a central actor may be important to enable learning in networks, particularly in brokering across diverse forms of knowledge, and building a common language and vision among participants (Heikkila and Gerlak, 2012; Crona and Parker, 2012). Such central entities must be impartial and trusted by all parties involved

(Koppenjan and Klijn, 2004; Leach and Sabatier, 2003). If a central actor favours its own interests over others, the network's capacity for deliberation may be compromised, limiting learning (Newig et al, 2010).

Networks in the context of hierarchy

In recent years, there has been greater attention to the role of government agencies in supporting collaboration (Koontz et al, 2004). An emerging literature on the meta-governance of networks suggests that to be effective, governments should avoid imposing stringent requirements, and instead rely upon 'soft' approaches such as providing financial and technical support to networks (Martin and Guarneros-Meza, 2013; Sorensen and Torfing, 2009). Nonetheless, hierarchy is still deeply embedded within current institutional structures (Olsen, 2008). As public agencies face pressure to maintain accountability to legislative mandates, they may seek to impose formal rules and standards on collaborative processes. Bureaucratic approaches that emphasise rule compliance may constrain opportunities for dialogue and creativity, and limit learning (Innes and Booher, 2010; Lejano and Ingram, 2009; Currie and Suhomlinova, 2006).

Several scholars have suggested that network managers may play a role in reconciling rule compliance with openness to new ideas and skills, and in building vertical connections as well as horizontal ones (Weber and Khademian, 2008; Cash et al, 2006; Hahn et al, 2006). However, empirical examinations of these effects have been limited. By comparing learning in two regional water planning networks in California, I explore the hypothesis that the presence of a trusted central actor can support learning within a network by allowing flexibility and informality to flourish, while still maintaining compliance with external requirements. Both networks are subject to the same statewide rules, but one is managed by well-resourced and trusted lead agency, while the other operates without a lead agency under a shared governance model. I expect that the lead agency network will support learning in response to the state's requirements, whereas the network without a lead agency will generate less learning. While acknowledging that other factors also play a role in shaping learning outcomes, the focus of this analysis is on identifying the mechanisms through which lead agencies can help establish the conditions for learning, while also engaging externally to comply with state requirements.

Integrated regional water management in California

California faces considerable challenges in managing its highly variable water resources to meet the needs of 38 million people, a massive agricultural industry, and the environment. For many decades, the state has relied upon snowpack in the Sierra Nevada mountains and reservoirs to store water for dry periods, and upon extensive infrastructure to send water from the wet north to the dry south (Hundley, 2001). However, it has become increasingly clear that these strategies are insufficient, and there is increasing agreement that solutions lie in promoting regional scale approaches to water management that address water needs in an integrated manner (DWR, 2013). However, achieving this requires greater coordination among the over 1,000 special districts, counties and cities responsible for water management in California.

Initiated through an act of the state legislature in 2002, the Integrated Regional Water Management (IRWM) process has become the centerpiece of the state's efforts to prepare for an increasingly water-constrained future (DWR, 2013). The IRWM Planning Act established a process whereby local agencies could form a region and jointly prepare an integrated plan for managing their water resources, referred to as an IRWM plan. In 2002 and 2006, California voters approved a total of $1.5 billion in grant funding for implementing IRWM plans, administered by the California Department of Water Resources (DWR), which provides the incentive for local agencies to participate. By 2012, 48 IRWM regions had been created, covering 87 per cent of the state's area and ranging in size from 680 to over 50,000 square kilometers. In keeping with California's tradition of local control over water resources, IRWM regions have largely been self-organised, and vary in their participants, decision-making structures and approaches to network management.

While the initial phase of the programme allowed local agencies considerable flexibility, over time the state refined its expectations of the IRWM process, and established increasingly complex rules designed to ensure that the functioning of IRWM regions follows legislative mandates. This was partly in response to concerns within DWR and among civil society organisations that the IRWM programme was dominated by water supply interests, and did not adequately address environmental or other aspects of water management. In particular, some advocates were concerned about equitable access to funding for poor communities, particularly in rural areas. For example, in the Central Valley, many small, low-income communities rely on water sources contaminated with nitrates (Balazs et al, 2011). In 2008, the IRWM Planning Act was updated, requiring that regions conduct outreach to 13 specific stakeholder groups, and that 10 per cent of all grant funds be allocated to projects meeting the water supply or quality needs of 'disadvantaged communities' (DACs).[1]

Implementation of the IRWM programme has been strongly affected by pressures to maintain accountability to legislative requirements. In 2010, DWR developed guidelines containing 16 detailed standards that IRWM plans must meet in order to be eligible for funding (DWR, 2010). IRWM grant proposals and reporting requirements are also extremely complex. From the perspective of IRWM regions, these requirements are constraining. One IRWM participant described them as 'by far the most laborious, difficult, and labyrinthine…exponentially more time consuming than any other funding source'. DWR staff, however, view them as necessary to ensure that public funds are spent as intended.

IRWM participants are clearly grappling with the tension between collaborative and hierarchical modes of governance. Interviews with the designers of the programme revealed that the overall intention of the IRWM process was to change how local agencies think about the problems they face and re-define their relationships with one another – in other words, to stimulate learning. However, the programme's creators lamented its bureaucratic implementation, particularly following the 2008 legislative update, which they believe has constrained the development of truly innovative partnerships and projects. A widespread joke among those involved in water planning is that the acronym IRWMP, instead of referring to an 'IRWM plan', actually stands for 'I really want money please'. Can learning occur within IRWM regions in the context of the state's rules, and under what conditions? In particular, are regions with a centralised structure better equipped to mediate this interface than are decentralised ones? Answers to these questions have important implications for the future management of the IRWM process, as well as for the design of other collaborative governance arrangements.

Methods

Using a multiple case study design (Yin, 2003), two regions that differ in their approaches to network management were analysed and compared with respect to learning in response to the state's IRWM requirements. Regions A and B, referred to anonymously to maintain confidentiality, were selected as follows. Nineteen out of the 48 IRWM regions were selected at random across the state, and their governance structures were analysed according to the three modes identified by Provan and Kenis (2008). This analysis revealed that nine regions had a lead agency, four established a network administrative organisation, and six followed a shared governance approach. Of these regions, two were selected to maximise difference in governance structure, but to minimise other differences. Region A has a lead agency, and Region B uses a shared governance approach. Although other factors also play a role in learning, the comparison of these case studies helps to isolate the role of a central actor in supporting learning in the context of hierarchical rules.

Interviews, meeting observations and analysis of public documents were combined to assess learning in Regions A and B in response to DWR's 2010 guidelines, and to examine how this learning was influenced by the difference in approach to network management. Semi-structured interviews were conducted between June 2013 and June 2014 with participants in both regions, representing four key stakeholder interests (agriculture, urban water, environment and low-income communities), as well as lead agency staff, consultants involved in network management activities and DWR staff. In total, 17 interviews were conducted for Region A and 11 for Region B (in which participation was lower). Three meetings were observed in Region A, and one in Region B. Documents reviewed include IRWM plans, grant applications, meeting notes and material on each region's website. This analysis was also informed by 43 additional interviews with various actors involved in the IRWM process statewide.

To assess cognitive and strategic learning, respondents were asked to describe their level of understanding of regional water issues and relationships with other stakeholders before and after the initiation of the IRWM programme, and their views on how participation in IRWM planning contributed to any changes. Interviews were coded for instances of cognitive and strategic learning around themes related to the state's objectives for the IRWM programme, embodied in DWR's requirements. Wherever possible, triangulation using the perspectives of multiple stakeholders, supported by meeting observations, helped to confirm findings. To measure institutional learning, indicators of an increased predictability in network-level interactions were identified, including changes in the regularity of meetings, stability of finances and transparency of decision-making processes. Data sources included interviews, meeting observations, meeting notes and other public documents. To assess how learning in these two regions was affected by their different approaches to network management, I used process tracing to delineate the chain of events leading to specific learning outcomes and identify the specific role of network management activities (George and Bennett, 2005).

Case study regions

Table 1 summarises key background and governance features of Regions A and B. Both are located in California's Central Valley, have boundaries based on biophysical features and cover portions of multiple counties. Each involves four main stakeholder groups: agricultural water users, urban water users, environmental interests and rural low-income communities. Both regions rely on a combination of surface and groundwater, but differ in the severity and homogeneity of the water management problems that they face. In Region A, groundwater withdrawals have exceeded its sustainable yield for decades, and many communities face groundwater quality problems due to nitrates from fertilisers as well as naturally occurring contaminants (Balazs et al, 2011). In Region B, water sources vary across the region. Groundwater quality problems exist, but they vary across the region and are not as severe as in Region A.

Table 1 also summarises governance structures and entities undertaking network management in both regions. Region A began as a collaboration between three irrigation districts in 2001 and expanded to incorporate cities, counties and environmental interests. In 2009, Region A formalised its governance structure as a Joint Powers Authority, led by a board of directors composed of member agencies with input from an Advisory Committee.[2] Since 2001, the network has been managed by the same member agency, which has a service area covering the entire IRWM region, a broad mandate and stable revenue sources. According to one staff member, 'We don't have a dog in a lot of these fights. We are just there to support and collaborate and bring people together to try to solve bigger problems.' The agency invests considerable staff time and some of its own funds to undertake network management activities. Despite its relative neutrality, this agency also acts as a network member, representing its own interests. Therefore, this network is best described as a 'lead agency' network within the typology laid out by Provan and Kenis (2008), and will be referred to here as Lead A.[3]

Governance arrangements differ considerably in Region B. Beginning in 2002, counties within Region B each led their own IRWM planning processes. However, in 2009, DWR encouraged the counties to consolidate into a single region encompassing two watersheds. This new Region B is currently led by a four-member Coordinating Committee, composed of three public water agencies and one voluntary association of water suppliers, each of which represents the interests of one of the counties in the region. None of these entities has a mandate to act outside of their own county, and all have limited staff resources. Coordinating Committee members hired a consulting team to develop its IRWM plan, which was

Table 1: Overview of case study regions

	Region A	Region B
Regional Features		
Land area	2,400 sq km	7,770 sq km
Boundaries	Groundwater basin	Two watersheds
No of counties involved	3	4
Major water sources	Groundwater (replenished by surface supplies)	Surface and groundwater; sources vary across region
Water quality issues	Nitrates and naturally occurring pollutants, making water unsafe to drink in some rural communities	Surface: mercury, algae blooms Groundwater: naturally occurring pollutants, nitrates, dissolved solids
Major stakeholder groups	Agriculture, cities, environmental groups, rural low-income communities	Agriculture, cities, environmental groups, rural low-income communities
Governance		
Decision-making body (before and after 2009)	2001–09: all participants who signed memorandum of understanding 2009–present: Board of Directors and Advisory Committee	2002–09: one agency in each county led its own IRWM process 2009–present: Coordinating Committee, with one agency representing each county, and informal Stakeholder Group
Number of participants (in 2014)	16 voting Board members (cities, counties, irrigation districts), 40 non-voting Advisory Committee members (small cities, non-profits)	Four voting committee members (three water agencies, one non-profit association of water agencies); number of stakeholders varies
Average meeting attendance (2012–13)	27	19
Network management mode (Provan and Kenis, 2008)	Lead agency	Shared governance
Entity handling network management tasks	2001–present: Public agency with a broad, regional mandate	2002–09: each county led its own IRWM process 2009–13: shared by Coordinating Committee, tasks delegated to consultants 2013–present: small public agency contracted for administrative tasks
% full-time equivalent (FTE) staff dedicated to network management (in 2014)	Greater than 100%	Less than 50%
Funding for network management (in 2014)	Regular membership dues	One-time payments from Coordinating Committee, negotiated each year

completed in 2013. For on-going administrative support, the Committee hired a small, conservation-oriented public agency, whose mission meshes well with the IRWM process but whose mandate extends to only one of the counties involved. Its role has been limited to administrative activities, and leadership aspects of network management are the shared responsibility of Coordinating Committee members. Thus, Region B is best described as a 'shared governance' network.

Learning in case study regions

Interviews revealed significant differences between Regions A and B in cognitive, strategic and institutional learning. Three themes emerged for cognitive and strategic learning in response to the state's requirements for the IRWM process: 1) creation of an overall regional vision for water management; 2) incorporation of environmental stewardship into water management activities; and 3) consideration of the needs of low-income communities, referred to in state requirements as 'disadvantaged communities' (DACs). Analysis of interviews revealed that although cognitive and strategic learning are distinct aspects of the collective learning process, participants frequently experienced and described them together, and therefore they have been combined for this analysis. Institutional learning was assessed at the network level with respect to the overall development of new patterns of interaction between stakeholders within a region. Findings regarding all three types of learning are briefly described here, and summarised in Table 2.

Cognitive and strategic learning in Region A has been relatively high with regard to the three themes. With regard to a regional vision, one

Table 2: Learning in case study regions

	Region A	Region B
Cognitive/strategic learning		
Regional perspective on water management	High	Moderate
Environmental stewardship	Moderate	Low
Low-income community needs	High	Low
Institutional learning		
Routine meetings	High	Moderate
Transparent decision-making process	High	Low
Stable financing	High	Low

participant commented, 'Before, we didn't even know what the regional issues were. At least now we can think about regional-scale projects.' Learning regarding the role of environmental stewardship was moderate, with both environmental representatives and irrigation districts reporting that they had already recognised the need to work together. With respect to the needs of low-income communities, Region A experienced a high degree of cognitive and strategic learning in response to DWR's 2010 requirements. Irrigation districts, cities, counties and non-profits reported gaining a better understanding of the drinking water quality problems in these communities, the interests of community representatives and opportunities to work together. The director of an irrigation district remarked upon this shift, saying, 'Ten years ago, we weren't thinking about DACs…Originally, the process was developed to address the overdraft problem. As the years went on, water quality became a bigger issue, and we are doing some projects on that now. And it's a good thing.' Non-profit advocates agreed that the dialogue has changed.

Region B appears to have experienced more limited cognitive and strategic learning. While the IRWM process did help participants identify a common interest in addressing invasive species, which affect water quality upstream and downstream, most commented that they had not discovered many other common concerns. As one participant put it, 'there isn't really a single cementing issue that bring us together, as of yet. But there are ways we can help each other out, so I don't think it's a wasted effort.' With respect to environmental stewardship, a few environmental groups have participated in the process, but interviews did not reveal any significant changes in their relationships with water agencies. Finally, the process does not appear to have generated a shared understanding or interest in addressing the needs of low-income communities and tribes. According to one participant, 'it hasn't been too much of an issue…it's not like we think they shouldn't have a voice, but we each really have a full plate.'

Research also revealed different levels of institutional learning in the two regions. In Region A, predictable patterns of interaction have emerged at the network level. Region A's Board of Directors and Advisory Committee meet four times per year, with dates announced a year ahead of time. There are clear procedures for joining the group, and annual membership dues from Board members provide financial support for the collaborative process. These new rules and norms appear to have fostered trust among participants and helped enable a number of new partnerships and joint projects. On the other hand, in Region B, Coordinating Committee meetings are relatively frequent but are typically planned only a few weeks ahead of time. Three out of the four agencies participating in the Coordinating Committee have not established routine patterns of interaction with stakeholders in the counties that they represent, leaving avenues for stakeholder participation unclear. Coordinating Committee members have made one-time payments to cover costs for the current year, but an on-going mechanism for sustaining the collaboration has not been established.

Bridging the collaborative–hierarchical divide: the role of lead agencies in supporting learning

Multiple factors have likely contributed to the differences in learning in Regions A and B. For example, differences in the geographic size of the regions, as well as in the homogeneity and severity of water management problems, may have affected the degree of interaction between stakeholders, and their motivation to participate. However, all regions faced the challenge of complying the state's requirements, while still enabling learning among regional stakeholders. A comparison of experiences in Regions A and B suggests that this requires mediation between the interests of the state, as expressed in IRWM programme rules, and the interests of stakeholders. A trusted lead agency appears to have helped enable this in Region A in three ways. First, Lead A set the stage for learning by helping to establish a vision for regional water management that accommodated state rules as well as regional interests. Second, Lead A's administrative capacities enabled it to turn the rule-heavy grant proposal process into an opportunity for practical, problem-oriented engagement among participants. Third, Lead A's stable and trusted presence provided the environment needed to allow the development of informal rules and norms that are crucial to institutional learning in a collaborative setting.

Setting the stage for learning: brokering across state and regional interests

The state's IRWM requirements regarding the involvement of a specific set of stakeholder groups were intended to stimulate the creation of a regional vision for water management, eventually leading to the development of multi-benefit projects. Region A's lead agency used its position as a trusted, neutral convener to broker conflict between the state's requirements and powerful water rights interests in the region, setting the stage for cognitive and strategic learning about the needs of the region as a whole. In Region B, the absence of a lead agency with brokering capacity appears to have resulted in a process defined by the state's guidelines but lacking deep stakeholder engagement, leading to only moderate learning about the region's needs.

Prior to 2010, Region A's IRWM process was primarily focused on the groundwater overdraft problem, and involved irrigation districts, cities, counties and environmental organisations. In 2010, DWR new rules required more extensive stakeholder engagement, particularly regarding disadvantaged communities (DACs). However, broadening the tent was controversial. Many irrigation districts and cities were aware of the drinking water quality problems faced by many small, unincorporated communities, but most viewed it as the responsibility of the county and the communities themselves to seek assistance from the Department of Public Health. Irrigation districts and cities were concerned that attention to these new issues would divert resources from the group's primary focus on groundwater overdraft.

Recognising the political salience of the problems faced by DACs and the need to include them in order to be eligible for IRWM funding, Lead A used its role as network manager to reframe the purpose of the collaboration. Lead A staff met individually with members who were opposed to the involvement of DACs, laying out a rationale for why working pro-actively to find solutions would reduce threats to their own water rights. One Lead A staff member commented that they 'had to, at some times, pull one of our member agencies aside and say, what you're trying to do is not consistent with where we want to go…casting them out isn't the solution, so what are the conditions for bringing them back into the process?' Lead A also met with non-profit advocates and low-income community representatives, encouraging them to formally join the IRWM process. Over time, perspectives changed. As one Lead A staff member commented, 'I think the DAC community sees [Region A's IRWM process] less as an enemy and more as an opportunity, and I think the irrigation districts have come to recognise this potential conflict or threat, and the opportunity to mitigate it by engagement…so, that's been a big evolution.' Although a few participants remain sceptical, vast majority of interviews with stakeholders confirmed this shift. This change was formally acknowledged when Region A updated its IRWM plan in 2012 to state that the group's priorities included groundwater quality as well as overdraft.

In Region B, the consultants, rather than participating agencies, played a leadership role in setting the vision for the IRWM process. The consulting team designed a stakeholder engagement process involving a series of public meetings and consultations focused on required components of IRWM plans. Participants did develop a shared understanding of a few common priorities, but significant differences in perspectives remained unaddressed. Public meetings appear to have been framed around state requirements rather than local or regional concerns. As one participant involved in the Coordinating Committee described it, 'public participation was not so good. A few people would show up, and they would want to do things that were beyond what we could do. So we'd explain that to them, and then they wouldn't come back.' The process of complying with DWR requirements also did not appear to generate mutual understanding between the Coordinating Committee agencies and disadvantaged communities and tribes in the region.

The lack of a trusted agency to lead the development of a regional vision that engaged local stakeholders appears to have been one reason why learning outcomes were different from those in Region A. Consultants could ensure compliance with state requirements, but without leadership from agencies in the Coordinating Committee, generating deep stakeholder engagement was difficult. One participant commented, 'We hired consultants, and no one could afford to invest in ownership. We relied on [the facilitator] to drive things…[it] was more of a "check the box" process – did we have all the required chapters to meet the standards?'

The fact that participants in Region B had heterogeneous interests may have contributed to its difficulties in building stakeholder engagement around a regional vision for water management. However, as Ansell (2011) argues, not all interdependencies are immediately apparent when a collaboration begins. The comparison of Regions A and B indicates that a trusted lead agency may be important for helping create shared meaning in the process, particularly in the presence of external requirements. It also suggests that, as others have also found, leadership requires a sustained local presence; external facilitators or consultants can play a complementary role, but they are not a replacement (Margerum, 2002; Leach and Sabatier, 2003).

Developing collaborative processes that transform requirements into learning opportunities

One of the most significant changes brought about by the IRWM programme was to require each region to submit a single grant proposal addressing regional needs. Previously, local agencies had applied individually to DWR for funding, but under the IRWM programme, each region's decision-making body determines which projects to include in a consolidated proposal. Further, proposal development is one of the most rule-intensive aspects of the IRWM process. Regions A and B illustrate two different approaches to developing proposals, and highlight the crucial role of a committed lead agency in enabling practical engagement of network participants in the process of meeting DWR's requirements.

Initially, participants in Region A were not closely involved in developing IRWM proposals, and Lead A handled most of the process.

However, after DWR's 2010 guidelines were issued, Lead A established a project review workgroup composed of a small number of participating agencies. The workgroup adapted DWR's proposal requirements into criteria and decided which projects to include in the proposal. Lead A would then prepare a proposal including these projects, investing significantly in translating DWR's requirements to make them accessible to participants. For example, an environmental non-profit representative commented, 'the project scoring process has changed two or three times, and…each time you have to re-format. That is where we have depended heavily on [Lead A]. If it weren't for them, we wouldn't have had the time and experience to put it all together.'

The workgroup also offered committee members an opportunity to learn about the work of other participants, think concretely about the region's needs, and reconcile these with the state's priorities. As one committee member described it, 'obviously, some people aren't happy if their project doesn't get in. But…we have to look at what projects will score the best with the state and also meet the needs of the region…it's really complicated and difficult.' Consultants working with Region A recognised the workgroup's value. One commented:

> [During the first round of funding], there were maybe 2–3 people understanding what the plan says, what the requirements were, etc. [In the next funding round], we had a workgroup reviewing and scoring internally. That has been a major success in my mind…previously, I think the process was too dependent on consultants or others who weren't as vested in the process.

In Region B, instead of providing an opportunity for learning among network participants, DWR's requirements became a barrier to collaboration. During the 2011 funding round, one member of the Coordinating Committee volunteered to assemble the proposal, but lacked adequate staff time and knowledge of the requirements. Without help in understanding the requirements, agencies whose projects were to be included struggled to produce the necessary materials, and one project proposed by a tribe had to be pulled out because materials were not ready in time. The resulting proposal did not score well and was not funded. This led participants to become increasingly frustrated with DWR's rules. For their next proposal, the Coordinating Committee hired consultants, who handled the entire process, including developing scoring criteria and ranking projects. This left limited opportunities for stakeholder interaction around the process of reconciling the needs of the region with the state's requirements.

Providing stability and support for institutional learning

Institutional learning involves the creation of predictable patterns of interaction, reducing uncertainty so that participants can invest in the process (Koppenjan and Klijn, 2004). In particular, informal norms are often critical for collaboration, enabling open exchange of information among participants and the flexibility needed for creativity (Innes et al, 2007). However, informal dynamics do not always mesh well with formalised, top-down rules. The experiences of Regions A and B demonstrate that a trusted lead agency can play a crucial role in providing the stability needed to develop predictable interactions and create opportunities for informal dynamics to guide network functions, despite externally imposed requirements.

Prior to DWR's 2010 guidelines, Region A operated under a memorandum of understanding that provided everyone with an equal voice in decisions. However, as the group expanded, it became clear that a new structure was needed to balance stakeholder interests, some of which were in tension with the state's new requirements. First, some irrigation districts and larger cities were concerned that their water rights might be threatened in a broad coalition involving environmental interests and low-income communities. Yet, DWR's guidelines required the involvement of these groups. Second, there was a need to build sustainable financing for managing the IRWM process. This could be achieved through member contributions, but DWR guidelines required that the process be accessible to all groups, regardless of their ability to pay. The group eventually decided to form a Joint Powers Authority (JPA), with a Board of Directors composed of a representative from each member agency. Under California law, only public agencies can hold decision-making authority in JPAs, which relieved some of the concerns of water rights holders. The Board hired Lead A to continue to manage the network, with costs covered by annual membership dues.

This new formal structure, however, did not allow non-profit organisations to be voting members, and the membership dues were beyond the reach of some small communities. To sustain their engagement, another category of participation was created, called Interested Parties, which did not require a membership fee and could include non-profits. Interested Parties would provide input to the Board through Advisory Committee meetings. This did not provide them with a formal vote in decisions, but evidence regarding the functioning of this arrangement over the past several years suggests that informal norms have emerged such that the decisions of the Board have always followed the recommendations

---

of the Advisory Committee, such that in practice, Interested Parties participate meaningfully in decision-making.

Lead A played a crucial role in enabling this compromise. Non-profits dropped their initial resistance to the arrangement when one environmental representative stood up in a meeting to express his confidence in Lead A, based on his previous experience working with them. Initially, trust between Lead A and DACs was low, but this changed as Lead A consistently encouraged DAC participation in Advisory Committee meetings and took actions to support their interests, including obtaining funding for a study of disadvantaged community needs. Over time, the tone of Advisory Committee meetings changed. Meeting observations in 2013 revealed a camaraderie and humour among participants, and active participation on the part of DAC representatives.

In contrast, Region B's experience reveals that institutional learning can be quite difficult to sustain without a lead agency, particularly when networks face significant external demands. Region B's governance structure was designed by its consulting team based on a successful approach in an IRWM region in southern California. In that region, the formal decision-making body was a small committee representing core participants, but in practice, all decisions were made in close consultation with a larger Stakeholder Group. Because the lead agency of the southern California IRWM region invested significantly in relationship building, it was able to maintain robust, informal engagement in the Stakeholder Group, alongside the small, formal decision-making body.

The consultants sought to replicate this in Region B, but the results were quite different. Although the group's IRWM plan specifies that decisions are to be made by the Coordinating Committee in consultation with a Stakeholder Group, the informal norms to put this into practice have not emerged. The four agencies involved in the Coordinating Committee have each been responsible for representing the interests of their respective counties. One agency had already developed routine interactions within among stakeholders in its country through a previous county-level IRWM process. However, similar consultation processes have not emerged in the other counties. One reason for this is the lack of staff time dedicated to outreach. When the consultants' contract ended, the Coordinating Committee hired a small public agency to provide basic administrative support. Operating on a minimal budget and a one-year contract, this agency had neither the resources nor the mandate to invest in the relationship building needed to build predictable patterns of engagement outside of Coordinating Committee meetings.

Conclusion

Research suggests that collaborative networks support learning by enabling flexible, informal dynamics, problem-oriented dialogue and leadership to promote integration across different forms of knowledge (Innes and Booher, 2010; Weber and Khademian, 2008). These conditions are difficult to cultivate in the context of hierarchical structures that tend to separate problems and establish standardised, top-down procedures to demonstrate accountability. Yet, given the persistence of hierarchy, in order for networks to contribute to addressing problems at large scales, some interface is needed to reconcile tensions between these two modes of governance.

Building upon network and resilience literature, this chapter presents evidence that network managers play a crucial role in mediating these tensions. Three specific roles for a lead agency emerge. First, this research confirms the findings of Weber and Khademian (2008), Hahn et al (2006), and others that leadership is a crucial ingredient for learning. A lead agency with brokering capacity can help to reconcile state interests with those of stakeholders within a regional network, building a sense of purpose that enables dialogue and learning, rather than a sole focus on compliance. Second, lead agencies may be able to use externally imposed rules as a platform around which to engage participants in practical problem solving. Without a lead entity with administrative capacity to both comply with requirements and manage collaboration, stakeholder engagement may be limited, focusing largely around compliance. Third, a lead agency helps enable institutional learning by supporting the development of informal dynamics necessary for a collaborative process that complies with rules, but is not limited by them. Although this research effort has focused on a lead agency mode of network governance, findings are also likely to apply to network administrative organisations (NAOs). As other research has shown, a crucial condition for success is that the central entity be trusted and responsive to all interests involved (Koppenjan and Klijn, 2004). According to Provan and Kenis (2008), NAOs may have less trouble meeting this condition than would lead agencies.

Other factors also play a role in determining learning outcomes. More limited biophysical interdependence, less severe problems, and a larger geographic size may have contributed to lower levels of learning in Region B than in Region A. However, this chapter argues that the presence of a trusted, well-resourced lead agency is an additional factor to consider, and in some cases, may even mitigate the effects of other factors. For example, a trusted lead agency's efforts to establish a vision and support dialogue might help participants discover interdependencies that they had not previously recognised. Further research is needed to explore how the presence of a lead agency interacts with other factors affecting learning.

This chapter highlights the importance of understanding how networks function within their broader institutional context. Many researchers have emphasised that if collaborative processes are to yield learning and other benefits, adequate resources must be dedicated to network management (Klijn et al, 2010; Imperial, 2005). My findings indicate that when networks operate within the context of externally imposed rules, resources for network management are even more crucial. In particular, resources must be available to support staff – not just consultants on short-term contracts – who can provide the leadership and administrative capacity needed to achieve both rule compliance and dynamic, problem-oriented stakeholder engagement. Yet, staffing at public agencies has become thinner as more work is contracted out (Terry, 2005). In the context of water management in California, in addition to a heavy reliance on contracting, responsibility for water management is decentralised and fragmented, leaving relatively few public agencies with mandates or service areas broad enough to take on management of a regional-scale network. Out of the 19 IRWM regions sampled for this study, six followed a shared governance model, mainly because there was no trusted, regional-scale entity willing to serve as a lead. This has important implications for the design of network governance approaches for resource management. In defining the scale of networks, it is important to consider whether capacity exists for adequate network management. While organising collaborations along watershed boundaries is often encouraged for integrated water management efforts, this may not yield the necessary coordination across jurisdictional boundaries (Blomquist and Schlager, 2005). For example, in Region B, DWR pushed individual counties to collaborate in forming a region based on watershed boundaries, even though no entity was in place to coordinate the process at that scale.

This study takes an important step toward understanding how hybrid governance structures can support the management of multi-scalar environmental problems. When networks provide a space for stakeholders to interact collaboratively and engage in dialogue around what state rules actually mean in their own regional context, then cross-scale linkages can occur. This chapter argues that within a regional network, adequately resourced and trusted central actors play a crucial role in enabling this. However, in order to fully address the challenges of governing complexity across scales, several other questions not addressed here need to be explored. For example, do hybrid governance arrangements enable regional networks to influence decision-making at larger scales? What conditions are needed for regional networks to interact with and learn from one another? In addition, this study has explored how networks operating with a hierarchical environment might be designed and supported to generate learning around complex problems. Yet, hierarchical rules may not always be appropriate instruments for maintaining accountability in these settings (Ansell, 2011; Innes and Booher, 2010). Research is needed to evaluate new approaches to accountability and how public agencies can transition toward them. Managers of regional-scale networks may play a role in this regard. If lead agencies can act as mediators between collaborative and hierarchical governance modes, as suggested by this chapter, then perhaps they can also serve as catalysts in processes of large-scale institutional change.

Notes

[1] A disadvantaged community is defined as having 80 per cent or less than the state's average income (California Water Code §79505.5).

[2] Under California law, two or more public agencies may form a Joint Powers Authority to carry out joint activities (California State Government Code §6502).

[3] Region A also has some characteristics of a NAO-managed network. This analysis does not attempt to distinguish between lead agency and NAO models, but instead focuses on comparing a relatively centralised network with a decentralised, shared governance mode.

References

Agranoff, R, 2006, Inside collaborative networks: Ten lessons for public managers, *Public Administration Review* 66, s1, 56–65

Ansell, C, 2011, *Pragmatist democracy: Evolutionary learning as public philosophy*, Oxford: Oxford University Press

Balazs, C, Morello-Frosch, R, Hubbard A, Ray I, 2011, Social disparities in nitrate-contaminated drinking water in California's San Joaquin Valley, *Environmental Health Perspectives* 119, 9, 1272–8

Blomquist, W, Schlager, E, 2005, Political pitfalls of integrated watershed management, *Society and Natural Resources* 18, 2, 101–17

Cash, DW, Adger, WN, Berkes, F, Garden, P, Lebel, L, Olsson, P, Pritchard, L, Young, O, 2006, Scale and cross-scale dynamics: governance and information in a multilevel world, *Ecology and Society* 11, 2, 8

Crona, B, Parker, JN, 2012, Learning in support of governance: Theories, methods, and a framework to assess how bridging organizations contribute to adaptive resource governance, *Ecology and Society* 17, 1, 32

Currie, G, Suhomlinova, O, 2006, The impact of institutional forces upon knowledge sharing in the UK NHS: The triumph of professional power and the inconsistency of policy, *Public Administration* 84, 1, 1–30

DWR (Department of Water Resources), 2010, *Proposition 84 and Proposition 1E: Integrated regional water management guidelines,* Sacramento, CA: California Natural Resources Agency

DWR (Department of Water Resources), 2013, *California Water Plan update 2013*, Bulletin 160–03, Sacramento, CA: California Natural Resources Agency

Folke, C, Hahn, T, Olsson, P, Norberg, J, 2005, Adaptive governance of socio-ecological systems, *Annual Review of Environment and Resources* 30, 441–73

George, AL, Bennett, A, 2005, *Case studies and theory development in the social sciences,* Cambridge, MA: MIT Press

Gerlak, AK, 2008, Today's pragmatic water policy: Restoration, collaboration and adaptive management along US rivers, *Society and Natural Resources* 21, 6, 538–45

Hahn, T, Olsson, P, Folke, C, 2006, Trust-building, knowledge generation and organizational innovations: The role of a bridging organization for adaptive comanagement of a wetland landscape around Kristianstad, Sweden, *Human Ecology* 34, 4, 573–92

Heikkila, T, Gerlak, A, 2012, In search of an integrative framework of learning in collective action settings, *Annual Meeting of the Midwest Political Science Association,* April 12–15, Chicago, IL

Hundley Jr., N, 2001, *The great thirst: Californians and water – A history,* Berkeley, CA: University of California Press

Imperial, M, 2005, Using collaboration as a governance strategy: Lessons from six watershed management programs, *Administration and Society* 37, 3, 281–320

Innes, J, Booher, D, 2010, *Planning with complexity: An introduction to collaborative rationality for public policy,* New York: Routledge

Innes, J, Connick, S, Booher, D, 2007, Informality as a planning strategy, *Journal of the American Planning Association* 73, 2, 195–210

Kettl, D, 2006, Managing boundaries in American administration: The collaboration imperative, *Public Administration Review* 66, s1, 10–19

Klijn, E, Steijn, B, Edelenbos, J, 2010, The impact of network management on outcomes in governance networks, *Public Administration* 88, 4, 1063–82

Koontz, TM, Steelman, TA, Carmin, J, Korfmacher, KS, Moseley, C, Thomas, CW, 2004, *Collaborative environmental management: What roles for government?* Washington, DC: Resources for the Future

Koppenjan, J, Klijn, E, 2004, *Managing uncertainties in networks,* New York: Routledge

Leach, WD, Sabatier, PA, 2003, Facilitators, coordinators, and outcomes, in R O'Leary, RB Bingham (eds) *The promise and performance of environmental conflict resolution*, Washington, DC: Resources for the Future

Lejano, R, Ingram, H, 2009, Collaborative networks and new ways of knowing, *Environmental Science and Policy* 12, 6, 652–62

Margerum, RD, 2002, Collaborative planning: Building consensus, and building a distinct model for practice, *Journal of Planning and Education Research* 21, 2, 237–53

Martin, S, Guarneros-Meza, V, 2013, Governing local partnerships: Does external steering help local agencies address wicked problems? *Policy and Politics* 41, 4, 585–603

Newig, J, Fritsch, O, 2009, Environmental governance: Participatory, multi-level – and effective?, *Environmental Policy and Governance* 19, 3, 197–214

Newig, J, Gunther, D, Pahl-Wostl, C, 2010, Synapses in the network: Learning in governance networks in the context of environmental management, *Ecology and Society* 15, 4, 24

Olsen, JP, 2008, The ups and downs of bureaucratic organization, *Annual Review of Political Science* 11, 13–37

Provan, K, Kenis, P, 2008, Modes of network governance: Structure, management, and effectiveness, *Journal of Public Administration Research and Theory* 18, 2, 229–52

Reed, MS, Evely, AC, Cundhill, G, Fazey, I, Glass, J, Liang, A, Newig, J, Parrish, B, Prell, C, Raymond, C, Stringer, LC, 2010, What is social learning?, *Ecology and Society* 15, 4, 1

Sabatier, PA, Focht, W, Lubell, M, Trachtenberg, Z, Vedlitz, A, Matlock, M (eds), 2005, *Swimming upstream: Collaborative approaches to watershed management*, Cambridge, MA: MIT Press

Sorensen, E, Torfing, J, 2009, Making governance networks effective and democratic through metagovernance, *Public Administration* 87, 2, 234–58

Terry, L, 2005, The thinning of administrative institutions in the hollow state, *Administration and Society* 37, 4, 426–44

Torfing, J, Peters, BG, Pierre, J, Sorensen, E, 2012, *Interactive governance: Advancing the paradigm*, Oxford: Oxford University Press

Weber, EP, Khademian, AM, 2008, Wicked problems, knowledge challenges, and collaborative capacity builders in network settings, *Public Administration Review* 68, 2, 334–49

Williams, P, 2002, The competent boundary spanner, *Public Administration* 80, 1, 103–24

Yin, RK, 2003, *Case study research: Design and methods*, 3rd edn, Thousand Oaks, CA: Sage

---

Scale and intensity of collaboration as determinants of performance management gaps in polycentric governance networks: evidence from a national survey of metropolitan planning organisations

Asim Zia, Christopher Koliba, Jack Meek
and Anna Schulz

Introduction

A growing number of studies characterise multi-level public–public and public–private inter-organisational partnerships as 'governance networks' (Klijn,1996; Jones et al, 1997; Kickert et al, 1997; Lowndes and Skelcher, 1998; Torfing, 2005; Klijn and Skelcher, 2007; Provan and Kenis, 2007; Koliba et al, 2010). While multi-disciplinary enthusiasm about the characterisation and analysis of governance networks has grown considerably in recent literature, much more theoretical and empirical work remains to be done to understand how performance management systems are institutionalised in multi-scale and polycentric governance networks (Kettl, 1996; Bardach and Lesser, 1996; Milward, 1996; Frederickson, 1997; Milward and Provan, 1998; Agranoff and McGuire, 2001; Papadopoulos, 2003; Benner et al, 2004; Scholte, 2004; Papadopoulos, 2007; Harlow and Rawlings, 2007; Koliba et al, 2011a). Page (2004) notes that while accountability and performance management are closely linked, the latter focuses on narrower, more measureable targets that are linked to specific goals. Performance management systems are often part of larger accountability regimes; both face challenges in the context of collaborative governance networks (Page, 2004; Ansell and Gash, 2008). Papadopoulos (2007, 2010) argues that multi-level governance may improve accountability to stakeholders while simultaneously reducing accountability to the general citizenry. The issues of scale, both the jurisdictional scale of inter-organisational network as well as the scale of vertical and horizontal collaboration in which a given inter-organisational network engages, are critical for assessing performance of polycentric governance networks.

The application of fair and effective performance measurement in 'traditional' vertical public administration and policy studies is no easy task. Beryl Radin, for instance, warns that, 'despite the attractive quality of the rhetoric of the performance movement, one should not be surprised that its clarity and siren call mask a much more complex reality' (2006, 235). Performance management is a complicated matter within *individual* organisations, let alone inter-organisational networks. Herbert Simon (1957) and Charles Lindblom (1959) were some of the first to discuss the limits of rationality within social organisations. We argue that the same factors that lead to 'bounded rationality' and incrementalism in the course of day-to-day management and policy making cloud performance measurement in polycentric governance networks.

Theodore Poister (2003) describes performance measurement as a continuous cycle of inquiry that encompasses the collection and processing of data, the analysis of this data, and the utilisation of this analysis to adjust actions and behaviours. Poister posits that the analysis of data is carried out through the act of rendering comparisons over time, against internal targets, across units and against external benchmarks (2003, 16). The analysis of data may lead to decisions regarding strategy, programme delivery, service delivery, day-to-day operations, resource allocation, goals and objectives, and performance targets, standards and indicators (2003, 16). Performance measurement implies certain assumptions regarding causality, namely that inputs into the system (however defined) shape the processes undertaken, which in turn, produce certain outputs leading to short, intermediate and long-term outcomes. The model of systems dynamics, in terms of inputs, processes, outputs and outcomes, has been adopted in some types of performance measurement initiatives, particularly those associated with the evaluation of programmes. The input, process, output, outcome model is often called the 'logic model' (Poister, 1978; 2003). The logic model is a commonly adopted form of performance evaluation used in government and non-profit organisations.

Input measures are often framed in terms of resources contributed to the system that may take any number of different forms of capital (financial, physical, human, social, natural and knowledge). Advocates of performance measurement argue that inputs themselves do not equate to success, but their value can be judged according to their contribution to measurable results (Poister, 1978; Savas, 2005). *Process measures* may involve information collected about activities undertaken within the social system, variables relating to organisational behavior and management, or actors' perceptions of practices. The wide array of process dynamics leads to inconsistency (Radin, 2006). We argue that more attention needs to focus on the development of process measures that are constructed around democratic norms and rules (Klijn and Skelcher, 2007), horizontal versus vertical authorities of governance networks (Weir et al, 2009) and collaborative and technical capacities of multi-level governance networks (Zia and Koliba, 2011).

Output measures hinge on results that may be directly ascribed to the activities undertaken within the system. Outputs are generally the most tangibly visible, often most measurable representation of 'the amount of work performed or the volume of activity completed' (Poister, 2003, 40). Outputs can be considered 'necessary but insufficient conditions for success' (Poister, 2003, 38–9). *Outcome measures*, however, are often the most difficult to determine because they are constructed out of a chain of causality that must take into account all of the input, processes and outputs implicated in the social system. Their impact-based nature requires the use of separate outcome indicators, which typically rely on the frequency of a particular outcome (Radin, 2006). Often implicated in society's most 'wicked problems', governance networks operate in highly politicised environment through which policy outcomes get framed by stakeholders differently (Stone, 2002). Broadly speaking, however, outcome measures indicate progress – either short- or long-term – toward accomplishing a programme or the organisation's overall mission or objectives (Radin, 2006).

Viewed outside the context of governance networks, performance measurement initiatives face a number of challenges that have been summarised by Durant as:

> confusion around outputs and outcomes; inadequate training and technical know-how for developing performance measures; lack of resources for measurement design, data collection and monitoring; different expectations about what performance measures are designed to do and for what they will be used; fear by agencies that they will be asked to develop outcomes measures for results that are not easily measured, that are shaped by factors outside their control…and, that are not amenable to assigning responsibility to particular actors. (Durant, 2001, 702–3)

Studies of performance measurement initiatives across governance networks accentuate all of these factors as being major challenges to applying performance measurement frameworks to the networks (Posner, 2002; Page, 2004; Frederickson and Frederickson, 2006).

Empirical analysis of polycentric governance networks that cut across multiple scales of governance (local to regional and national to international) is warranted to understand the institutionalisation of performance management systems in increasingly hollowed-out nation-states. The shift in the locus of power from federal and state authorities to regional and local governments does not necessarily translate into more effective and equitable governance. Weir et al (2009), for example, found that vertical authority is probably as critical as horizontal expansion for effective and meaningful transportation policy implementation processes. Early on, Ostrom's (2009) Institutional Analysis and Development (IAD) framework laid out theoretical foundations to study polycentric governance networks across increasingly complex vertical and horizontal inter-mingling of governance actors in so-called 'action arenas'. A clear empirical understanding of the scale and intensity of collaboration across vertical and horizontal actors in polycentric governance networks is thus needed to improve the broader governance network theory. In this chapter, we explore this empirically by studying the performance management issues faced by MPOs in the US.

In the US context, Metropolitan Planning Organizations (MPOs) present a unique opportunity as real-world laboratories to investigate the dynamics of accountability and performance management in polycentric governance networks. While MPOs are funded and regulated through federal agencies and legislation such as the Intermodal Surface Transportation Efficiency Act of 1991 (ISTEA) and the subsequent SAFETEA-LU act of 2006, local and regional scale governments, businesses and NGOs work formally and informally with MPOs to design and implement projects at the intersection of land-use, transportation and environment. Performance management practices within metropolitan planning organisations (MPOs) have been indelibly shaped by both ISTEA and SAFETEA-LU. Given the inter-modal short- to medium- and long-range transportation planning responsibilities of MPOs, their performance measures must not only capture conventional efficiency measures, but also capture broader social, economic and environmental impacts of regional transportation planning choices. The construction and use of a region's transportation infrastructure affects environmental, social and economic conditions (Codd and Walton, 1996) including energy consumption, air quality, impact on natural resources, safety, neighbourhood integrity, employment and economic output. These impacts are vital components of an accurate representation of the transportation system's performance. Traditionally, these impacts have not been captured by conventional/vertical governance-based output measures. Yet, ISTEA recognises the importance of these outcomes of the transportation system: the desired social and economic ends of the system's users, and the environmental, social and economic impacts resulting from the use of the system. Any performance management system under ISTEA must measure these outcomes.

—

MPOs sit at the intersection of regional transportation planning networks (Koliba et al, 2011a). As officially sanctioned quasi-governmental 'special districts', MPOs fall within vertically integrated intergovernmental networks. As our research bears out (Zia and Koliba, 2013), MPOs serve to aggregate the preferences of local governments in their regions and pass along those preferences to state DOTs. The governing bodies of MPOs are required to have elected or appointed representation from local governments, as well as representatives from regional FHWA and state DOTs. MPOs also sit at the juncture of regional planning networks that may include a variety of other nonprofit and even for-profit actors. In these instances, MPOs are horizontally aligned with stakeholders outside of the intergovernmental axis and will, to varying degrees, act as collaborators and partners within regionally aligned partnership networks. As actors that forge both vertical and horizontal ties with stakeholders, the capacity of MPOs to collect, report and use performance measurement data is particularly complex. Meyer (2002) conceptualised performance management for MPOs as inherently tied to the demands of transportation system users. Under this demand–driven approach, a way to improve management and operations strategies aimed at enhancing transportation performance is to collect data on system performance. As Meyer (2002, 155) noted:

> By monitoring key performance measures that reflect what is of greatest concern to the users of the transportation system, state, regional and local officials can link this understanding with the types of strategies and actions that best improve this performance…by providing meaningful system performance information at the national level, system-based management and operations could become an important element of a federal programme for improving the nation's transportation system.

In contrast to this demand–driven approach, which uses public perception surveys to prioritise performance measures (Meyer, 2002), other studies have focused on the use of specific performance measures prioritised by the MPO or agency itself. Among them are equity and environmental justice (Duthie et al, 2007), travel time reliability (Lyman and Bertini, 2008), and safety (Montes de Oca and Levinson, 2006); some consider a small set of uniform performance measures, such as the 'total amount of vehicle miles traveled, the amount of the network experiencing congestion during peak periods, the total amount of delay in the network, and the level of airborne emissions' proposed for Puget Sound Regional Council (Reinke and Malarkey, 2006, 75).

Accountability frameworks are often structured around the roles and relationships of the actors in a given governance network (Koliba et al, 2011b); whether performance measures are established according to user demand or initiated as a top-down approach by MPOs may have influence over the accountability framing. Page (2004) has noted that improved interagency collaboration is typically beneficial for accountability and performance management, indicating that increased collaborative capacity at MPOs could have positive accountability ramifications. The relationship between performance management and accountability lies in the capacity of stakeholders to not only collect and report performance measures, but to use those measures to inform project prioritisation and programme implementation. In this study, we look into the extent to which the size of an MPO affects the ability to collect and use performance measurement data of value to them.

Both theoretically and practically, the US federal and state governments are challenged to institutionalise performance management systems for MPOs, in particular small- and medium-scale MPOs (for example, see current challenges postulated by Transportation Research Board's TRB ADA30 committee on small and medium MPOs). Using a 2009 Government Accountability Office (GAO) survey of all 381 MPOs (response rate of 86 per cent), this study examines whether the scale and intensity of collaboration of an MPO across vertical (federal, state and local governments) and horizontal (regional planning commissions, businesses, citizen advocacy) stakeholder groups influences performance management gaps. The variability in how MPOs and their regions use and value performance data contributes to a 'performance management gap', manifested as the differences between what performance data is collected and what performance data is valued. This study formally defines the performance management gap as the statistical distance between the values ascribed to performance measures (normative performance measures) and the current practices for measuring performance (descriptive performance measures). We test the hypothesis: *Small-scale MPOs have a significant performance management gap compared with large-scale MPOs in the US*. Scale and intensity of collaboration with vertical and horizontal stakeholders, both of which are mediated by an MPO's spatial scale, are contributing factors that influence the MPO's ability to collect and utilise performance data to inform planning. This leads us to test a second hypothesis: *The performance management gap is inversely affected by the scale of MPOs as polycentric governance networks; that is, larger-scale MPOs with higher scale and intensity of collaboration have a smaller performance management gap.*

Research design and methodology

We use a GAO survey of all 381 MPOs in the United States with a response rate of 86 per cent. The GAO survey questionnaire is available online (GAO, 2009). The survey asked the directors of MPOs (or their designees) to respond to a series of 45 questions regarding a variety of factors that shape an MPO's structures and functioning. From the survey, we focus on the set of questions that specifically relate to the MPO's spatial scale, their scale and intensity of collaboration with other agencies and stakeholders, the operational challenges that MPOs face, and the performance management gap. Table 1 provides descriptive statistics for specific variables that measure these constructs. Specific measurement approach that was used to construct each of the variables in Table 1 is described below in greater detail.

Spatial scale

The role that spatial scale and sheer size of an MPO play within virtually any study of inter-organisational governance networks needs to be taken into consideration. In the transportation planning arena, we represent this spatial scale in terms of the size of an MPO's regional population, the extent to which the MPO region spanned more than one state, and whether the MPO's region is in an air quality non-attainment area (meaning whether the region had been identified by US EPA as having poor air quality). The spatial scale variables (SS1–3) for this study were measured from responses to different survey questions, as described below.

Population (SS1): Question no 28 of the GAO survey asked respondents: 'Is your MPO part of a transportation management area (TMA), that is, an urbanised area larger than 200,000 population?' If respondents answered 'Yes', we coded it as an MPO with a large population, otherwise, it was coded as an MPO with a small- or medium-sized population for CV1. Table 1 shows that 45 per cent of the MPO respondents are large and the remaining 55 per cent are based in small- or medium-sized communities. The size of the MPO's metropolitan region plays a significant role in determining the depth and breadth of the regional transportation network and the kinds of resources that it uses.

Area of Representation (SS2): Similarly, Question no 3 in the survey enabled us to code SS2, whether the MPO represents a multi-state area. Table 1 shows that 12 per cent of the MPOs in the sample (N=327) represent multi-state areas. This factor could play a significant role in MPO governance, as government agencies, rules and regulation from multiple states must be accounted for.

Table 1: Descriptive statistics for the variables measured through GAO survey data

Variable	Symbol	N	Min	Max	Mean	Standard deviation
SPATIAL SCALE						
TMA Urban (>200K)	SS1	327	0	1	0.45	0.498
Multi-state area	SS2	327	0	1	0.12	0.328
Located within an air quality non-attainment or maintenance area	SS3	328	0	1	0.50	0.501
Air Quality Non-Attainment Area and >200K	SS1*SS3	327	.00	1.00	0.3242	0.4687
SCALE & INTENSITY OF COLLABORATION						
FHWA Board Member	SC1	328	0	1	0.43	0.495
FHWA Committee Member	SC2	328	0	1	0.55	0.498
FTA Board Member	SC3	328	0	1	0.32	0.466
FTA Committee Member	SC4	328	0	1	0.41	0.492
StDOT Board Member	SC5	328	0	1	0.79	0.406
StDOT Committee Member	SC6	328	0	1	0.76	0.430
State Env. Agency Board Member	SC7	328	0	1	0.16	0.366
State Env. Agency Committee Member	SC8	328	0	1	0.47	0.500
Transit Operator Board Member	SC9	328	0	1	0.59	0.492
Transit Operator Committee Member	SC10	328	0	1	0.76	0.426
Local Govt. Elected Board Member	SC11	328	0	1	0.95	0.222
Local Govt. Elected Committee Member	SC12	328	0	1	0.48	0.500
Local Govt. Non-elected Board Member	SC13	328	0	1	0.48	0.501
Local Govt. Non-elected Committee Member	SC14	328	0	1	0.78	0.417
Other Regional Authority Board Member	SC15	328	0	1	0.38	0.487
Other Regional Authority Committee Member	SC16	328	0	1	0.59	0.493
Environmental Advocacy Org. Board Member	SC17	328	0	1	0.05	0.209
Environmental Advocacy Org. Committee Member	SC18	328	0	1	0.34	0.476
Business Advisory Groups Board Member	SC19	328	0	1	0.13	0.335

Business Advisory Groups Committee Member	SC20	328	0	1	0.45	0.499
Citizen Participation Groups Board Member	SC21	328	0	1	0.10	0.305
Citizen Participation Groups Committee Member	SC22	328	0	1	0.56	0.497
Private Sector Board Member	SC23	328	0	1	0.13	0.338
Private Sector Committee Member	SC24	328	0	1	0.48	0.500
Other Officials Board Member	SC25	328	0	1	0.19	0.392
Other Officials Committee Member	SC26	328	0	1	0.20	0.402
Intensity of Collaboration Index	ICI	328	0.00	100.00	44.7866	21.9686
CAPACITY CHALLENGES						
Lack of funding	CC1	326	0.00	4.00	2.6840	1.1508
Competing Priorities	CC2	322	0.00	4.00	1.9752	1.1731
Obtaining public input	CC3	321	0.00	4.00	2.2991	1.0417
Lack of flexibility	CC4	317	0.00	4.00	1.8486	1.2638
Lack of ability to find local match	CC5	324	0.00	4.00	2.2006	1.3213
Fiscal Constraints	CC6	327	0.00	4.00	2.5719	1.1378
Limited authority	CC7	312	0.00	4.00	2.3942	1.0914
Limitations in TDM Capacity	CC8	317	0.00	4.00	1.7634	1.0984
Data limitations	CC9	321	0.00	4.00	2.0436	1.0237
Coordination with land-use agencies	CC10	321	0.00	4.00	1.6168	1.0721
Coordination with other regions	CC11	311	0.00	4.00	1.0161	.9348
Coordination with state DOT	CC12	326	0.00	4.00	1.4448	1.1156
Lack of trained staff	CC13	322	0.00	4.00	1.5497	1.1269
PERFORMANCE MEASURE GAP						
Project Implementation	PMG1	306	-4.00	4.00	0.6503	1.55509
Travel Demand Model Accuracy	PMG2	287	-3.00	4.00	0.9826	1.52016
Transportation System Safety	PMG3	305	-4.00	4.00	0.7115	1.39855
Transportation System Reliability	PMG4	299	-4.00	4.00	0.7926	1.44838
Transportation System Accessibility	PMG5	301	-4.00	4.00	0.7143	1.43228
Transportation System Security	PMG6	285	-4.00	4.00	0.7333	1.50788
Compliance with federal and state rules	PMG7	315	-3.00	4.00	-0.1556	1.24073
Satisfaction among local stakeholders	PMG8	306	-3.00	4.00	0.1895	1.02590

Satisfaction among general public	PMG9	308	-3.00	3.00	0.4610	1.10747
Extent of coordination and stakeholder involvement	PMG10	311	-3.00	4.00	0.3312	1.12864
Measure of public participation	PMG11	308	-4.00	4.00	0.4708	1.27713
Level of highway congestion	PMG12	300	-4.00	4.00	0.4700	1.52869
Air quality	PMG13	245	-4.00	4.00	0.5224	1.97227
Mobility for disadvantaged populations	PMG14	301	-4.00	4.00	0.6379	1.31089
Condition of transportation network	PMG15	300	-4.00	4.00	0.7433	1.44837

Air Quality Non-Attainment Area (SS3): Question no 6 provided an answer for SS3: 50 per cent of the MPOs are located in air quality non-attainment areas, meaning that they have been identified as having poor air quality. We also generated an interaction term between the size of the MPO (SS1) and the air quality non-attainment area (SS3), which tells us that 32.42 per cent of MPOs in the sample are large in size (TMA>200K) and located in air quality non-attainment areas. The designation of air quality non-attainment is an important feature of the Clean Air Act.

Scale of collaboration (SC)

As regional organisations, MPOs are required to collaborate with a variety of other institutional actors cutting across vertical and horizontal levels of governance, including their state DOTs, the local governments of their region, federal agencies and a host of other regional organisations from the nonprofit and business sectors. Many of these interests are formally integrated into the internal governance structure of the MPO. MPO boards of directors and technical committees are often comprised of representatives from local governments, state DOTs and federal agencies and often have other interests integrated into their board governance structure. The scale of their external collaboration with these entities may be measured in terms of the representation of vertical and horizontal stakeholders on MPO's governing boards and committees.

The GAO survey asks a question relating to the MPO's internal governance structure – specifically the range of crosscutting organisational backgrounds of MPO board members. Question no 4 in the survey asked respondents: 'Which of the following types of officials are members (including both voting and non-voting) of your MPO's board?' The GAO survey provided a list of the following 12 stakeholder groups: FHWA, FTA, State DOT, State or local environmental agency, transit operator, local government (elected), local government (non-elected), other regional agency, environmental advocacy organisations, business advocacy groups, citizen participation groups, and private sector. In addition, a thirteenth category, 'other stakeholders', was asked as an open-ended question. Text analysis of this open-ended question reveals that these 'other stakeholders' are typically represented by local universities, port authorities, freight industry, FAA, US Air Force, school districts and airport authorities. The survey respondents also provided similar binary responses for these 13 stakeholder groups vis-à-vis their representation on the technical advisory committees of MPOs. Using these responses, we measured 26 binary variables [SC1…SC26] that represent an MPO's scale of collaboration across vertical and horizontal stakeholders. We find that FHWA is represented on 43 per cent of MPO boards and 55 per cent of MPO committees. The remaining 24 'scale of collaboration' variables shown in Table 1 could be interpreted along these lines. We recognise the many measures of scale of collaboration may be identified through additional means, including measuring the collaborative capacity of critical committees, teams and other communities of practice (Gajda and Koliba, 2007), the collaborative dispositions of staff, and the strength of weak and strong ties across vertical and horizontal stakeholders (Weir et al, 2009).

Intensity of collaboration index (ICI)

For measuring intensity of collaboration index (ICI), we used Question no. 8 in the GAO survey: 'How, if at all, does your MPO coordinate its planning activities with the following types of organisations?' The GAO survey provided a list of the following ten organisations: Federal DOT (FHWA and FTA), State DOT, city and county entities (for example, planning boards), adjacent MPOs, councils of government/regional council, regional transit operators, environmental agency (for example, EPA or state department of natural resources), air quality organisation (for example, regional air quality management district), regional civic organisation(s), and advocacy group(s) (for example, business-oriented or environmental-oriented interest groups). For reporting coordination mechanisms with each of these ten organisations, respondents reported whether coordination took place through representation on MPO committees (which we assigned a weight of 4), through regular meetings (weight of 3), through regular correspondence (weight of 2), solicitation of input/feedback on an ad-hoc basis (weight of 1) or does not coordinate (weight of 0). If an MPO coordinates with an organisation through all four coordination mechanisms, it will get an ICI score of 10, if none then 0. Since the respondents reported for ten different organisations, each

MPO's ICI is measured on a scale from 0 to 100, where 100 implies that MPOs have the highest ICI (meaning they are coordinating with all ten organisations at all four levels). The mean ICI (N=328) is 44.78 per cent points with a standard deviation of 21.96 per cent points.

Operational challenges

The GAO survey asked MPO respondents to indicate the extent to which their MPO faces certain operational challenges. This list of challenges is comprised of some of the widely recognised factors that have been cited as barriers to effective performance for public sector organisations more generally. Many of these operational challenges, such as limited funding, difficulties around garnering public input, as well as challenging relationships with state level and local level actors are common to many organisations operating with networked environments. Operational Challenges (CC1-13) were measured through question no. 27 in the survey: 'In your opinion, how much of a challenge, if any, do the following issues present for your MPO in carrying out the federal requirements for transportation planning?' The respondents ranked 13 issues (variables CC1–CC13 in Table 1) on a likert scale: very great challenge (coded as 4), great challenge (3), moderate challenge (2), some or little challenge (1) and no challenge (0). From Table 1, we can determine that the lack of funding provides the greatest challenge with a mean score of 2.68 (on a scale from 4 to 0), while coordination with other regions is the least challenging issue (mean score of 1.01).

Use and valuation of performance measures and the estimation of performance management gaps

The range of performance measures that matter to MPOs and their networks include a fairly well developed set of metrics that are commonly acceptable forms of performance measures found within the transportation planning field (Koliba et al, 2011a). In the GAO survey, performance measures were identified along the following parameters: the extent to which project implementation evaluations were conducted, travel demand models were used, the safety, accessibility and security of the regional transportation system, the level of compliance with federal and state rules, local stakeholder and general public satisfaction, the extent of coordination with stakeholders, measures of public participation, levels of traffic congestion, air quality and mobility for disadvantaged populations, and assessments of the condition of the regional transportation network.

Space precludes a detailed description of responses for each of these categories. Interested readers may explore the GAO (2009) report.

Data pertaining to the descriptive performance measures was gathered through question 37 of the GAO survey: 'To what extent, if at all, does your MPO use the following indicators to evaluate its effectiveness?' The survey instrument provided a list of 15 performance measures and asked respondents to select one answer from 'very great extent, great extent, moderate extent, some or little extent to no extent and no basis to judge'. Data pertaining to the normative performance measures was gathered

Figure 1a: Variability in the prioritisation of descriptive performance measures (mean response has been re-scaled on a binary scale)

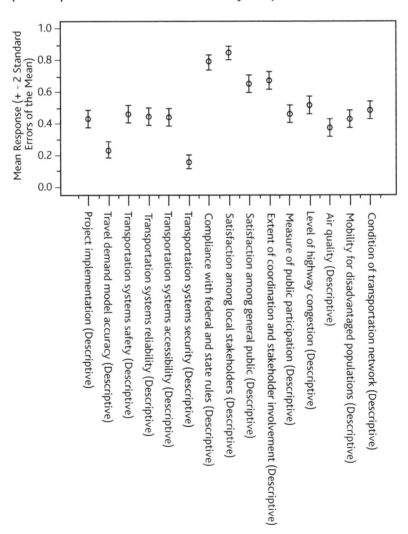

through question 38 of the GAO survey: 'Regardless of your individual answers to question 37, from your perspective, how useful, if at all, could the following indicators be for evaluating the effectiveness of MPOs?' The same list of 15 performance measures that was given in Q37 was provided to the respondents, who were asked to select an answer from very useful, useful, moderately useful, of some or little use, of no use, to no opinion or no basis to judge. Normative performance measures thus solicit what survey respondents value, while descriptive performance measures solicit what survey respondents practice. Figure 1a shows the mean and the standard error of the mean for the responses to the 15 descriptive performance measure listed in the GAO survey. Figure 1b shows similar statistics for the 15 normative performance measures. Figure 1a shows that the satisfaction among local stakeholders and compliance with federal and state rules are accorded significantly high priorities as the performance measures that are being used by MPOs. Transportation system security

Figure 1b: Variability in the prioritisation of normative performance measures (mean response has been re-scaled on a binary scale)

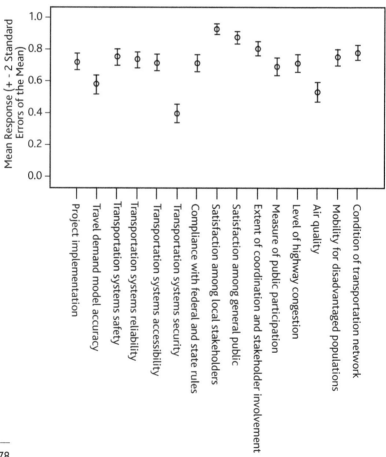

and travel demand model accuracy are ranked the lowest in terms of their utility as performance measures. Figures 1b shows similar patterns for the normative/desirable performance measures, except that satisfaction among the general public is ranked almost as high as the satisfaction among the local stakeholders.

We formally define the performance management gap as the statistical distance between the values ascribed to performance measures (normative performance measures) and the current practices for measuring performance (descriptive performance measures). In Table 1, 15 variables (PMG1...PMG15) represent the continuous scale for performance management gaps for each of the 15 performance measures considered relevant by GAO. Figure 2 shows a box plot of performance management gap variables. Figure 2 reveals that performance measures such as travel demand model accuracy and condition of transportation network are perceived by public managers to have a higher performance management

Figure 2: Box plot of 15 performance management gap variables (positive values show higher gap)

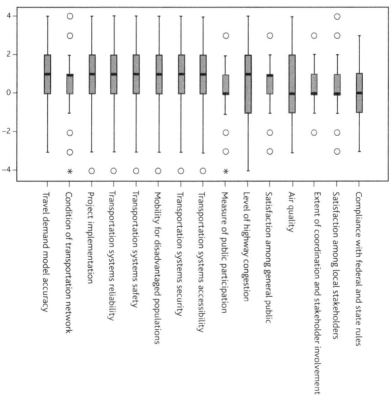

gap, while compliance with federal and state rules and satisfaction among local stakeholders have minimal gap.

The implications of this apparent gap will need to be explored in greater detail through additional research. It should be noted that the GAO survey was completed by the executive director of the MPO or her or his designee. We may presume that responses related to performance indicator use have a greater likelihood of being grounded in actual practice. Responses to question 38 concerning the relative value of specific performance measures may be viewed as statement of opinion and perception that may (or may not) be informed by reasoned consideration. Thus, the apparent gap between the performance measures that are used and those that are valued needs to be couched in terms of the opinions of those completing the survey itself. However, the potential of such a gap may be an important signal in ascertaining the extent to which a performance management culture persists across the transportation planning networks in this study, a point that we will return to in our conclusion.

In an effort to gather qualitative data to help explain our findings, we contacted several MPOs in Maine and Vermont and requested short interviews. Rob Kenerson, director of the Bangor Area Comprehensive Transportation System (BACTS), and Tom Reinauer, director of the Kittery Area Comprehensive Transportation System (KACTS) provided what insight they could (Kenerson, personal communication, 22 April 2015; Reinauer, personal communication, 30 April 2015). Both MPOs are very small compared to many national counterparts, having a full-time staff of three and two, respectively. BACTS gauges performance primarily by assessing pavement condition and does not employ federally defined performance measures. Kenerson cited limited funding, not conceptions of value, as the primary factor that restricted staff time and overall MPO ability to employ performance measures. In late 2014, KACTS began to formally measure performance regarding incident clearance, roadway clearance and incident public notification time on its major highways. Of those, only incident public notification time is specifically linked to nationally used measures. Reinauer expressed interest in employing federally defined performance measures, particularly those pertaining to safety. Similar to BACTS, the size of KACTS and associated funding levels were identified as the primary impediments to employing additional performance measures, federally defined or not. Both interviewees cited a gap between federal guidelines and small-scale MPO capacity to engage in adequate tracking even a very limited number of performance measures.

To test the study hypotheses, we estimated 15 OLS regression models that deploy spatial scale, the scale and intensity of collaboration and operational challenges as independent variables to explain the variation in the performance management gap for each of the 15 performance indicators.

Findings

Table 2 shows estimated coefficients for 15 OLS regression models that predict MPO performance management gaps for each of the 15 performance indicators discussed above. The R^2 values for the estimated regression models range from a low value of 15.2 per cent to a high value of 34.7 per cent. We report standardised coefficients in Table 2 to enable comparison of the magnitude and direction of effect sizes across 15 regression models for each of the performance indicators. The estimated standardised coefficients can be used to test the two study hypotheses for each of the 15 performance indicators, as discussed below.

Regarding the first hypothesis that small-scale MPOs have a significant performance management gap compared with large-scale MPOs in the US, we find that there is mixed evidence for the postulated difference after we control for the confounding effects of air quality non–attainment areas, multi–state areas, and other independent variables in the regression models shown in Table 2. Due to the interaction term 'air quality non–attainment area and >200K' in the model, the coefficient on TMA Urban (>200K) shows the standardised effect size for the large–scale MPOs as compared with small–scale MPOs that are both located in air quality attainment areas. Further, the coefficient on the interaction term must be interpreted to estimate the effect of spatial scale: larger MPOs located in air quality non–attainment areas must be compared with smaller MPOs that are also located in non–attainment areas. Let us consider the 'travel demand model accuracy' performance indicator for interpretation and testing of the first hypothesis. We find that large–scale MPOs located in air quality attainment areas have a statistically significant (p<0.05) higher performance management gap for travel demand model accuracy indicator compared with small–scale MPOs that are also located in air quality attainment areas. In contrast, small–scale MPOs that are located in air quality non–attainment areas have a relatively higher performance management gap for travel demand model accuracy indicator compared with large–scale MPOs that are also located in air quality non–attainment areas. Similarly, for the performance indicator of satisfaction among general public, we find that in large–scale MPOs that are located in air quality non–attainment areas, there is a relatively higher performance management gap (p<0.1) compared with small–scale MPOs that are also located in air quality non–attainment areas. Further, small–scale MPOs located within an air quality non–attainment area have a relatively high performance management gap for the performance indicator of mobility for disadvantaged populations (p<0.05) compared with small–scale MPOs that are located in air quality attainment areas. Finally, we find that large–scale MPOs located in air quality attainment area have a relatively high performance management gap (p<0.05) for the performance indicator of transportation network condition compared with small–scale MPOs that are also located in air quality attainment areas.

Table 2: Results from 15 OLS regression models predicting performance management gap for 15 performance measures: Standardised Coefficients (effect sizes) with * show significance with 10%; ** shows significance with 5% and *** shows significance with 1% Type I probability error.

	Project implementation	Travel demand model accuracy	Transportation system safety	Transportation system reliability	Transportation system accessibility
TMA Urban (>200K)	0.129	0.324**	0.127	0.152	0.095
Multi-state area	0.056	-0.038	-0.019	0.022	-0.068
Located within an air quality non-attainment area	0.060	0.245**	0.142	0.135	0.193*
Air Quality Non-Attainment Area and >200K	-0.042	-0.413**	-0.076	-0.070	-0.097
FHWA Board Member	-0.172	0.029	0.094	0.135	0.051
FHWA Committee Member	-0.074	-0.052	-0.163	-0.095	-0.176*
FTA Board Member	0.248**	-0.061	0.010	-0.106	0.002
FTA Committee Member	0.090	0.065	0.166	0.178*	0.171*
StDOT Board Member	0.049	0.078	0.049	0.014	0.137
StDOT Committee Member	-0.069	-0.106	0.133	-0.070	0.100
State Env. Agency Board Member	-0.101	-0.014	0.025	0.007	0.030
State Env. Agency Committee Member	0.080	-0.170*	0.019	-0.126	-0.076
Transit Operator Board Member	-0.077	-0.125	-0.086	-0.076	-0.089
Transit Operator Committee Member	0.192*	-0.060	0.091	0.126	-0.010
Local Govt. Elected Board Member	-0.006	-0.029	0.027	-0.004	-0.008
Local Govt. Elected Committee Member	0.029	0.055	0.031	-0.017	0.064
Local Govt. Non-elected Board Member	0.040	0.063	-0.014	-0.035	0.040
Local Govt. Non-elected Committee Member	-0.142	0.054	-0.035	-0.001	0.003

Other Regional Authority Board Member	-0.054	0.128*	-0.028	-0.039	-0.041
Other Regional Authority Committee Member	0.040	0.122	-0.068	0.030	0.041
Environmental Advocacy Org. Board Member	-0.058	0.043	0.024	0.016	0.103
Environmental Advocacy Org. Committee Member	-0.027	0.095	-0.032	-0.062	-0.019
Business Advisory Groups Board Member	0.026	0.026	0.021	0.135	-0.061
Business Advisory Groups Committee Member	0.007	-0.071	0.052	-0.086	-0.068
Citizen Participation Groups Board Member	0.037	-0.066	0.051	0.015	-0.018
Citizen Participation Groups Committee Member	0.003	-0.030	-0.054	0.044	-0.037
Private Sector Board Member	-0.018	0.006	0.000	0.032	0.136
Private Sector Committee Member	-0.170*	-0.117	-0.053	0.017	0.005
Other Officials Board Member	-0.007	-0.117*	-0.020	-0.072	-0.032
Other Officials Committee Member	-0.020	0.160**	-0.034	0.021	-0.008
Intensity of Collaboration Index	-0.237***	-0.204**	-0.211**	-0.190**	-0.224**
Lack of funding	-0.061	-0.047	-0.121	-0.185**	-0.088
Competing Priorities	-0.042	-0.109	0.057	0.124	0.085
Obtaining public input	0.019	0.045	0.007	-0.059	-0.042
Lack of flexibility	0.007	0.011	-0.136	-0.078	-0.135
Lack of ability to find local match	-0.019	-0.007	-0.007	-0.130	-0.150*
Fiscal Constraints	0.102	0.059	0.055	0.107	0.140*
Limited authority	-0.014	-0.115	-0.016	-0.036	-0.027
Limitations in TDM Capacity	-0.271**	-0.104	-0.173*	-0.190**	-0.139
Data limitations	0.233	0.097	0.190*	0.063	0.140
Coordination with land-use agencies	0.004	-0.031	0.001	0.138*	0.078
Coordination with other regions	0.068	-0.172**	0.013	0.014	0.007
Coordination with state DOT	0.169**	0.193**	0.064	0.102	0.076
Lack of trained staff	-0.035	0.099	0.037	0.116	0.085
N	254	239	251	246	249
R^2	23.3%	27.1%	19.2%	24.7%	25.0%

	Transportation system security	Compliance with federal and state rules	Satisfaction among local stakeholders	Satisfaction among general public	Extent of coordination and stakeholder involvement
TMA Urban (>200K)	0.109	0.084	0.040	-0.026	0.074
Multi-state area	-0.020	0.036	-0.127	0.042	-0.023
Located within an air quality non-attainment area	0.128	-0.018	-0.032	0.044	0.054
Air Quality Non-Attainment Area and >200K	0.030	-0.003	0.086	0.257*	0.067
FHWA Board Member	-0.027	-0.044	0.050	0.090	0.126
FHWA Committee Member	0.088	-0.173	-0.155	-0.023	-0.030
FTA Board Member	0.152	0.021	0.021	0.007	-0.094
FTA Committee Member	-0.012	0.138	0.132	0.030	0.130
StDOT Board Member	0.033	-0.030	-0.036	-0.047	-0.062
StDOT Committee Member	-0.118	0.020	0.148	0.181*	0.187*
State Env. Agency Board Member	-0.003	-0.030	0.123	-0.071	-0.059
State Env. Agency Committee Member	-0.063	-0.137	-0.001	0.071	-0.008
Transit Operator Board Member	-0.023	-0.079	-0.105	-0.046	-0.126
Transit Operator Committee Member	0.205*	0.036	-0.103	0.160	-0.066
Local Govt. Elected Board Member	-0.035	-0.068	-0.045	0.033	0.046
Local Govt. Elected Committee Member	0.103	0.064	-0.062	-0.165	-0.120
Local Govt. Non-elected Board Member	0.038	0.121	0.015	0.031	0.126
Local Govt. Non-elected Committee Member	-0.031	0.010	-0.008	-0.039	-0.003
Other Regional Authority Board Member	0.056	0.040	0.031	0.042	0.034
Other Regional Authority Committee Member	0.051	-0.056	-0.020	-0.043	-0.054
Environmental Advocacy Org. Board Member	-0.025	-0.006	0.061	0.010	-0.048
Environmental Advocacy Org. Committee Member	-0.062	0.072	0.021	0.023	0.089
Business Advisory Groups Board Member	0.011	-0.025	0.194**	0.081	0.068
Business Advisory Groups Committee Member	-0.054	-0.065	-0.023	-0.084	-0.114
Citizen Participation Groups Board Member	0.005	-0.094	-0.176**	-0.098	-0.018

Citizen Participation Groups Committee Member	0.078	0.078	0.000	-0.061	0.091
Private Sector Board Member	0.104	0.074	0.021	0.102	-0.060
Private Sector Committee Member	0.002	0.070	0.032	0.074	-0.103
Other Officials Board Member	-0.047	0.032	0.018	0.109	0.029
Other Officials Committee Member	-0.117	-0.097	0.056	0.032	-0.003
Intensity of Collaboration Index	-0.191**	-0.127*	-0.172**	-0.147**	-0.161**
Lack of funding	-0.040	0.050	-0.034	-0.170**	-0.124
Competing Priorities	-0.028	-0.078	0.022	0.044	-0.049
Obtaining public input	0.001	0.027	0.011	0.046	0.048
Lack of flexibility	-0.091	-0.045	-0.087	-0.068	-0.008
Lack of ability to find local match	-0.168**	-0.129	0.045	-0.025	-0.032
Fiscal Constraints	0.124	-0.045	0.012	-0.023	0.063
Limited authority	-0.003	0.067	-0.057	0.053	-0.086
Limitations in TDM Capacity	-0.126	-0.117	0.033	-0.041	-0.011
Data limitations	0.166*	-0.053	-0.030	0.074	0.037
Coordination with land-use agencies	0.074	0.054	-0.068	-0.007	-0.016
Coordination with other regions	-0.023	0.004	0.080	0.004	-0.028
Coordination with state DOT	0.033	0.119	0.027	-0.023	-0.060
Lack of trained staff	0.001	0.091	-0.007	0.091	0.197**
N	237	260	254	253	256
R²	22.7%	15.2%	16.3%	22.6%	20.8%

	Measure of public participation	Level of highway congestion	Air quality	Mobility for disadvantaged populations	Condition of transportation network
TMA Urban (>200K)	0.198	0.092	0.085	0.075	0.252**
Multi-state area	0.096	0.017	0.045	0.037	0.011
Located within an air quality non-attainment area	0.105	0.053	-0.327	0.199**	0.062
Air Quality Non-Attainment Area and >200K	-0.157	-0.038	0.026	-0.073	0.038
FHWA Board Member	0.062	0.121	0.157	0.221**	0.140
FHWA Committee Member	0.087	-0.080	-0.221*	-0.220**	-0.048
FTA Board Member	0.052	0.054	-0.048	-0.009	-0.068
FTA Committee Member	-0.002	-0.001	0.114	0.109	-0.032
StDOT Board Member	-0.048	0.085	0.060	0.045	0.063
StDOT Committee Member	-0.062	-0.054	0.036	0.220**	-0.150
State Env. Agency Board Member	-0.043	0.020	0.045	0.092	-0.010
State Env. Agency Committee Member	0.016	-0.049	-0.202**	-0.100	-0.010

Transit Operator Board Member	-0.102	-0.084	-0.161*	-0.112	-0.145*
Transit Operator Committee Member	0.185*	0.134	0.086	0.155	0.254**
Local Govt. Elected Board Member	0.038	-0.057	-0.058	0.074	0.015
Local Govt. Elected Committee Member	0.002	-0.077	-0.057	-0.025	0.019
Local Govt. Non-elected Board Member	0.184**	-0.011	0.104	-0.091	-0.033
Local Govt. Non-elected Committee Member	-0.061	-0.027	-0.061	-0.100	-0.008
Other Regional Authority Board Member	-0.003	0.082	0.012	-0.012	-0.029
Other Regional Authority Committee Member	0.016	-0.018	0.159*	-0.014	-0.130
Environmental Advocacy Org. Board Member	-0.077	0.041	0.153*	-0.022	0.042
Environmental Advocacy Org. Committee Member	0.033	0.100	-0.037	0.090	-0.126
Business Advisory Groups Board Member	0.066	0.185**	-0.036	-0.014	0.049
Business Advisory Groups Committee Member	-0.008	-0.036	-0.044	-0.105	0.072
Citizen Participation Groups Board Member	0.013	-0.111	-0.141*	-0.099	0.022
Citizen Participation Groups Committee Member	-0.137	-0.110	0.022	-0.107	-0.025
Private Sector Board Member	0.026	-0.022	0.016	0.079	-0.084
Private Sector Committee Member	-0.097	0.058	0.006	0.064	0.033
Other Officials Board Member	0.046	0.056	-0.108	0.095	-0.001
Other Officials Committee Member	-0.028	0.124*	0.035	0.014	-0.042
Intensity of Collaboration Index	-0.115	-0.052	-0.138*	-0.190**	-0.175**
Lack of funding	-0.089	-0.119	-0.040	-0.070	-0.045
Competing Priorities	-0.026	0.000	0.003	0.055	-0.064
Obtaining public input	-0.046	0.026	0.009	-0.028	0.049
Lack of flexibility	-0.009	-0.079	-0.096	-0.206**	-0.114
Lack of ability to find local match	-0.116	-0.080	-0.143*	-0.089	-0.120
Fiscal Constraints	0.107	-0.127*	0.012	0.050	0.050
Limited authority	-0.110	-0.010	0.047	-0.039	0.042
Limitations in TDM Capacity	-0.050	-0.047	-0.161*	-0.134	0.074
Data limitations	0.052	-0.007	0.139	0.115	-0.013
Coordination with land-use agencies	-0.031	-0.003	-0.016	0.056	0.030
Coordination with other regions	0.104	-0.014	0.020	0.008	0.075
Coordination with state DOT	-0.082	0.090	-0.054	0.062	-0.035
Lack of trained staff	0.201**	0.128*	0.034	0.062	0.046
N	253	247	205	250	249
R^2	22.1%	23.9%	33.7%	34.7%	24.3%

Table 2 models can also be used for testing the second hypothesis that the performance management gap is inversely affected by the scale of MPOs as polycentric governance networks; that is, larger-scale MPOs with higher scale and intensity of collaboration have a smaller performance management gap. The scale of collaboration effects on performance management gaps for each of the 15 performance indicators, after controlling for their spatial scales and operational challenges, can be elicited from the coefficients on 26 variables that test the effects of MPO board and committee memberships of different vertical and horizontal stakeholders. More specifically, from the perspective of vertical stakeholders, we find that the presence of FHWA on MPO boards increases the performance management gap for the performance indicator on mobility of disadvantaged populations; however, the presence of FHWA on MPO committees decreases the performance gap for the indicators of air quality and mobility for disadvantaged populations. Having FTA board members increases the gap for project implementation, while having FTA committee members on committees marginally increases the gap for transportation system reliability and accessibility indicators (p<0.1). Having state DOT committee members increases the performance gap for the indicators on satisfaction among general public and the extent of coordination and stakeholder involvement, as well as mobility for disadvantaged populations. In contrast, having state environmental agency committee members decreases the performance gap for air quality indicators. Having transit operator committee members increases the performance gap for project implementation, transportation system security, measure of public participation and condition of transportation network. Finally, having non-elected local government members on MPO boards increases the performance gap for the indicator on public participation.

Horizontally, the scale of collaboration across different stakeholders also affects performance gap. Presence of other regional authorities on MPO board increases performance gap for travel demand model accuracy and their presence on MPO committee increases gap for air quality. Environmental advocacy representatives on MPO boards also increase gap for air quality indicator. The presence of business advisory groups on MPO boards increases performance gap for the indicators on satisfaction among general public and level of highway congestion. In stark contrast, the presence of citizen participation groups on MPO boards decreases performance gap for the indicators on satisfaction among general public and air quality. Further, we find that the presence of private sector members on MPO boards decreases performance gap for project implementation.

The strongest finding of this study pertains to the inverse relationship hypothesis postulated and tested between the intensity of collaboration and the size of the performance management gap. The standardised coefficient on the intensity of collaboration index is statistically significant (p<0.05) for 11 out of 15 performance indicators. Two indicators are marginally significant (p<0.1). We are thus confident to confirm the part of the second hypothesis that as the intensity of collaboration by an MPO across vertical and horizontal stakeholders goes up, after controlling for all other factors in the model, the performance management gap across the board goes down. In other words, if MPOs aim to decrease their performance management gaps, one strategy could be to increase their intensity of collaboration with both vertical and horizontal stakeholders. In our qualitative research, both interviewees noted that the small-scale of their MPOs necessitates both vertical and horizontal collaboration to accomplish basic initiatives. KACTS is uniquely situated at a state border and collaborates regularly with nearby MPOs in New Hampshire, while BACTS relies on partnerships with local organisations, such as the University of Maine, to make progress toward shared goals. The directors of both MPOs were unsurprised by our findings regarding scale and intensity of collaboration as, in their experience, collaboration has contributed to positive performance overall. Additionally, Reinauer noted that collaboration has contributed to his MPO's understanding of how to employ specific performance measures. The absence of the use or explicit valuation of many specific performance measures at either MPO renders the qualitative evidence largely anecdotal.

Finally, among the control factors, the operational challenges such as data limitations, coordination with state DOT and lack of trained staff can increase the performance management gap for some performance measures. One surprising finding among the operational challenges concerns the effect of limitations in travel demand modelling (TDM) capacity. We find that the limited TDM capacity decreases performance gap for the indicators on project implementation and transportation system reliability (p<0.05), as well as a marginal decreasing effect on transportation system safety and air quality indicators. Perhaps this finding is an artifact of the expectations game caused by limited TDM capacity, which in turn reflexively leads to lower expectations on the desirability of setting higher performance standards for project implementation and transportation system reliability. More qualitative research is warranted to explain this surprising finding from the GAO survey data. In both of the interviews we conducted, the respondents' MPOs had limited TDM capacity.

Implications and conclusions

Evidence confirms MPO leaders' perception that a 'performance management gap' persists for their organisations and the wider networks that their organisations serve. We also find that, after controlling for MPO spatial scale, air quality attainment status and operational challenges, the higher intensity of collaboration of an MPO across vertical and horizontal stakeholders significantly decreases the perceived performance management gap. In contrast, larger vertical scale of collaboration measured through federal and state agency representation on MPO boards and committees can potentially increase the performance management gap for some performance measures. A theoretical implication of this empirical research is that MPOs are clearly embedded in cross-cutting polycentric governance networks, and that these network ties can potentially minimise performance management gaps by improving the strength of their ties with external stakeholders and partners across both vertical scales (ranging from local governments to federal government) and horizontal scales (ranging from public sector agencies to private sector firms and advocacy groups).

The disparities between the performance measures that are actually used and those performance measures that are valued suggests that those performance measures that are most *used* may not be found to be the most *useful*. We recognise that we have grounded the evidence of a performance management gap in an analysis of the perceptions of the survey respondents: MPO executives directors or their designees. The extent to which the gap is a perception held by just this population of responders, a perception that is held by MPO governing boards, or a perception widely held across the regional network is a distinction worth noting. Given the limited scope of our qualitative data, we are only comfortable saying perception of a performance management gap exists for those responding to the GAO survey. In our two interviews, however, both MPO directors noted that, anecdotally, small MPOs struggle with the performance management gap because resources are too limited to effectively consider the range of performance measures that are perceived to be valuable.

Our findings about the scale and intensity of collaboration are also relevant to the matter of the perceptions of a performance management gap because the 'culture of performance' that exists within MPOs and across MPOs and their network ties will likely exist within the context of *using* performance data, but not necessarily *valuing* performance data. These findings have important implications for understanding the role that performance management systems play as governors of systems-level feedback (Koliba et al, 2011a). This observation begs for a deeper, more nuanced explanation that will only be answered through extensive additional research. The use of performance measures may be predicated on the institutional rules that shape network ties. The value of performance measures will likely be predicated on the mental models and belief systems of critical actors in the system. Those completing the GAO survey rendered a value judgement concerning which performance measures were most valuable. It becomes very important, then, to determine how the belief systems of various actors combine, comingle and compete in these settings. Because of the high degree of efficacy that the scale and intensity of collaboration brings to performance measurement use, it stands to reason that this matter of values versus use is one that calls for more inquiry in a large variety of inter-organisational governance network policy settings along the lines suggested above.

Because it can no longer be assumed that the nation-state possesses the same kind of authority as traditionally ascribed to public organisations, governing the actors in inter-organisational networks gives rise to new performance management and accountability challenges. These challenges arise when nation-states are displaced as central actors; market forces are considered; and cooperation and collaboration across vertical and horizontal scales is recognised as an integral administrative activity. Discerning the accountability structures amid the complexity that emerges in cross-sector, cross-jurisdictional settings requires us to consider the dynamics at work when the accountability structures of one network actor comingle, compete or complement the accountability structures of other network actors. In confronting the accountability challenges presented by the shift toward networked and collaborative systems of governance, many public organisations have refocused their attention on performance measurement and management (Kersbergen and Waarden, 2004), which is also confirmed by this study of MPOs. However, the definition of what constitutes effective set of performance indicators for a given governance network remains a critical question to be addressed. Some previous studies have examined the efficacy of network structures in achieving ascribed outputs or outcomes (see as a representative: Marsh and Rhodes, 1992; Heinrich and Lynn, 2000; Koontz et al, 2004; Frederickson and Frederickson, 2006; Rodriguez et al, 2007; Koliba et al, 2011a). The highly contextual nature of the environments that governance networks operate within, coupled with the highly contextual nature of most of the perceptions of the network actors within the network, render the development of consensus around common definitions of viable network performance indicators very difficult to achieve. MPOs of varying sizes, spatial scales, operational challenges and scales and intensities of collaboration face similar challenges that is manifested in the heterogeneity of 15 performance indicators analysed in this study. Future empirical research can replicate the testing of our study hypotheses by surveying and interviewing other types of polycentric/cross-cutting governance networks, such as watershed partnerships, airshed partnerships, food provision networks and health provision networks.

Acknowledgements

We gratefully acknowledge funding from the United States Department of Transportation via the University of Vermont Transportation Research Center and National Science Foundation EPS-1101317. We are also thankful to GAO for providing access to their survey data. The authors bear complete responsibility for all the analysis and information provided in this chapter.

References

Agranoff, R, McGuire, M, 2001, Big questions in public network management research, *Journal of Public Administration Research and Theory* 11, 3, 295–326.

Ansell, C, Gash, A, 2008, Collaborative governance in theory and practice, *Journal of Public Administration Theory and Research* 18, 4, 543–71

Bardach, E, Lesser, C, 1996, Accountability in human services collaboratives: For what? And for whom?, *Journal of Public Administration Research and Theory* 6, 197–224

Benner, T, Reinicke, WH, Witte, JM, 2004, Multisectoral networks in global governance: Towards a pluralistic system of accountability, *Government and Opposition* 39, 2, 191–210

Codd, N, Walton, MC, 1996, Performance measures and framework for decision making under the national transportation system, *Transportation Research Record* 1518, 70–7

Durant, RF, 2001, A way out of no way? Strategy, structure, and the 'new governance', *Public Administration and Public Policy* 87, 689–724

Duthie J, Cervenka, K, Waller, ST, 2007, Environmental justice analysis: challenges for metropolitan transportation planning, *Transportation Research Record* 2013, 8–12, http://trrjournalonline.trb.org/doi/10.3141/2013-02

Frederickson, GD, Frederickson, HG, 2006, *Measuring the performance of the hollow state*, Washington, DC: Georgetown University Press

Frederickson, HG, 1997, *The spirit of public administration*, San Francisco, CA: Jossey-Bass

Gajda, R, Koliba, C, 2007, Evaluating the imperative of intra–organization collaboration: A school improvement perspective, *American Journal of Evaluation* 28, 1, 26–44

GAO (Government Accountability Office), 2009, Transportation planning: Survey of metropolitan planning organizations, GAO-09-867SP, an E-supplement to GAO-09-868, www.gao.gov/special.pubs/gao-09-867sp/09-867sp4.html.

Harlow, C, Rawlings, R, 2007, Promoting accountability in multilevel governance: A network approach, *European Law Journal* 13, 4, 542–62

Heinrich, CJ, Lynn, LE Jr (eds), 2000, *Governance and performance: New perspectives*, Washington, DC: Georgetown University Press

Jones, C, Hesterly, WS, Borgatti, SP, 1997, A general theory of network governance: Exchange conditions and social mechanisms, *Academy of Management Review* 22, 4, 911–45

Kersbergen, KV, Van Waarden, F, 2004, 'Governance' as a bridge between disciplines: Cross-disciplinary inspiration regarding shifts in governance and problems of governability, accountability and legitimacy, *European Journal of Political Research* 43, 2, 143–71

Kettl, DF, 1996, Governing at the millennium, in L Perry (ed) *Handbook of public administration*, San Francisco, CA: Jossey-Bass

Kickert, WJM, Klijn, E, Koppenjan, JFM, 1997, Introduction: A management perspective on policy networks, in WJM Kickert, E Klijn, JFM Koppenjan (eds) *Managing Complex Networks*, London: Sage

Klijn, E, 1996, Analyzing and managing policy processes in complex networks, *Administration and Society* 28, 90–119

Klijn, E, Skelcher C, 2007, Democracy and governance networks: Compatible or not?, *Public Administration* 85, 3, 587–608

Koliba, C, Meek, J, Zia, A, 2010, *Governance networks in public administration policy*, Boca Raton, FL: CRC Press

Koliba C, Campbell, E, Zia, A, 2011a, Performance measurement considerations in congestion management networks: Aligning data and network accountability, *Public Performance Management Review* 34, 4, 520–48

Koliba, C, Mills, RM, Zia, A, 2011b, Accountability in governance networks: An assessment of public, private, and nonprofit emergency management practices following Hurricane Katrina, *Public Administration Review* 71, 2, 210–20

Koontz, TM, Steelman, TA, Carmin, J, Korfmacher, KS, Moseley, C, Thomas, CW, 2004, *Collaborative environmental management: What roles for government?*, Washington, DC: Resources for the Future (RFF) Press

Lindblom, C, 1959, The science of 'muddling through', *Public Administration Review* 19, 2, 79–88

Lowndes, V, Skelcher, C, 1998, The dynamics of multi-organizational partnerships: An analysis of changing modes of governance, *Public Administration* 76, 313–33

Lyman, K, Bertini, RL, 2008, Using travel time reliability measures to improve regional transportation planning and operations, *Transportation Research Record* 2046, 1–10

Marsh, D, Rhodes, RAW, 1992, *Policy networks in British government*, Oxford: Oxford University Press

Meyer, M, 2002, Measuring system performance: key to establishing operations as a core agency mission, *Transportation Research Record* 1817, 155–62

Milward, HB, 1996, Symposium on the hollow state: Capacity, control, and performance in interorganizational settings, *Journal of Public Administration Research and Theory* 6, 193–5

Milward, HB, Provan, KG, 1998, Principles for controlling agents: The political economy of network structure, *Journal of Public Administration Research and Theory* 8, 203–21

Montes de Oca, N, Levinson, D, 2006, Network expansion decision making in Minnesota's Twin Cities, *Transportation Research Record* 1981, 1–11

Ostrom, E, 2009, *Understanding institutional diversity*, Princeton, NJ: Princeton University Press

Page, S, 2004, Measuring accountability for results in interagency collaboratives, *Public Administration Review* 64, 5, 591–606

Papadopoulos, Y, 2003, Cooperative forms of governance: problems of democratic accountability in complex environments, *European Journal of Political Research* 42, 473–501

Papadopoulos, Y, 2007, Problems of democratic accountability in network and multilevel governance, *European Law Journal* 13, 4, 469–86

Papadopoulos, Y, 2010, Accountability and multi-level governance: More accountability, less democracy?, *West European Politics* 33, 5, 1030–49

Poister, TH, 1978, *Public program analysis: Applied research methods*, Baltimore, MD: University Park Press

Poister, TH, 2003, *Measuring performance in public and nonprofit organizations*, San Francisco, CA: Jossey-Bass

Posner, P, 2002, Accountability challenges of third–party government, in L Salamon (ed) *The tools of government: A guide to the new governance*, New York: Oxford

Provan, KG, Kenis, P, 2007, Modes of network governance: Structure, management, and effectiveness, *Journal of Public Administration Research and Theory* 18, 2, 229–52

Radin, B, 2006, *Challenging the performance movement: Accountability, complexity and democratic values*, Washington, DC: Georgetown University Press

Reinke, D, Malarkey, D, 2006, Implementing integrated transportation planning in metropolitan planning organizations: Procedural and analytical issues, *Transportation Research Record* 1552, 71–8

Rodriguez, C, Langley, A, Beland, F, Denis, J, 2007, Governance, power, and mandated collaboration in an interorganizational network, *Administration and Society* 39, 2, 150–93

Savas, ES, 2005, *Privatization in the city: Successes, failures, lessons*, Washington DC: CQ Press

Scholte, JA, 2004, Civil society and democratically accountable global governance, *Government and Opposition* 39, 2, 211–33

Simon, HA, 1957, *Models of man: Social and rational*, Oxford: Wiley.

Stone, D, 2002, *Policy paradox: The art of political decision making*, New York: Norton

Torfing, J, 2005, Governance network theory: Towards a second generation, *European Political Science* 4: 305–15

Weir, M, Rongerude, J, Ansell, CK, 2009, Collaboration is not enough: Virtuous cycles of reform in transportation policy, *Urban Affairs Review* 44, 4, 455–89

Zia, A, Koliba, C, 2011, Accountable climate governance: Dilemmas of performance management across complex governance networks, *Journal of Comparative Policy Analysis: Research and Practice* 13, 5, 479–97

Zia, A, Koliba, C, 2013, The emergence of attractors under multi-level institutional designs: Agent-based modeling of intergovernmental decision making for funding transportation projects, *AI & society: Knowledge, Culture and Communication*, doi: 10.1007/s00146-013-0527-2

When collaborative governance scales up: lessons from global public health about compound collaboration

Chris Ansell

Introduction

A disease that has spread across the world represents an enormous governance challenge. It is a challenge to healthcare systems who must deliver medicines and treatment to a remote mountain village lacking roads or electricity. It is a challenge to scientists and firms who must produce effective vaccines at realistic prices. It is a challenge to governments and to donors who must prioritise budgets and raise money to effectively administer disease prevention and treatment programmes. Overarching all these challenges is the challenge of collaboration, because healthcare workers, scientists, private drug companies, government ministers and donors must concert their efforts in order to be effective. A promising new drug cannot be effective unless it can be delivered and it cannot be delivered if the healthcare system has no budget.

Given these challenges of operating on a large scale and at multiple scales, global public health campaigns to slow or eradicate particular diseases are good places to investigate the effects of scale on collaboration. How does collaboration scale up to the global level and how does it scale down to provide support for national and local public health programmes? This chapter examines the experience of three international collaborations created to respond to major diseases – UNAIDS, the Stop TB Partnership, and the Roll Back Malaria Partnership. Each of them has been at least modestly successful in fostering collaboration on a global scale, but their experiences also call attention to the complexities of conducting a concerted global campaign to slow or stop a major disease.

These three global collaborations were selected for investigation for several reasons. First, they represent some of the most serious global diseases. The numbers are, in fact, staggering. In 2012, 35 million people were living with AIDS and 1.7 million died of the disease that year. In the same year, 207 million people contracted malaria and 667,000 died. And there were also 1.2 million deaths from tuberculosis (TB) and 8.3 million

---

95

new cases in 2012.[1] Regarded as both preventable and treatable, these three diseases have hit low-income countries particularly hard (notably Africa), but their scale is clearly global. Controlling them by 2015 was one of the UN's eight Millennium Development Goals.

A second reason to study these three diseases is that each of them led, at approximately the same time, to the formation of a major international partnership charged with orchestrating global collaboration to stop and reverse the disease. UNAIDS was created in 1996, followed by the Roll Back Malaria Partnership in 1998, and the Stop TB Partnership in 2000. These partnerships are structurally similar in many respects and a comparison of them may allow us to draw stronger conclusions about global collaboration.[2] Yet they also represent slightly different institutional models for achieving collaboration. UNAIDS is a unique 'cosponsored' programme of the UN System – a joint programme of 11 UN agencies. The Stop TB Partnership and the Roll Back Malaria Partnership are public–private partnerships. They were both initiatives of the UN's World Health Organization (WHO), are currently hosted by WHO, and have a large number of both public and private partners. They differ, however, in some of the particulars of their governance arrangements.

A third reason to study these three examples of global public health collaboration is that each of them has been subjected to at least two major evaluation studies. These evaluations offer detailed insight into how these partnerships function as collaborative institutions, particularly in terms of governance. Each evaluation team conducted interviews, multiple country visits, and documentary analysis, and some of them also included surveys of stakeholders and observational analysis (see Table 1 for details). Spaced at least five years apart, these evaluations help us to understand the developmental challenges faced by collaboration on a global scale.

One of the points brought into relief by examining these partnerships is that global scale collaboration must really be understood as *compound collaboration*. Each of these three global partnerships tries to facilitate collaboration within countries and between countries, among global institutions, and between global institutions and national and regional collaborations. In addition, they must facilitate cooperation for a diverse set of scientific, technical, financial and administrative needs, with each of them possibly requiring its own distinctive collaborative process. Collaboration on a global scale is, in large part, about aligning multiple forms of collaboration that operate at different geographic and operational scales, which may themselves be composites of various forms of collaboration. As scale increases, so too does the compound nature of collaboration, becoming a *collaboration-of-collaborations*.

Governance and international relations scholars have, of course, been highly attuned to the institutional fragmentation and complexity of contemporary governance for a long time. They have extensively explored the role of governance networks and collaborative governance to address this fragmentation and complexity. Much less attention has been paid, however, to the specific challenges that arise when governance networks or collaborative governance becomes compound in nature. How do we align the efforts of multiple governance networks? How do we collaboratively manage many interdependent forums for collaboration? The discussions of meta-governance in the governance literature (Sørensen and Torfing, 2009) and orchestration in the international relations literature (Abbot and Snidal, 2010) have begun to describe the leadership dimensions of compound governance and the literature on democratic experimentalism (De Burca et al, 2014) offers important insights into the role of general framework goals and reporting and monitoring as a strategy for compound coordination. Yet we still know relatively little about large-scale compound modes of governance.

To explore these issues of scale and compound collaboration, this chapter examines conclusions drawn from the evaluation studies of each of these global collaborations – UNAIDS, the Stop TB Partnership, and the Roll Back Malaria Partnership. As the evaluations reveal, each partnership is complex in structure and function. After presenting a narrative summary of the evaluations for each partnership, a discussion section considers the common features of the cases, with a focus on the common challenges of scale and compound collaboration for in global public health.

UNAIDS

UNAIDS was established in 1996 to provide better coordination to UN efforts to combat AIDS after a 1993 evaluation found the WHO Global Programme on AIDS to be inadequate. With pressure from donors and activists to create a body that would provide stronger leadership for the international response, UNAIDS took the novel form of a 'cosponsored' programme created by a Memorandum of Understanding between UN agencies. One of the key goals of the new programme was to improve the multi-sectoral response to the AIDS epidemic at the country level. The first two to three years of UNAIDS were characterised as 'gathering momentum by cosponsors,' which gradually resulted in a sense of 'joint ownership' by the sponsoring agencies (UNAIDS, 2002, 6).

Table 1: Evaluation studies

Evaluation study	Period analysed	Key elements of study methodology
UNAIDS 2002	1996–2002	Four person core team plus extended country evaluation team; stakeholder workshop to design evaluation; meetings with UNAIDS staff, cosponsors, and donors; telephone and email contact with wide range of NGOs and private sector institutions; 9 country study visits (Argentina, Namibia, Burkina Faso, Mozambique, Trinidad & Tobago, Eritria, India, Indonesia, Ukraine) with interviews, group meetings, and self-evaluation survey
UNAIDS 2008	2002–08	Joint ITAD-HLSP 3 person evaluation team; 3 stakeholder workshops; global and regional meetings; web-based surveys of secretariat/board members (117 responses of 199 contacted) and stakeholders (657 responses of 2000 sent); 12 country visits (Côte d'Ivoire, Democratic Republic of Congo, Ethiopia, Swaziland, Kazakhstan, Ukraine, Iran, India, Indonesia, Vietnam, Peru, Haiti) with semi-structured interviews and focus groups; document analysis
STOP TB 2003	2000–03	Nine member evaluation team from Institute for Health Sector Development; 94 global interviews; 6 country visits (Russia, Cambodia, South Africa, Indonesia, Brazil, Afghanistan); document analysis; meeting observation
STOP TB 2008	2001–06	McKinsey & Co evaluation team; 94 interviews at global level; 8 country visits (Burkina Faso, China, India, Indonesia, Kenya, Morocco, Peru, Uzbekistan) totaling 150 interviews; internet survey of 1336 stakeholders (17% overall response rate); document review; meeting observation
Roll Back Malaria 2002	1998–02	Six member evaluation team chaired by Professor Richard Feachem of Institute for Global Health, University of California, San Francisco and Berkeley; Interviews with partners and stakeholders; 3 country visits (Cambodia, Cameroon, Tanzania); document review
Roll Back Malaria 2009	2004–08	200 stakeholder interviews at global and country level (including 60 current and former board members, working group chairs and members); global and country level surveys (120 global level and 102 country level respondents); document review
Roll Back Malaria 2013	2009–13	Five member evaluation team from Center for Global Health and Development (Boston University); 95 interviews with key informants in 45 institutions; on-line survey of 952 key partners (219 respondents); 4 country visits (Kenya, Zimbabwe, Senegal, Cameroon); document review

The first evaluation of UNAIDS gives it – particularly the Secretariat – credit for advocacy and lobbying that helped to build a deeper consensus around AIDS at the global level (UNAIDS, 2002, xi). It is worth quoting the report on this success, since it offers an important insight:

> Where technical knowledge is uncertain and has complex ramifications…or where the political context denies high-risk groups…or when an entrenched bureaucracy fights multi-sectoralism, the task is much harder. In such an environment, a wise strategy is to obtain agreement on goals and then take a flexible approach to achieving them. That has been the approach of the Secretariat by winning consensus on a global framework. (UNAIDS, 2002, 15, §4.30)

In building this consensus, UNAIDS adopted a strategy of building support from top world leaders, which then trickled down to a greater working consensus at the agency level.

In terms of governance, the UN's Economic and Social Council (ECOSOC) had formal oversight authority over UNAIDS, but strategic direction and oversight fell in practice to two UNAIDS governing bodies – the Committee of Cosponsoring Organizations (CCO) and the Programme Coordination Board (PCB) (UNAIDS, 2002, 38, §6.31). Cosponsors treated the CCO as more of a consultative forum than a decision-making body and, as a result, decision-making eventually shifted to the PCB.

Early fundraising and budgeting efforts were also challenging because cosponsors did not contribute directly to UNAIDS. Thus, a 'consolidated appeal' proved unsuccessful. A programme innovation called the Unified Budget and Work (UBW) Plan, however, did improve coordination by making individual agency budgets and tasks subject to collective approval. This integrated planning process also designated a 'convening agency' to coordinate interagency efforts in different areas (UNAIDS, 2002, 22, §4.60). The Secretariat took responsibility for raising money for this overall budget and work plan, which proved to be a great success because the Secretariat's efforts significantly increased the total pool of money available to the agencies (UNAIDS, 2002, 34, §6.10–12). However, a survey of stakeholders conducted by the second evaluation found that UNAIDS was not as successful in driving the UBW down to the country level (UNAIDS, 2009, 12–13, §2.21).

The first evaluation suggests that UNAIDS made more progress in areas where the Secretariat had direct control over resources and programmes (UNAIDS, 2009, 12, §2.18). The Secretariat also received high marks for serving as the critical broker between the cosponsors. The first evaluation argues that the Memorandum of Understanding had created 'ambiguity and incompleteness' in the roles of the cosponsors. Through the facilitation of the Secretariat, these responsibilities were clarified (UNAIDS, 2002, 35, §6.15) and a survey conducted by the second evaluation found that a majority of stakeholders surveyed felt that progress had been made in clarifying roles (UNAIDS 2009, 12–13, §2.21).

The Secretariat operated according to a hub and spoke model and became the 'primary partner of each of the cosponsors' (2002, 35–6, §6.18). This hub-and-spoke model persisted and the second evaluation describes the Secretariat as 'running separate consultation processes with individual constituencies, but little lateral consultation taking place among the constituencies' (UNAIDS, 2009, 49, §3.52). It also noted that the Secretariat tended to be driven by a crisis management style that encouraged a 'short term' strategic focus (UNAIDS, 2009, 83 §5.43). However, the second evaluation also noted that the Secretariat had created global coordinator positions that served as liaisons between the cosponsors and the Secretariat and that this had been an effective mechanism of coordination.

Despite this growing collaborative success at the global level, meta-governance of country-level UN coordination proved quite challenging (UNAIDS, 2002, ix). UN Agencies maintained separate programmes, facilities, and clients at the country level and these differences made it difficult to produce coordination. The institutional fix for this fragmentation was to create a 'UN theme group' at the country level administered by a resident coordinator (UNAIDS, 2002, 25, §4.74). These groups were generally effective at creating a common forum at country level, but less effective at producing effective programme coordination (UNAIDS, 2002, 26, §4.76). Their ambiguous role in relation to the authority of the line ministries made it difficult for them to be effective in coordinating local programming (UNAIDS, 2002, 26, §4.79).

The theme groups made some progress toward coordination at the country level by creating integrated work plans However, the first evaluation observed that these were ineffectual because they largely fit the programmes of the cosponsors to the national strategies rather than designing for country needs (UNAIDS, 2002, 27, §4.83). Moreover, the evaluation found that the UN system made few efforts to extend participation beyond a limited set of groups (UNAIDS, 2002, 30, §5.4). The second evaluation found that country level teams were still relatively ineffective and that country coordination had not improved significantly since the first evaluation (UNAIDS, 2009, 27, §2.75). Still, the second evaluation notes that UNAIDS had increased its focus on the national level and that the country coordinators were making a significant contribution to country-level coordination (UNAIDS, 2009, 38, §3.6). The UN Secretary General introduced a 'joint team approach' in 2005 to further improve country coordination and provided high level support for it.

The first evaluation found signs of attempts to expand the country-level response to AIDS, but with limited success (UNAIDS, 2002, x). It pointed to a number of barriers to expanded country-level efforts, including: 'the uncertain accountability of the theme groups; the absence of objectively monitorable targets for the theme groups; the limited influence of the [Programme Coordinating Board] over country-level activities and the lack of any incentives for the cosponsors to develop a genuinely integrated approach' (UNAIDS, 2002, xi). On the positive side, country programme advisors (CPA) – who represented the Secretariat at the country level – were found to be critical assets in making progress at the country level. Country visits found that resident coordinators and theme group chairpersons relied on these advisors to advance country efforts. Fifty-six CPAs had been recruited and trained by the end of 2001, with more in the pipeline (UNAIDS, 2002, 36, §6.19).

The second evaluation report notes that from 2003 the Secretariat increasingly used high-level 'country coordinators' to facilitate coordination at the national level. This evaluation also finds evidence of greater country-level UN coordination (UNAIDS, 2009, 64, §4.33). Not surprisingly, leadership was found to be a key factor in the success of joint teams (UNAIDS, 2009, 66, 4.45). A survey of coordinators in 2008 found that progress had been achieved in clarifying a division of labor at the country level. However, the concept of a 'lead agency' at the country level was not clearly working (UNAIDS, 2009, 67, §4.53–4).

One strategy UNAIDS took to facilitate country-level efforts was to encourage countries to develop national strategic plans for fighting AIDS. These plans were intended to bring together public and private actors to identify priorities and strategies for addressing AIDS and were seen as a positive way that UNAIDS could intervene to facilitate greater country-based coordination (UNAIDS, 2002, 24, §4.69). The second evaluation, however, found limited progress at the country level in terms of fulfilling the recommendations of the first evaluation (UNAIDS, 2009, 13, §2.22). It also found that the roles of the Secretariat, UNDP and the World Bank remained unclear in relation to the development of national plans (UNAIDS, 2009, 16, §2.38).

Finally, the first evaluation pointed to the lack of data as a significant factor limiting the expansion of efforts at the country level. It argued that data was a key mechanism of scaling:

Scaling up typically involves both vertical and horizontal processes. Vertical is the development of institutional and policy changes to support the context under which innovations are successful; horizontal is the process of replication. Both require evidence of what works and in what context (effectiveness), and analysis of the resource implications to plan for wider application (efficiency). (UNAIDS, 2002, 31, §5.11)

As a result, UNAIDS has mounted a serious effort to collect and manage data on the pandemic and the second evaluation recognised the Monitoring & Evaluation Reference Group for its work in producing harmonised indicators for monitoring country-level progress (UNAIDS, 2009, xxx). UNAIDS also helped to focus its country-level efforts by adopting a 'three ones' strategy that recognises a single country plan, coordinating body, and monitoring and evaluation (M&E) framework.

Stop TB Partnership

The Stop TB Partnership was created in 2000 in response to concerns about the global resurgence of tuberculosis. The first evaluation generally praises the Stop TB Partnership, observing that it had quickly established itself as a well-respected global health partnership (Stop TB Partnership, 2003, 65, §343–4). It is worth quoting one of the first evaluation's summary judgments about the Partnership's early years:

In terms of relevance and efficiency, it rates extremely high. On efficacy, the Partnership has scored some major achievements in only three years. It has built and is sustaining a broad network of partners; established a partnership architecture which commands broad support; heightened political commitment and marshalled widespread commitment to a detailed Global Plan to Stop TB; made significant progress against TB, even in difficult environments; highlighted work on new diagnostics, drugs and vaccines; and operationalised in a remarkably short time the Green Light Committee for second-line TB drugs and a complex Global Drug Facility covering grant-making, procurement and partner mobilisation for technical assistance for first-line drugs. This is a formidable record. (Stop TB Partnership, 2003, 65, §344)

A notable achievement, according to the evaluation, was bringing together a wide group of diverse actors under a common agenda and strategy – the Global Plan to Stop TB, 2001–05 (Stop

TB Partnership, 2003, 8, §36). The second evaluation noted '[t]he foundation of any effective global public health effort is a common agenda within a unified framework of action' (Stop TB Partnership 2008, 15). The Partnership's 'distinctive contribution,' it noted 'has been in broadening the agenda for tuberculosis control and research, increasing consensus on this agenda, and strengthening guidance for TB control' (Stop TB Partnership, 2008, 15). Thus, like UNAIDS, the Stop TB Partnership successfully brought together partners on a global scale to collaboratively address the global resurgence of TB.

The Partnership's focus on giving 'high burden' countries the responsibility and capacity to control TB has been an effective strategy for building commitment to this global plan. In the past, such countries have not had the capacity to implement successful TB control programmes (Stop TB Partnership, 2003, 10, §47). The Partnership has therefore encouraged the importance of country coordination as a way to improve access, set priorities and build sustainable programmes. The first evaluation notes that 19 of 22 high burden countries had formal coordinating bodies by 2002 (Stop TB Partnership, 2003, 10, §44). The second evaluation generally praises the Partnership's contribution to country-level efforts, but does not directly address the efficacy of country-level coordination.

The Partnership meta-governed the country TB programmes in various ways. Through working groups, it provided technical support and expertise. It has also sought to mobilise 'in-kind support' from partners as a way of keeping costs low for national programmes (Stop TB Partnership, 2003, 10, §47). In 2001, a Memorandum of Understanding between WHO and the Partnership created the Global Drug Facility (GDF) to make TB drugs more accessible and inexpensive for countries. The second evaluation praised the innovative business model of the GDF (Stop TB Partnership, 2008, 33), but also noted that the GDF has not been as effective in getting countries to develop their own sustainable sources of TB drugs (Stop TB Partnership, 2008, 37).

Working Groups are important features of the Partnership and were described in interviews as 'the engines or the pillars of the Partnership' (Stop TB Partnership, 2003, 32, §153). Their activities provide direct support to countries. Several of the Working Groups actually predated the partnership and had their own funding and governance structure; they were then folded into the Partnership with little adaptation to their working arrangements (Stop TB Partnership, 2003, 33, §160). Although the Global Plan provides an overarching framework for the Working Groups, the first evaluation notes that the Global Plan is in fact 'a compilation of individual Working Group work plans rather than a synthesis' (Stop TB Partnership, 2003, 33, §163). The second evaluation concludes that the

Working Groups operated as effective forums and serve a critical role in the Partnership (Stop TB Partnership, 2008, 40–1, 46).

The second evaluation finds that the Secretariat has been effective at coordinating the efforts that went into creating the two Global Plans, though it was less effective in getting partners to articulate their own agendas in relationship to these plans (2008, 29). The first evaluation raises an interesting challenge that global health partnerships face in 'balancing the need for inclusiveness and loosely-knit structures with a necessary minimum of business–like approaches and oversight' (Stop TB Partnership, 2003, 65, §348). The evaluation noted that this tension between loose-knit inclusiveness and a business-like approach had become more pronounced as the Partnership developed. The Partnership succeeded in building a broad-based partnership that grew from seven initial partners to 40 in 2001. But the first evaluation noted 'two recurring themes' in interviews: the need for more business-like operations and more transparent and open governance (Stop TB Partnership, 2003, 65, §348).

The Stop TB Partnership's 'Global Plans' have been praised for establishing a common framework of action on TB (Stop TB Partnership, 2008, 15). The Partnership has also been successful in strengthening technical guidance. Advocacy efforts are also widely recognised as successful at producing sustainable funding for TB control efforts. Country visits by the second evaluation suggested that the Partnership's contributions have produced significant country-level impacts (Stop TB Partnership, 2008, 20–1). The evaluation concludes that the success of the Stop TB Partnership has been facilitated by four factors: a technical consensus established before the Partnership began, but which it successfully built upon; its ability to balance an inclusive, collaborative relationship with partners without infringing on their affairs; its focus on where it could add value to what the partners were already doing; and its effort to bring innovative approaches to bear on TB control (it notes the Global Drug Facility as a prime example). Yet this somewhat 'loose' approach also points to some of the challenges that the Partnership has faced in establishing a clear performance management regime that can be used to drive the success of the overall Partnership (Stop TB Partnership, 2008, 47).

Roll Back Malaria

Roll Back Malaria (RBM) was created in 1998 to respond to the view that prior international programmes had not met expectations and in response to cynicism at the country-level – particularly in Africa – about the possibility of controlling malaria. It has been described as a 'cabinet project' of the then Secretary-General of WHO, Gro Brundtland (Roll

Back Malaria, 2002, 16). The initial founders of RBM – WHO, the World Bank, UNICEF, and UNDP – sought to create a 'broad-based and comprehensive effort to tackle malaria', but they deliberately designed it as a 'loosely constructed' partnership that would preserve the discretion of partners (Roll Back Malaria, 2002, 5, 7). The first evaluation notes that the partnership was successful in mobilising the global community against malaria:

> The most significant accomplishment of Phase I has been that the world has embraced the problem of tackling malaria with renewed vigour and optimism. Against great odds, the Roll Back Malaria movement successfully mobilised the collective efforts of the international agencies, bilaterals, the NGO community and others to promote a 'can-do' attitude that represents a sea-change in perspective compared with the fatalism of just a decade before. (Roll Back Malaria, 2002, 11)

Like UNAIDS and the Stop TB Partnership, RBM helped to build a consensus framework to guide global efforts. The RBM Partnership currently has over 500 partners (Roll Back Malaria, 2013, 7).

Like UNAIDS, the Roll Back Malaria Partnership has also faced significant challenges in meta-governing national Malaria efforts. The first evaluation notes that RBM helped 15 African countries create 'Country Strategic Plans' and upgraded the technical support that the international community brought to countries (Roll Back Malaria, 2002, 14). However, the evaluation also concludes that the RBM's progress at country level was 'suboptimal' (Roll Back Malaria, 2002, 18). In a number of cases, this is because of the low status of malaria programmes within country institutions and the weak institutional links between malaria control programmes and national health planning and institutions, a situation that makes it very difficult to mount ambitious country-level campaigns (Roll Back Malaria, 2002, 19–21, 31, 36).

The first evaluation also notes that 'weaknesses in the global and regional structures' of RBM had hindered its ability to support country-level planning (Roll Back Malaria, 2002, 16). The evaluation links this failure back to the decision to keep the partnership's structures 'loose and somewhat informal' (Roll Back Malaria, 2002, 16). The idea behind this loose and informal conception of the partnership was that it would allow greater flexibility in mobilising and adapting support for a changing situation. However, it also produced 'dissatisfaction and frustration', because the actual meaning and responsibilities of partnership remained ambiguous (Roll Back Malaria, 2002, 16). Most importantly, this arrangement led partners to avoid responsibility and to blame the lead agency – WHO – for failures. The result was that RBM became a 'WHO programme with friends, rather than a true partnership of equals' (Roll Back Malaria, 2002, 16).[3] This situation, in turn, encouraged a unilateral style of decision-making without wide consultation or consensus-building. The evaluation observes that '[t]oday, those involved in RBM, and particularly the core partners, unanimously feel that this model is not appropriate as RBM moves forward' (Roll Back Malaria, 2002, 16).

In response to the negative criticism of the first evaluation, RBM underwent a significant institutional transformation. Its first step was to create a board to govern its activities. In 2005, this board produced a 10-year strategic plan – the Global Strategic Plan 2005–15. In 2006, it went through a significant 'change management' process, creating an Executive Committee, new Working Groups, clarifying the meaning of partnership, and forging a Memorandum of Understanding with WHO. In 2008, RBM issued the Global Malaria Action Plan (GMAP), which was based on partner agreement on universal coverage goals and a goal of eliminating malaria in eight to ten countries by 2015 (Roll Back Malaria, 2009, vii). The plan was developed through a highly collaborative process that incorporated input from countries, international institutions, and experts (Roll Back Malaria, 2013, 9).

A 'harmonised work plan' was also created in 2008 as an operational guide to achieving the GMAP (Roll Back Malaria, 2009, 3–4) and four 'Sub-Regional Networks' (SRNs) were created in Africa to facilitate coordination among country and regional partner organisation (Roll Back Malaria, 2009, 5). The regional networks emerged during the second evaluation period as important institutions for linking the global institutions to country-level efforts. The SRNs were coordinated by an RBM secretariat focal point and hosted by one of the RBM partners (Roll Back Malaria, 2009, 35–6). Although the Partnership's success in delivering technical assistance was still modest, the short missions of the SRNs to aid countries with grant-writing and monitoring were deemed successful (Roll Back Malaria, 2009, 16–18). The third evaluation also concluded that the RBM's sub-regional networks (SRNs) serve a key role in linking global level and country level (Roll Back Malaria, 2013, 27). The evaluation report praises the 'focal point' coordinators of the SRNs, who must operate in contexts characterised by considerable constraint and uncertainty (Roll Back Malaria, 2013, 28).

Although country-level activities still received mixed reviews in the third evaluation, some countries had been successful in establishing country-level partnerships (Roll Back Malaria, 2009, 19). The six country visits by the evaluation team suggested that the National Malaria Country

Programme managers generally worked well with the RBM partnership and they were receiving support from their SRNs (Roll Back Malaria, 2009, 19–20). RBM global partners proved useful to country programmes as interlocutors with the Global Fund or the World Bank and the RBM Executive Director and Secretariat were regarded as valuable country-level advocates (Roll Back Malaria, 2009, 20).

The third evaluation notes that RBM 'prioritised support to in-country planning to scale up and sustain key malarial interventions' (Roll Back Malaria, 2013, 14). It had done this through its Harmonization Working Group and the SRNs, with support from the Secretariat. This finding suggests that RBM had learned from prior evaluations and experiences how to facilitate and mobilise country-level efforts. It had done this in part by supporting a 'three ones' strategy – one national plan, one M&E system, and one coordinating body (Roll Back Malaria, 2013, 14). The third evaluation concludes, however, by stressing the need for RBM to better prioritise its efforts at the country level (Roll Back Malaria, 2013, 41).

The second evaluation credited the RBM reforms with moving the Partnership in a much more positive direction, creating clear roles and responsibilities for partners and governance institutions (Roll Back Malaria, 2009, 27). After overcoming some early challenges with management, the Board achieved wide representation of constituencies and established legitimacy (Roll Back Malaria, 2009, 28). Its growing effectiveness allowed it to negotiate the Global Strategy, 2005–15 and the Global Malaria Action Plan (GMAP). In the third evaluation, the importance of the RBM Board – with its 'remarkable and committed members' – is again noted (Roll Back Malaria, 2013, 22).

During the third evaluation period, the RBM updated its global framework – the Global Malaria Action Plan (GMAP). The third evaluation gives the RBM high marks for advocacy and for keeping malaria a priority issue, which it notes 'is a very important accomplishment given the many competing global health and development priorities' (Roll Back Malaria, 2013, 10). This advocacy kept resources flowing to malaria control – in part, by helping countries to prepare successful Global Fund proposals (Roll Back Malaria 2013, 11). Overall, the evaluation notes that RBM 'has successfully carried out its mandate to Convene, Coordinate, and Facilitate Communication with key stakeholders' which 'has led to a significant contribution to the impressive progress made towards achieving the objectives of the GMAP' (Roll Back Malaria, 2013, 20).

Discussion

UNAIDS, the Stop TB Partnership and the Roll Back Malaria Partnership have each succeeded in establishing collaboration on a global scale. They have successfully mobilised the international community's energies and maintained its focus on three global diseases – AIDS, TB, and Malaria. Each partnership has helped to forge a global strategic consensus on how to halt or eradicate the disease and has generally been successful in coordinating and aligning budgets and programmes of different global partner institutions. The Achilles heel of these global collaborations is country-level coordination, which is perhaps ironic from the perspective of scaling. It seems to be easier to scale up collaboration to the global level than to scale it down to the national or local level.

While the experience of these three partnerships demonstrates the capacity for global scale collaboration, this experience also illustrates the challenges of multi-scale collaboration. It is in fact misleading to see these partnerships as a single collaboration; they are *compound collaborations*. These compound collaborations fit the model of 'orchestration' described by Abbott and Snidal (2010), in the sense that these global public health partnerships operate as intermediaries who indirectly govern national 'target' institutions. These partnerships utilise the techniques of meta-governance described in the literature on network governance to facilitate and steer the country-level efforts (Sørensen and Torfing, 2009) and the mechanisms described by the literature on global democratic experimentalism – broad framework goals and M&E – to try to unify decentralised country-level efforts (De Burca et al, 2014). Compound collaborations utilise a variety of modes of governance.

The evaluations reveal that 'looseness' or 'flexibility' of global public health partnerships is both an advantage and a disadvantage. Where partners have relatively weak commitments to the joint enterprise, where they are highly sensitive about maintaining control over their own programmes and budgets, or where their commitments to the partnership vary significantly, 'loose' partnership arrangements strategically allow for variable commitment and participation and preserve partner sovereignty. Loose arrangements include informal working rules, self-defined levels of member commitment and participation, member-initiated ad hoc projects and broad or ambiguous goals and performance measures. Such loose or flexible arrangements can be a functional organisational property that allows partnerships to get off the ground and move forward with a minimum or variable level of buy-in and joint ownership.

The evaluations also make it clear that loose institutional arrangements are a barrier to deeper and more consequential collaboration. In each case, we therefore see a push to develop tighter organisational arrangements over time. These tighter institutional arrangements lead to greater formalisation of the partnership, clearer specification of partner roles, attempts to encourage more integrated planning processes and joint programming, and more precise specification of goals and performance measures. Table 2 summarises this contrast between loose and tight coupling in global collaboration. The development of each of the global partnerships leads toward tighter coupling, a movement made possible by the deeper buy-in and commitment by partners.

Table 2: Loose–tight principles of global collaborations

	Looser coupling	Tighter coupling
Basis of collaboration	Informal	Formal
Partner roles	Self-defined	Collectively specified
Dominant mode of action	Distributed action	Joint, integrated action
Patterns of coordination	Ad hoc coordination	Programmed
Collective goals	Weakly defined	Well defined
Performance measurement	Weak articulation; poor data collection	Well-articulated; systematic data collection

Tensions between loose and tight coupling can be observed in collaborations operating at any scale, but are magnified in compound collaborations operating at multiple scales. Each scale or mode of collaboration mobilises a certain group of stakeholders with different agendas and relationships. To accommodate this diversity, each scale or mode of collaboration is at least partially self-organising. Looseness is thus inherent in the non-hierarchical nature of compound collaboration. At the same time, looseness will be a very attractive organisational property for managing cooperation among these interdependent, but semi-autonomous collaborations, since strong attempts to prescribe common agendas or rules of action can undermine voluntary participation and cooperation. Yet this looseness also encourages centrifugal tendencies in compound collaborations, making it difficult to generate synergies or common direction in multi-scalar collaboration.

The tensions between loose and tight coupling in global public health partnerships appears to be managed through *focal institutions*. In each global partnership, the evaluations note the key focal role played by the secretariat, a point previously noted in the international relations literature (Abbott and Snidal, 2010). While the partnership board may provide overarching strategic steering, boards themselves are often quite weak where collaborations are loosely structured. This is because board action can bring conflict to the surface and deepen it. As a focusing institution, the secretariat can align the inputs of different partners (or partnership institutions) without exacerbating conflict and thereby build workable coalitions for different tasks.[4] From the perspective of the literature on collaborative governance, the secretariat's play a crucial 'facilitative' role (Ansell and Gash, 2008).

The logic of focal institutions will vary according to variations in the autonomy, commitment and participation of stakeholders. Where stakeholders are sensitive about their sovereignty, distrustful of other stakeholders, or uneven in their commitment to the partnership, a secretariat must play a highly selective role of aligning and building action where it can, often on a relatively ad hoc basis. In the evaluation of UNAIDS, we saw that the secretariat was described as engaging in a 'hub and spoke' relationship with partners. The secretariat engaged in bilateral communication with partners, building support for a common agenda. In general, it was quite successful in doing this, but it was also accused of a reactive style of management that probably reflected the 'shuttle diplomacy' it had to engage in. In the case of UNAIDS, we even see that this practice becomes somewhat formalised in the creation of 'global coordinators' who serve as permanent liaisons between partners and the secretariat. It should not be too surprising that communication and decision-making are not very transparent in this type of situation.

The role of focal institutions can degrade and become self-defeating under some circumstances. In the RBM case, the Partnership was criticised for becoming a 'WHO programme with friends' rather than a true partnership. The evaluation of RBM noted that this situation had the deleterious effect of absolving partners of responsibility for the programme while giving them a platform to criticise the WHO. Collaborative success is therefore likely to depend heavily on the energy and skill of the Secretariat. This may seem almost contradictory, since this point suggests that the more networked and distributed action is, the more the executive action of a single focal actor becomes necessary for getting anything done.[5]

While Secretariats are probably the most important single focal institution in global partnerships, we can also see this focusing and facilitating logic gradually extended much more widely in these compound collaborations. Notably, we see the logic of focal institutions used at the regional and local levels to facilitate country-level coordination. In RBM, sub-regional networks (SRNs) played a key role in helping to align partner actions at the country and regional levels. SRNs were themselves staffed by a 'focal point' coordinator who reported to the global secretariat. As described above, a focal role may be exercised through bilateral hub-and-spoke communication and shuttle diplomacy, especially where open deliberation among Board members accentuates conflict. But the sub-regional networks also suggest an alternative role for focal points. In the case of the SRN's, they were praised for creating a forum for open communication and engagement among local partners. Such a role moves the focal institution beyond bilateral communication and shuttle diplomacy to facilitating multilateral deliberation.

Another interesting lesson from global public health partnerships is related to how commitment in compound collaborations may cascade down from high-level agreements. In each partnership, high-level agreement on goals or strategies was achieved relatively early in the history of the partnership. Although these agreements did not translate easily or immediately into coordinated delivery of services on the ground, they did create important frameworks for operational collaboration. High-level strategic goals also provide the necessary framework for establishing an M&E regime for each partnership, as suggested by the literature on global experimentalist governance (De Burca et al, 2014) An M&E regime is, of course, a way of measuring progress toward the achievement of a partnership's goals. However, the history of each of these Partnerships also suggests that M&E regimes may help to integrate compound collaborations. Common metrics and evaluative tools help to create a common platform for action and coordination. By providing M&E support to country-level collaborations, the partnership helps to integrate countries into the global framework while also helping countries to integrate their own activities.

A final observation is related to the vertical and horizontal integration of global partnerships. Each of the partnerships improved integration and alignment by creating intermediary structures that linked partners and institutions together either vertically, horizontally, or both. UNAIDS created Country Programme Advisors to encourage country-level collaboration and to the link these efforts to the Secretariat. The Stop TB Partnership's Working Groups were described as the 'pillars' of the partnership and Roll Back Malaria's Sub-regional Networks were critical for supporting country-level coordination.

Conclusion

The experiences of UNAIDS, the Stop TB Partnership, and the Roll Back Malaria Partnership each exhibit the challenges of compound collaboration – the need to facilitate collaboration among collaborations. Notably, each partnership must facilitate cooperation of efforts among international institutions in order to provide support to country-level collaborations. Although continuing tensions among international partners is visible in all three cases, each of the partnerships has generally been successful in bringing together its partners around a common strategic framework. These partnerships have also been quite successful in advocating at the global for attention and resources. However, the partnerships face greater challenges in facilitating collaboration at the country-level. This is not really surprising in the sense that global institutions have only a supporting role – and not a direct steering role – at the national level. Yet each of the partnerships appears to have been successful in delivering technical support to country-level efforts, establishing M&E frameworks, and institutionalising some level of cooperation among international partners at the country level.

We can also draw some interesting lessons from the structuring principles of these global partnerships. We see tensions in each of them between loose and tight coupling. The partnerships tend to start out favouring looser coupling because it preserves the autonomy and flexibility of partners. If the coupling is too loose, however, it tends to make collaboration difficult and can create a vicious cycle of disappointment and disengagement. As a result, we see that each of the partnerships responds to early challenges by tightening up partnership arrangements. They do this by formalising relationships, elaborating collective goals, clarifying partner roles and responsibilities, creating mechanisms for joint and integrated action, and establishing clearer performance management systems. These observations suggest that compound collaboration can be conceived in terms of a developmental dynamic conditioned by the commitments of partners to joint programming.

These cases also suggest that tight coupling can only go so far as a solution because partners still want to preserve their autonomy and flexibility. The experience of these partnerships suggest that focal institutions are an intermediate solution that manages between loose and tight coupling. The most important focal institution is the secretariat, which can help to align the agendas of different partners and governance bodies. If partner demand for autonomy and flexibility is high, the Secretariat may engage in a 'hub and spoke' relationship with partners, communicating bilaterally with partners and running shuttle diplomacy between them. This may be effective, but can also lead to a reactive, crisis-oriented style of management. However, we also saw some hints that focal institutions may also encourage multilateral deliberation. Finally, we saw that the logic of focal institutions can be extended more widely throughout the partnership. Country-level collaboration can also be facilitated through focal points and these focal points can in turn be aligned with the Secretariat. Focal institutions are therefore an important mechanism for addressing the challenges of large-scale compound collaboration.

Notes

[1] World Health Organization website, MDG 6: Combat AIDS, Malaria, and Other Diseases.

[2] The Stop TB Partnership, and the Roll Back Malaria Partnership exemplify 'global public–private partnerships', (GPPPs) which have become an important institutional mechanism for delivering global public goods, particularly in the field of public health (Buse and Walt, 2002; Börzel and Risse, 2005; Buse and Harmer, 2007; Buse and Tanaka, 2011). Buse and Walt define global health partnerships as 'collaborative relationships that transcend national boundaries and bring together at least three parties – among them a corporation or industry association and an intergovernmental organisation – so as to achieve a shared, health-creating goal on the basis of a mutually agreed and explicitly defined division of labor' (2002, 171). UNAIDS is not strictly a 'public–private partnership', since it is formally a public partnership of UN agencies. However, it partners with private groups (Buse and Walt, 2000) and is seen as a particularly good example of the UN system's increasing embrace of multistakeholder processes that incorporate NGOs and civil society into policy-making processes (Dodds, 2002).

[3] This erosion of a partnership as the result of becoming too narrowly identified with 'WHO' can also be seen in the Global Outbreak Alert and Response Network (Ansell et al, 2012).

[4] Such an organisational role is sometimes referred to as a 'bridging' or 'boundary' organisation (Brown, 1991; 1993; Lawrence and Hardy, 1999; Berkes, 2009).

[5] However, Provan and Kenis's (2008) discussion of the importance of network administrative organisations and lead organisations provides useful insights here.

References

Abbott, KW, Snidal, D, 2010, International regulation without international government: Improving IO performance through orchestration, *The Review of International Organizations* 5, 3, 315–44

Ansell, C, Gash, A, 2008, Collaborative governance in theory and practice, *Journal of Public Administration Research and Theory* 18, 4, 543–71

Ansell, C, Sondorp, E, Stevens, RH, 2012, The promise and challenge of global network governance: The global outbreak alert and response network, *Global Governance: A Review of Multilateralism and International Organizations* 18, 3, 317–37

Berkes, F, 2009, Evolution of co-management: Role of knowledge generation, bridging organizations and social learning, *Journal of Environmental Management* 90, 5, 1692–702

Börzel, TA, Risse, T, 2005, Public–private partnerships: Effective and legitimate tools of international governance, Grande, E, Pauly, LW, (eds), *Complex sovereignty: On the reconstitution of political authority in the 21st century*, pp 195–215, Toronto: University of Toronto Press

Brown, LD, 1991, Bridging organizations and sustainable development, *Human relations* 44, 8, 807–31

Brown, LD, 1993, Development bridging organizations and strategic management for social change, *Advances in Strategic Management* 9, 381–405

Buse, K, Harmer, AM, 2007, Seven habits of highly effective global public–private health partnerships: Practice and potential, *Social Science and Medicine* 64, 2, 259–71

Buse, K, Tanaka, S, 2011, Global public–private health partnerships: Lessons learned from ten years of experience and evaluation, *International dental journal* 61, s2, 2–10

Buse, K, Walt, G, 2000, Global public–private partnerships: Part I – A new development in health?, *Bulletin of the World Health Organization* 78, 4, 549–61

Buse, K, Walt, G, 2002, The World Health Organization and global public–private health partnerships: In search of 'good' global health governance, in M Reich (ed) *Public–private: Partnerships for public health*, pp 169–95, Cambridge, MA: Harvard Center for Population and Development Studies

De Burca, G, Keohane, RO, Sabel, C, 2014, Global experimentalist governance, *British Journal of Political Science* 44, 3, 477–86

Dodds, F, 2002, The context: Multi-stakeholder processes and global governance, in M Hemmati (ed) *Multi-stakeholder processes: Beyond deadlock and conflict*, pp 26–38, London: Earthscan

Lawrence, TB, Hardy, C, 1999, Building bridges for refugees: Toward a typology of bridging organizations, *The Journal of Applied Behavioral Science* 35, 1, 48–70

Provan, KG, Kenis, P, 2008, Modes of network governance: Structure, management, and effectiveness, *Journal of Public Administration Research and Theory* 18, 2, 229–52

Roll Back Malaria, 2002, *Final report of the external evaluation of Roll Back Malaria*, www.rollbackmalaria.org/cmc_upload/0/000/015/905/ ee_toc.htm

Roll Back Malaria, 2009, Independent evaluation of the Roll Back Malaria Partnership 2004–2008, Final evaluation report, Prepared by Dahlberg, Global Development Advisors, 30 September, Geneva: Roll Back Malaria

Roll Back Malaria, 2013, *External evaluation of the Roll Back Malaria (RBM) Partnership 2009–2013*, Submitted to the RBM Secretariat 31 December, Boston, MA: Boston University Center for Global Health and Development

Sørensen, E, Torfing, J, 2009, Making governance networks effective and democratic through metagovernance, *Public administration* 87, 2, 234–58

Stop TB Partnership, 2003, Independent external evaluation of the global Stop TB Partnership, Submitted by the Institute for Health Sector Development, December, Geneva: Stop TB Partnership

Stop TB Partnership, 2008, *Independent evaluation of the Stop TB Partnership*, Final report, McKinsey and Company, 21 April, Geneva: Stop TB Partnership

UNAIDS, 2002, Five year evaluation, Final report, UNAIDS/PCB(13)/02.2, Geneva: UNAIDS

UNAIDS, 2009, *UNAIDS second independent evaluation 2002-2008*, Final Report, UNAIDS/PCB(25)/09.18, 2 October, Geneva: UNAIDS

The 'Milky Way' of intermediary organisations: a transnational field of university governance

Kerstin Sahlin, Filip Wijkström, Lisa Dellmuth,
Torbjörn Einarsson and Achim Oberg[1]

A transnational network of university governance

In recent decades, we have witnessed a profound transformation of what is now commonly perceived to be a global university field (for example, Drori et al, 2012; Frank and Meyer, 2007). Universities are typically governed and financed within national systems of higher education and they differ widely in terms of type (for example, private or public) and funding structure. The governing, performance monitoring, and organisation of universities varies considerably locally yet follows global themes (Ramirez, 2010; Hedmo et al, 2006; Sahlin, 2013). Furthermore, the wider global university field is shaped by transnational networks and collaborative arenas of governance (see Beech, 2009; 2011; Maasen and Olsen, 2007; Ramirez, 2012; Krücken and Meier, 2006): a growing number of transnational intermediary organisations form important arenas for actors from different countries that compare and assess universities, and form as well as translate ideas for how to manage universities and measure university performance (for example, Sahlin, 2013). This chapter focuses on the role and position of transnational intermediary organisations. Typically, those intermediary organisations are actively involved in transnational university governance without having formal access to or control over policy or governmental funding. Intermediaries can be placed, analytically, between those who aim to govern and those who are governed. In this position, these organisations function as organisational bridges between these two different communities. This chapter conceptualises transnational intermediaries and provides systematic empirical evidence for the importance of intermediaries in the scaling up of collaborative governance.

The growing importance and complexity of transnational governance has received increased scholarly attention during the last decade. Especially since the end of the cold war, the diversity of actors involved in global governance has increased, ranging from multinational corporations, professional associations, to non-governmental organisations (NGOs). These actors differ widely in terms of functions. Broadly speaking, they 'create issues, set agendas, establish and implement rules or programs, and evaluate and/or adjudicate outcomes' (Avant et al, 2010, 10). Moreover, transnational governance is highly organised (Drori et al, 2009, 17). Organisations have emerged and risen in both number and activity worldwide to the extent that our contemporary society has been described as 'the organised society' (Perrow, 1991; 2002; see also Meyer and Bromley, 2013). Particularly noteworthy is the continuous growth of international organisations (for example, Boli and Thomas, 1997; Drori et al, 2009). This is especially true for international non-governmental organisations, whose members largely comprise a mix of governmental units, corporations and NGOs and various nonprofit and voluntary associations (for example, Tallberg et al, 2013). Transnational governance also tends to be organised in the sense that the links and relations among those many and different organisations are largely organised in the form of transnational networks (Torfing, 2012; Marcussen and Torfing, 2007).

Transnational networks transcend national boundaries, even if governmental bodies and intergovernmental bodies constitute important parts of those networks. A defining characteristic of transnational networks is, as argued by Djelic and Sahlin (2011), the blurring of the distinction between national and international, governmental and non-governmental, public and private. This blurring of boundaries between sectors was identified by Stoker (1998) who identified it as a defining characteristic for our understanding of governance, as there is a 'baseline agreement that governance refers to the development of governing styles in which boundaries between and within public and private sectors have become blurred' (Stoker, 1998, 17). In this way, transnational networks form core parts of a mode of governance that relies on mechanisms not directly associated with state authority or sanctioning power (see also Risse, 2012). Not only actors and organisational boundaries, but also modes and mechanisms of governing tend to be blurred and to rely on combinations of authorities. Such modes of governance have been shown to follow complex patterns of an interplay between soft and hard law (Mörth, 2004) and between ideational norms and financial measures (Avant et al, 2010; Finnemore and Sikkink, 1998), and of the linking between rules, to each other, to organising and to expertise (Djelic and Sahlin-Andersson 2006).

In this chapter we used a web-crawler technique to map transnational intermediaries concerned with higher education and research, and their linkages with each other. We created an original data set of more than 400 intermediary organisations active in the global university field during 2014. Based on network analysis of these data, we argue that these transnational intermediaries form an organised field of their own, where actors are attuned to and interact with each other based on a shared understanding of the field, its rules and actors as well as agreement among the actors of what is at stake. This implies that they together perform important roles in the travelling and translation of global themes for how to govern and define universities, and that they are crucial for the scaling up of transnational collaborative governance. Against the backdrop of existing literature, the broader purpose of our analysis is to open up an agenda for the future study of fields of transnational intermediaries.

The remainder of this chapter proceeds as follows. The ensuing section develops a conceptualisation of intermediary organisations. The following section briefly describes the globalised university landscape and the importance of and interactions between transnational intermediaries by drawing on previous studies about the globalised university field. We then present the analytical framework of organised fields, followed by an account of the methods applied in this project, and the empirical results. The concluding section expands on the broader implications of our empirical results for existing research on transnational networks and future research on intermediaries in collaborative governance.

Transnational intermediaries

Previous studies have highlighted a large array of normative and ideational functions of different types international organisations, pertaining to the diffusion of norms and ideas (Boli and Thomas, 1997; 1999; Finnemore, 1993; Finnemore and Sikkink, 1998; Reuter et al, 2014; Marcussen, 2000; 2004; Brunsson and Jacobsson 2000). International organisations largely reflect what is happening in a particular field, but they also shape and disseminate ideas and conceptualisations, establish and strengthen core institutions and they are important meeting places of the field. John Meyer has used the term 'others' to describe the features and functions of these organisations, paving the way for research on such organisations and their role in processes of idea circulation and transnational governance:

> Others, in this scheme loosely derived from George Herbert Mead, do not take action responsibility for organisational behavior and outcomes. They discuss, interpret, advise, suggest, codify, and sometimes pronounce and legislate. They develop, promulgate, and certify some ideas as proper reforms, and ignore and stigmatise other ideas. Who are these Others, and why are there so many of them, out there in the modern organisational environment? (Meyer, 1996, 244)

Subsequent studies built on Meyer's distinction and focused on those kinds of 'other- organisations' and on their role in transnational governance, and in the circulation of ideas. Terminology, however, has shifted. Such organisations have been termed 'carriers', in analyses of how they promote and circulate management ideas (Sahlin-Andersson and Engwall, 2002), and 'editors', in analyses of how they not only promulgate, certify and circulate ideas, but also how they edit those ideas as they circulate them (Sahlin-Andersson, 1996; Sahlin and Wedlin, 2008). The role of such organisations in the transfer, translation and editorial work has also been noted in research on university governance (for example, Beech, 2011; Sahlin and Wedlin, 2008; Drori et al, 2012).

Terminologies differ, but a common result from the above cited studies is that organisations that circulate, edit and mediate ideas are important in the formation of organised fields and in governance. We conceive of such organisations as intermediary organisations. The conceptualisation as intermediaries emphasises these organisations' spanning function and their role in bringing together and scaling up collaborative governance and networks (for a similar argument in global environmental governance, see Andonova and Mitchell, 2010).

Based on the previous research cited above, we argue that many transnational organisations play important roles as intermediaries: they develop ideas and norms; span organisational and national boundaries; and develop more globalised and rationalised cultures of university governance and university development. Through a better understanding of these organisations' roles and relationships with each other as well as other actors we can understand the governance dynamics in the wider, globalised university field. Yet previous works have been predominantly qualitative case studies of specific actors, global themes, or the growth of international organisations, failing to provide systematic knowledge about who these actors are and how they are linked to each other.

Intermediaries do not control or make ultimate decisions about policy, such as the allocation of resources or the shaping of legal frameworks. Neither do they possess the formal authority to compel compliance with different forms of regulatory systems. Rather, intermediaries function as organisational arenas in the transnational networks of university governance, bridging governing actors and governed institutions. Intermediary organisations also represent and develop various interests with stakes in the transnational governance network, that is, they are actors in their own interest and capacity. These interests may be rooted in the values or interests of the members or constituencies of the individual intermediary, yet intermediary organisations can also be expected to develop an interest in their own organisational survival, growth and position in the field.

An old observation in organisation theory is that organisations tend to develop an interest in their own survival and growth (for example, Selznick, 1949), and stabilise and formalise over time. Studies of intermediary organisations in the particular area of business schools have clearly shown that such dynamics are at play and partly explain some of the recent expansion of evaluation and monitoring schemes (Hedmo, 2004; Hedmo et al, 2006). These observations suggest that organisational activities and relations among intermediaries form important dynamics in the transnational governance of universities. Traditional examples of intermediaries in the university field are intergovernmental organisations; academic associations; assessing, ranking and accreditation agencies; think tanks, university networks and umbrella organisations consisting of, created by and for universities; and associations of industry, student and professional interests. These organisations are increasingly hybrid in their character as they cross and span different societal spheres and combine as well as merge those sector logics; that is, civil society, the private and public sectors (see Wijkström, 2011) and they also form boundary spanners across these societal sectors (see Hedmo and Sahlin-Andersson, 2006).

A global university landscape in transition

Universities worldwide have been reorganised in terms of organisation and management, largely inspired by globally diffused ideas. Extended demands are put on higher education and research to contribute to policy and to innovation and growth. The latter are concepts that are increasingly used by many national governments. This development has analytically been described in terms of universities having become increasingly rationalised at the same time as they are being increasingly embedded in society (for example, Ramirez, 2006; 2010; see also Maasen and Olsen, 2007). Global debates also show an increased demand for academic excellence, and 'blue sky' research, with intermediary organisations playing a crucial role for the diffusion of related ideas. We use these examples to illustrate that global themes and ideas on university governance are far from coherent and unidirectional.

The described developments are global in scope, and indeed, one of the most important transformations of the entire landscape of higher education and research is its increased degree of transnationalisation. Universities have of course from the very beginning worked in a highly global context and partly also been governed and controlled by a global regulatory framework. Today, however, new global themes of organising, governing and performance measurements largely transform the conditions for research and higher education in a more systematic and profound way. The on-going transnationalisation of the university landscape is influenced by widely circulated themes.

One such global theme that has evolved and circulated globally is that of university rankings. Studies of this global theme show the importance of a multitude of transnational intermediaries for spreading those ideas and ideals (see Sahlin, 2013). Rankings have come to be part of the broader frame of governance of universities and have at the same time spurred extensive organising efforts, among individual universities as well as among and between intermediary organisations. The spread of rankings have certainly been pursued by a multitude of interlinked intermediaries, and with this development intermediary organisations have developed links with each other.

Field models in organisational analysis

In the previous sections, we referred to previous research showing that intermediary organisations are crucial in transnational governance networks. Apart from having close linkages with those aiming to govern and those who are governed, intermediaries are connected with each other in many different ways. They compete with each other, but also collaborate and they imitate each other. This leads us to expect that the importance of intermediary organisations is largely due to interlinkages among them. With such dense linkages among intermediaries, they can be expected to form a recognisable field of their own.

What, then, is a field? How can it be conceptualised and mapped? Field models have a long history in the social sciences, although with slightly different emphasis in different traditions and disciplines (Lewin, 1951; Bourdieu, 1977; 1984; Meyer and Rowan, 1977; DiMaggio and Powell, 1983). A more strategic approach to organised fields has recently been developed by Fligstein and McAdam (2011; 2012) in their work on 'strategic action fields'.

Following Martin's (2003) and Mohr's (2005) overviews of field models in social sciences, Djelic and Sahlin-Andersson (2006) noted that in practice, many studies tend to reduce fields to networks of actors and interactions. However, field models typically emphasise that fields involve structured patterns of interaction as well as a meaning dimension – common beliefs in the importance of certain activities and a mutual awareness of what is at stake. Moreover, as emphasised by DiMaggio and Powell (1983, 148) 'The structure of an organisational field cannot be determined a priori but must be defined on the basis of empirical investigation.'

Building on this definition of a field, the following sections of this chapter analyse the field of transnational university governance intermediaries empirically. Our working hypothesis is that a large number of intermediary organisations is active in university governance, forming a recognisable organised field of their own, where the organisations are attuned to and interact with each other based on a shared understanding of this particular field, its rules and actors as well as a kind of agreement among the actors of what is at stake. Within this intense exchange, we also expect an active global circulation of norms, themes and ideas, with implications for national university systems and individual universities.

The empirical study

To map the transnational intermediaries and their linkages with each other, we use an original web-crawler technique. Using this technique, we map the links between websites of intermediaries. Such links can indicate interactions as well as mutual awareness and referencing. Hence, mapping their connections encompasses both aspects of field models – meaning and interaction.

To identify the population of intermediaries active in transnational university governance, we compiled a data set on organisations from a combination of sources. Our data collection strategy proceeded in several steps. To begin with, we derived data on 82 organisations defined as active in what is described as 'higher education' in the *Yearbook of international organizations* (Union of International Associations, 2014). The Yearbook is the largest and most encompassing catalogue of international organisations to date. The list of these 82 organisations encompasses active organisations that are not subsidiary or internal bodies of other international organisations.

This catalogue, however, does not capture all the organisations active in global university governance that we are seeking. To identify the population of intermediaries, we therefore used the list of organisations identified through the Yearbook as a starting point for a second-level mapping that relied on an iterative combination of a web-crawling technique and extensive manual data cleaning. Using this technique, we identified organisations through existing links on the web pages of the set of the 82 already identified organisations (the so-called 'seed' organisations) to web pages of other organisations. This snowballing technique is based on the assumption that the links that the 82 'seed' organisations provide on their web pages to other organisations' web pages are indicators for interaction and recognition between these organisations, thereby identifying other relevant organisations in the population. We ran the web-crawler and received a set of 19,795 domains referenced by the seed organisations.

In order to reduce the amount of irrelevant domains that are characterised by weak recognition by other organisations in the field, a cut-off limit of at least four incoming links to the domain were used in order for a new organisation to be included in the material. This resulted in a total list of 2,915 web domains, for which the webpages were analysed for signs of any kind of intermediary function at transnational level. This list included domains owned by intermediaries and other organisations in the university field, that is, close to our target group, but the list also contained many domains belonging to other types of organisations and different forms of web services, such as Facebook and Google. We manually inspected and evaluated each of the 2,915 candidate domains and kept only those 654 domains belonging to an organisation with a distinct relation to higher education or research and an indication of some kind of intermediary function. The purpose of the manual sorting and cleaning of the results yielded by the web-crawling technique was to arrive at a stable valid data set, while simultaneously ensuring a reliable data collection process.

This selection procedure obviously involved judgements regarding where to draw the boundary of the field; below we briefly describe how three such boundary considerations were handled. A first judgement concerned which organisations should be considered to be intermediaries. The majority of organisations on the list are the typical kinds of intermediary organisations as described above; they are actively involved in transnational university governance without having formal access to or control over the funds and legislation in the field. However, all relevant organisations are not single-purpose organisations, but many display a broad palette of functions, roles and activities. The decision was made to include all those organisations that clearly included intermediary functions in their presentations. This meant that the list also includes a limited number of organisations that primarily operate as research funding bodies, such as the British Council, Volkswagenstifung and The German Foundation (DFG). These three organisations can also exemplify boundary judgements of a second type, namely which organisations to define as transnational. Here, our web-crawling process was used as the selection criterion. As described above, we included in the field those intermediary organisations that on their website had at least four links with other organisations in the identified transnational field. A third boundary judgement prescribed which organisations should be considered as included in the field of transnational university governance, as opposed to other fields of society. In this respect, we excluded general domains, such as Facebook and Google, but also included some addresses that were not specific for university governance, such as the World Bank and the Organisation for Economic Co-operation and Development (OECD). Although these latter international organisations are actively involved in the university governance field, this is not their only or even primary field of interest as they are also active in other fields (see, for example, Marcussen, 2000; 2004; Avant et al, 2010).

In the final step of the data collection, we ran the web-crawler again for the 654 domains of intermediary organisations to collect all references between these organisations and kept only those organisations whose webpages yield both out-going and in-going references to and from other actors in the field. Furthermore, we increased the required number of ties to five or more and thus created a core set of 451 intermediary organisations, among which we were able to identify the pattern of linkages and the key players. This data collection strategy resulted in a networked population of intermediaries identified as the primary organisations of the transnational field of university governance.

The transnational field of intermediaries in university governance

This section presents the empirical results. We briefly describe the identified set of intermediaries and we present maps to display their mutual linkages. These maps, we argue depicts a core network of intermediaries within the field of transnational university governance.

A variety of organisational types and sectors

A first finding is that the 451 intermediary organisations in our data set represent a variety of types and that their many constituents come from different sectors in society. In terms of legal and organisational form, most intermediaries are NGOs with voluntary membership. The members or other forms of constituents are primarily either governmental, public agencies or other state bodies or they come from civil society, including interest organisations such as student unions, professional associations, scholarly societies and trade unions. We have identified a few corporations as members, although this is not a major component in our material. We further find a smaller number of intergovernmental organisations and also nationally-based organisations with clear transnational agendas. The intermediate organisations are largely hybrid in form as they span different societal sectors, for example, crossing the public–private divide or mediating between state and civil society.

The 'Milky Way' of intermediaries

The remainder of this section is confined to the mapping and analysis of the linkages among the identified intermediaries. More specifically, our analysis proceeds in three steps. First, we start with the population of 451 well-connected intermediary organisations with web links to other intermediaries on their webpages, where both organisations recognise each other. In total, 1,640 such bi-directional ties were identified within this system, where the size of the node in Figure 1 represents the total number of bi-directional ties for each node or organisation (the average number being 7.27). As described above, the bi-directional links are seen to signify interactions and/or mutual recognition between the intermediaries. Hence, we understand this network of nodes and ties to portray the core organisations in an organised transnational field of intermediaries. The field has no obvious single centre but instead a set of kept-together organisational constellations, illustrated in the stretched-out structure of the field with several more densely connected cores and some lesser but still well connected satellite organisations in the periphery (see Figure 1).[2] Our initial analysis indicates a field with a structure resembling a 'Milky Way' in view of the large number of organisations, the diversity in the field and the intense mutual recognition among the transnationally active university intermediaries. The high number of salient nodes in the pattern illustrates the intensity of mutual recognition among the many organisations in the field. Further, the stretched-out character of the field is due to more complex patterns of recognition among the organisations affecting the internal field structure (see next section).

Among the most recognised organisations in the field, we observe such organisations as the European University Association (EUA), the Academic Cooperation Association, but also an organisation like RePEc (Research Papers in Economics) run by scholars themselves serving as volunteers, and the World Bank (see also Appendix on core intermediaries). These examples illustrate well the spread and diverse character of the intermediaries involved in transnational university governance.

The core of the field

The initial analysis (illustrated in Figure 1) contains all 451 organisations that had at least one bidirectional reference to another intermediary organisation. In a second step we decided to increase the required number of bidirectional links to other actors to five or more to enhance the likelihood to identify the core of the field. This new core of the field comprises 243 organisations and the stretched-out Milky Way character is sustained (see Figure 2).

Figure 1: The 'Milky Way' of transnational university intermediaries

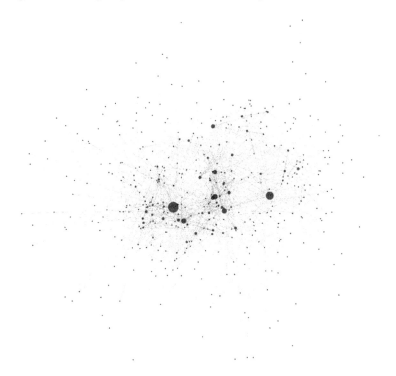

Nodes Intermediaries within the largest component (N = 451)
Relations   Bi-directional ties of intermediaries on the WWW (N = 1640)
Node size   Number of bi-directional ties (average degree = 7.27)

In total, 1,208 bi-directional relations among these 243 core organisations were identified and the average number of ties has now increased to 9.94 ties (from earlier 7.27). Each organisation thus has several links with others in the field. On the basis of this finding, we argue that these intermediary organisations recognise each other and can be expected to interact with each other. When it comes to the structure of the field, this core population of organisations remains stretched out in the same way as the field as a whole.

Figure 2: The core of the transnational field of university intermediaries

A structure of inter-connected sub-clusters

In a third step we have visualised how the inter-organisational linkages are distributed throughout the field (see Figure 3). With this visual analysis we were able to identify four main clusters containing more densely related and linked organisations.

In Figure 3, we can observe the very same 243 intermediaries also displayed in Figure 2, with the same number of ties (and an average of 9.94 ties per node). To enhance the analysis, we have, however, chosen to highlight the four potential clusters in the illustration and also add organisational labels for those of the core organisations that have 15 or more bi-directional ties, thus being even stronger recognised by the other intermediaries and potentially central organisations in the field (for lists of the most central intermediaries for each of the clusters, see Appendix).

Interestingly, we are able to identify fairly distinct features of each such cluster. To begin with, in the south-east/lower-right corner of the figure, we find a cluster where the organisations are centred around the European Union (EU). This is also the intermediary cluster with highest internal density with respect to the number of ties in-between organisations. We

Figure 3: Four clusters in the transnational field of university governance

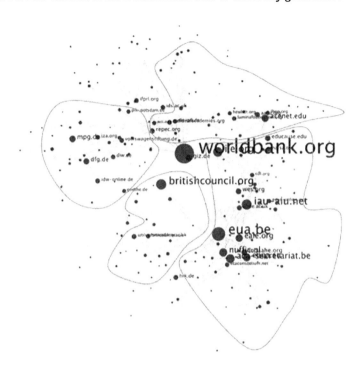

find a high degree of Brussels-based intermediaries at the very core of this cluster. Moreover, two of the other clusters contain a large number of organisations based in Europe, whereby one (north-east/upper-right corner) encompasses several organisations primarily based in Germany while the other (south-west/lower-left corner) instead is dominated by UK-based intermediaries. The fourth cluster, finally, resides in the north-west/upper-left corner of the illustration and contains a fair deal of organisations perhaps best described as 'international'. In each of the clusters we are able to identify a number of intermediaries that are more central than the others and the multi-centred structure of the field is thus confirmed.

Yet, the four sub-clusters are linked with each other through many linkages and in addition through a handful of intermediaries that link with all four sub-clusters but are themselves rather positioned between them. Among them we find one organisation that stands out in the material and represent something like a mother-hub in the field, namely the World Bank. The World Bank has several different web pages and web addresses for different parts or programmes of the organisation, and those were in the project technically merged manually as one single umbrella website for the continued analysis. This particular organisation exhibits a large number of ties with other actors in the field, as indicated by the sheer size of the node in the illustration (see Figure 3). What is more important, however, is that the World Bank cannot easily be subsumed into one or the other cluster through a denser set of ties with a particular cluster. Neither can the World Bank be said to serve as the centre of the field with its still polycentric character. The special position of the organisation as and interlinking node across the clusters in the field is, however, stable as it has more or less equally strong ties with members of all the four identified clusters and it is thus positioned in a unique in-between role potentially bridging the clusters.

Discussion and conclusions

This chapter uses the concept of intermediaries to direct our attention to the many organisations that populate the intermediate space between the many actors of the transnational governance field and between those who aim to govern and those who are governed. Intermediaries largely reflect what is happening in the field, but they also shape and disseminate ideas and conceptualisations, establish and strengthen institutions and they are important meeting places and boundary spanners of the field. This chapter takes the first steps in developing systematic knowledge on the roles and relations of such intermediary organisations, adding new knowledge about intermediary organisations and transnational networks of governance.

To begin with, our literature review showed the importance of intermediaries in disseminating global themes and ideas that shape policies and measures among governing bodies, universities and other research and higher education institutions. Furthermore, previous research has pointed to the expansion of intermediary organisations and their close linkages with each other, leading to the working hypothesis that intermediaries form an organised field of their own. To examine this hypothesis empirically, we created a dataset of intermediaries through an original method that builds, first, on primary information on organisations in the *Yearbook of international organizations*, and, second, identifies web-links to other intermediaries through stepwise web-crawlings.

Our empirical analysis yielded three main findings. First, we found a surprisingly large number of intermediary organisations that operate in the transnational network of university governance. The organisations in our data come in different types and forms, and span various societal sectors, such as civil society and the public sector. Our second finding confirms the working hypothesis that intermediaries are closely linked with each other. We took these links to indicate mutual recognition and interaction among and between the intermediaries. In this respect, intermediary organisations form an organised field of their own. A third finding is that this field exhibits a multi-centred and stretched-out structure, which we refer to as a 'Milky Way' pattern.

When manually scrutinising all websites, we could confirm that most organisations in our dataset are exclusively working with intermediary functions; they evaluate, coordinate, observe and seek to influence policy. However, some are also funding research and performing research themselves, others are clearly operating nationally while some are only partly active in the wider university field. These organisations were included in our dataset as they have sub-domains or exhibit additional roles that more clearly address intermediary functions in the field of transnational university governance.

A combination of continued web-crawlings and more qualitative cases studies of individual organisations and global themes will lead us to increased knowledge of the transnational field of intermediaries, their complex intra-organisational designs and, finally, also about their relations with other actors in transnational networks of governance.

Within this transnational field of intermediaries we identified a number of clusters or groups of organisations, possibly explaining some of the elongated structure of the field. These clusters seem to be geographically determined. Within each of these clusters, we identified a number of organisations with a more central position than the others. Further research will address the question why this is so. Is it simply because it is easier to mingle with nearby friends or are there deeper and more meaningful differences between the clusters? Could it be that the different clusters actually are dealing with or prioritising different issues or do they have different views on certain questions?

One of the clusters was clearly centred around Brussels. In this cluster, organisations can be expected to have close interactions with the European Union (EU), and in fact may be dependent on the EU for resources, legitimacy and attention. This finding points to promising avenues for future research on the development of the European Union and its impact. What is important is that to enhance our understanding of intermediaries, future studies could investigate whether intermediaries strengthen the voice of researchers, universities and professional bodies vis-à-vis the EU and other political institutions. Furthermore, future research could examine when and how intermediaries form venues to influence the European Union and other political bodies. Do intermediaries in other words contribute to an increased politicisation of the university field (see de Wilde and Zürn, 2012; Zürn et al, 2012)?

Interestingly, a number of organisations in central positions within the field appear, but without an obvious place in any of the identified clusters. They form nodes where sub-clusters of the field are interlinked. This observation indicates a potential structure of transnational governance sub-networks with dense regional clusters, embedded in and interlinked with other regional clusters. The European region is a special case – densely populated by intermediary organisations and many links among them.

This chapter provides a first glance of the field of transnational intermediaries active in the governance of universities, yet our inquiry is also characterised by limitations that point to potential future research. To begin with, the dataset may exhibit a European bias as the *Yearbook of international organizations* is Europe-based. We sought to control for this bias through the web-crawling and manual sorting of the lists. However, limitations in terms of mapping the hubs as well as the links between the organisations remain. The European bias in the *Yearbook* could still have some importance. Another bias concerns language. We can, for example, assume a number of Asian organisations with non-English websites and references among themselves. Clearly these fall outside our data. Furthermore, we cannot see ties that may develop 'under the radar' and informally without being reflected in links on the websites. Moreover, certain organisations might rather link to their 'preferred partners' in the field only, while just writing the names of (or completely omit mentioning) organisations with which they do not share the same ideas or even are in conflict, thus running the risk of reducing the field to only the like-minded. If this would be carried out systematically throughout the field, even with a relevant original set of organisations to start with, it would result in several clusters in the relevant 'web-crawler universe' without any ties in-between the clusters. These limitations suggest that future research would need to develop with extended web-crawling combined with qualitative studies of individual organisations, clusters and global themes.

We conclude by pointing at how our data set can be developed to explore four additional questions that follow from the cited literature on intermediaries, organised fields and transnational governance. First, previous studies have indicated an almost exponential growth of international non-governmental organisations, many of which we have defined to be pursuing intermediary functions. In subsequent work, we will be able to add more dynamic data to our dataset, most immediately by adding dates of when the different organisations in the field were founded. Second, studies of global governance have shown the multitude and diverse sets of actors involved in global governance. By coding our data according to type of actor and type of activities in which they involve, further empirical research will systematically show this diversity and also be able to map the hybridity of the field. Of specific interest will be to study the existing private–public links and overlaps in this particular field in more detail, not least related to ongoing discussions and research on the many aspects of privatisation of higher education and research. And last, one main background to this chapter was our interest in global themes that permeate and shape university governance. Using the web-crawling technique, we have collected all material available at the official websites, which means that we can search for specific words, key phrases and particular references other than links to the domains of other organisations. Through the mapping and analysis of the conceptual patterns created by the tracking of such key terms and phrases and the trajectories of them throughout the field of transnational intermediaries, we can empirically map and more clearly understand the emergence, circulation, clustering and travels of global themes in the transnational field of university governance.

Notes

[1] We would like to thank David Falk and Sara Edvinsson at the Centre for Civil Society Studies at Stockholm School of Economics, and Tino Schöllhorn at University of Mannheim, for valuable research assistance.

[2] The visual depiction of the data in this section is based on the Fruchterman-Reingold algorithm, which interprets a relation between two nodes as a force pulling these two nodes together. As nodes typically have many relations, they are pulled into various directions. The algorithm identifies the optimal solution where the different strengths are balanced. In a network that is characterised by many nodes and relations, more than one optimal solution may exist. Hence, each time the algorithm is started, solutions might differ. As there are different solutions, we do not visualise the data using Euclidean distances. Instead, the number of ties to get from one node to another node is a distance that is stable for all visualisations. For example, if two nodes are connected with each other, they are likely to be positioned in proximity to each other in each graph, but not necessarily with the exact same Euclidean distance.

References

Andonova, LB, Mitchell, RB, 2010, The rescaling of global environmental politics, *Annual Review of Environment and Resources* 35, 255–82

Ansell, C, Gash, A, 2008, Collaborative governance in theory and practice, *Journal of Public Administration Research and Theory* 18, 543–71

Avant, D, Finnemore, M, Sell, SK (eds), 2010, *Who governs the globe?*, Cambridge: Cambridge University Press

Beech, J, 2009, Policy spaces, mobile discourses, and the definition of educated identities, *Comparative Education* 45, 3, 347–64

Beech, J, 2011, *Global panaceas, local realities: International agencies and the future of education*, Frankfurt on the Main: Peter Lang

Boli, J, Thomas, GM, 1997, World culture in the world polity: A century of international non-governmental organization, *American Sociological Review* 62, 171–90

Boli, J, Thomas, GM (eds), 1999, *Constructing world culture: International nongovernmental organizations since 1875*, Stanford, CA: Stanford University Press

Boulton, G, Lucas, C, 2008, *What are universities for?*, Leuven: League of European Research Universities

Bourdieu, P, 1977, *Outline of a theory of practice*, Cambridge: Cambridge University Press

Bourdieu, P, 1984, *Distinction: A social critique of the judgement of taste*, Cambridge, MA: Harvard University Press

Brunsson, N, Ahrne, G, 2008, *Meta-organizations*, Cheltenham: Edward Elgar

Brunsson, NB Jacobsson, B, 2000, *A world of standards*, Oxford: Oxford University Press

Collini, S, 2012, *What are universities for?*, London: Penguin

DiMaggio, PJ, Powell, WW, 1983, The iron cage revisited: Institutional isomorphism and collective rationality in organizational fields, *American Sociological Review* 48, 2, 147–60

Djelic, M-L, Sahlin-Andersson, K (eds), 2006, *Transnational governance: Institutional dynamics of regulation*, pp 1–28, Cambridge: Cambridge University Press

Djelic, M-L, Sahlin, K, 2011, Reordering the world: Transnational regulatory governance and its challenges, in L Faur (ed) *The Oxford Handbook of Governance*, pp 745–58, Oxford: Oxford University Press

Drori, GS, Meyer, JW, Hwang, H, 2009, Global organization: Rationalization and actorhood as dominant scripts, in R Meyer, K Sahlin, M Ventresca, P Walgenbach (eds) *Research in the sociology of organizations: Institutions and ideology*, 27, pp 17–43, Bingley: Emerald

Drori, GS, Delmestri, G, Oberg, A, 2012, Branding the university: Relational strategy of identity construction in a competitive field, in L Engwall, P Scott (eds) *Trust in higher education institutions*, London: Portland Press

Finnemore, M, 1993, International organization as teachers of norms: The United Nations educational, scientific, and cultural organization and science policy, *International Organization* 47, 567–97

Finnemore, M, Sikkink, K, 1998, International norm dynamics and political change, *International Organization* 52, 4, 887–917

Fligstein, N, McAdam, D, 2011, Toward a general theory of strategic action fields, *Sociological Theory* 29, 1, 1–26

Fligstein, N, McAdam, D, 2012, *A theory of fields*, Oxford: Oxford University Press

Frank, DJ, Meyer, JW, 2007, University expansion and the knowledge society, *Theory and Society* 36, 4, 287–311

Hedmo, T, 2004, *Rule-making in the transnational space: The development of European accreditation of management education*, PhD dissertation, Uppsala: Uppsala University

Hedmo, T, Sahlin-Andersson K, 2006, The evolution of a European governance network of management education, in M Marcussen, J Torfing (eds) *Democratic network governance in Europe*, Basingstoke: Palgrave MacMillan

Hedmo, T, Sahlin-Andersson, K, Wedlin, L, 2006, Is a global organizational field of higher education emerging? Management education as an early example, in G Krücken, A Kosmütsky, M Torka (eds) *Towards a multiversity? Universities between global trends and national traditions*, Bielefeld: Transcript Verlag

Krücken, G, Meier, F, 2006, Turning the university into an organizational actor, in GS Drori, JW Meyer, H Hwang (eds) *Globalization and organization: World society and organizational change*, Oxford: Oxford University Press

Krücken, G, Kosmütsky, A, Torka, M (eds) 2007, *Towards a multiversity? Universities between global trends and national traditions*, Bielefeld: Transcript Verlag

Lewin, K, 1951, *Field theory in social science; selected theoretical papers*, D, Cartwright (ed), New York: Harper & Row

Maassen, P, Olsen, JP, 2007, *University dynamics and European integration*, Springer: Dordrecht

Marcussen, M, 2000, *Ideas and elites*, Denmark: AAlborg University Press

Marcussen, M, 2004, OECD governance through soft law, in U Mörth (ed) *Soft law in governance and regulation*, pp 103–28, Cheltenham: Edward Elgar

Marcussen, M, Torfing, J, 2007, *Democratic network governance in Europe*, Basingstoke: Palgrave Macmillan

Martin, JL, 2003, What is field theory?, *American Journal of Sociology* 109, 1–49

Meyer, J, 1996, Otherhood: The promulgation and transmission of ideas in the modern organizational environment, in B Czarniawska, G Sevón (eds) *Translating organizational change*, pp 241–52, de Gruyter Studies in Organization

Meyer, JW, Bromley, P, 2013, The worldwide expansion of 'organization', *Sociological Theory* 31, 4, 366–89

Meyer, JW, Rowan, B, 1977, Institutionalized organizations: Formal structure as myth and ceremony, *American Journal of Sociology* 83, 2, 340–63

Mohr, JW, 2005, Implicit terrains: Meaning, measurement, and spatial metaphors in organizational theory, in M Ventresca, J Porac (eds) *Constructing industries and markets*, New York: Elsevier.

Mörth, U, 2004, *Soft law in governance and regulation*, Cheltenham: Edward Elgar

O'Brien, R, Goetz, AM, Scholte, JA, Williams, M, 2000, *Contesting global governance: Multilateral economic institutions and global social movements*, Cambridge: Cambridge University Press

Perrow, C, 1991, A society of organizations, *Theory and society* 20, 6, 725–62

Perrow, C, 2002, *Organizing America: Wealth, power, and the origins of corporate capitalism*, Princeton, NJ: Princeton University Press

Ramirez, FO, 2006, The rationalization of universities, in M-L Djelic, K Sahlin-Anderson (eds) *Transnational governance: Institutional dynamics of regulation*, Cambridge: Cambridge University Press

Ramirez, FO, 2010, Accounting for excellence: Transforming universities into organizational actors, in VD Rust, LM Portnoi, SS Bagely (eds) *Higher education, policy, and the global competition phenomenon*, New York: Palgrave Macmillan

Ramirez, FO, 2012, The world society perspective: Concepts, assumptions, and strategies, *Comparative Education* 48, 4, 423–39

Risse, T, 2012, Governance in areas of limited statehood, in L Faur (ed) *The Oxford handbook of governance*, pp 699–716, Oxford: Oxford University Press

Reuter, M, Wijkström, F, Meyer, M, 2014, Who calls the shots? The real normative power of civil society, in M Freise, T Hallmann (eds) *Modernizing democracy: Associations and associating in the 21st century*, New York: Springer

Sahlin, K, 2013, Global themes and institutional ambiguity in the university field: Rankings and management models on the move, in GS Drori, M Höllerer, P Walgenbach (eds) *Global themes and local variations in organization and management: Perspectives on glocalization*, New York: Routledge

Sahlin, K, Wedlin, L, 2008, Circulating ideas: Imitation, translation and editing, in R Greenwood, C Oliver, K Sahlin, R Suddaby (eds) *Handbook of organizational institutionalism*, Los Angeles, CA: Sage

Sahlin-Andersson, K, 1996, Imitating by editing success: The construction of organizational fields, in B Czarniawska, G Sevón (eds) *Translating organizational change*, pp 69–92, Berlin: Walter de Gruyter

Sahlin-Andersson, K, Engwall, L, 2002, Carriers, flows, and resources of management, in K Sahlin-Andersson, L Engwall (eds) *The expansion of management knowledge: Carriers, flows, and sources*, pp 3–32, Stanford, CA: Stanford University Press

Selznick, P, 1949, *TVA and the Grass Roots*, Berkeley, CA: University of California Press

Stoker, G, 1998, Governance as theory: Five propositions, *International Social Science Journal* 50, 17–28

Tallberg, J, Sommerer, T, Squatrito, T, Jönsson, C, 2013, *The opening up of international organizations: Transnational access in global governance*, Cambridge: Cambridge University Press

Torfing, J, 2012, Governance networks, in L Faur (ed) *The Oxford handbook of governance*, pp 99–112, Oxford: Oxford University Press

Union of International Associations, 2014, *Yearbook of international organizations*, www.uia.be/yearbook-international-organizations-online

Wijkström, F, 2011, 'Charity speak' and 'business talk': The on-going (re) hybridization of civil society, in F Wijkström, A Zimmer (eds) *Nordic civil society at a cross-roads: Transforming the popular movement tradition*, Baden-Baden: Nomos

de Wilde, P, Zürn, M, 2012, Can the politicization of European integration be reversed, *Journal of Common Market Studies* 50, 1, 137–53

Zürn, M, Binder, M, Ecker-Erhardt, M, 2012, International authority and its politicization, *International Theory* 4, 1, 69–106

Appendix: Core intermediaries in the field

	Website and 'centrality'	
Cluster No 1: 'Europe' (top ten intermediaries)		
European University Association	eua.be	50
International Association of Universities	iau-aiu.net	37
Academic Cooperation Association	aca-secretariat.be	32
Nuffic	nuffic.nl	30
European Association for Quality Assurance in Higher Education	enqa.eu	28
European Association for International Education	eaie.org	27
International Network for Quality Assurance Agencies in Higher Education	inqaahe.org	22
World Education Services	wes.org	21
Observatory on Borderless Higher Education	obhe.ac.uk	18
European Consortium for Accreditation	ecaconsortium.net	16
Cluster No 2: 'UK' (top intermediaries)		
British Council	britishcouncil.org	38
Universities UK	universitiesuk.ac.uk	18
The Higher Education Academy	heacademy.ac.uk	16
The Association of Commonwealth Universities	acu.ac.uk	14
Cluster No 3: 'Germany' (top intermediaries)		
Max-Planck-Gesellschaft	mpg.de	24
Deutsche Forschungsgemeinschaft	dfg.de	22
Informationsdienst Wissenschaft	idw-online.de	18
Deutsches Institut für Wirtschaftsforschung	diw.de	17
Cluster No 4: 'US etc' (top intermediaries)		
Institute of International Education	iie.org	35
American Council on Education	acenet.edu	26
EDUCAUSE	educause.edu	20
Research Papers in Economics	repec.org	19
NAFSA: Association of International Educators	nafsa.org	18
Association of American Colleges & Universities	aacu.org	18
Influential organisations without obvious cluster membership		
World Bank	worldbank.org	73
Deutsche Gesellschaft Für Internationale Zusammenarbeit	giz.de	22
Hochschulrektorenkonferenz	hrk.de	18

CHAPTER SEVEN

Scaling up networks for starving artists

Ben Farr-Wharton and Robyn Keast

Introduction

An increasing number of countries are adopting a creative industries policy platform, combining the film, digital, media, music, performing arts and design segments under one banner to stimulate economic development. A key reason for this is that the innovation generated by those that work in the creative industries (henceforth 'creative workers') appears to produce significant spill-over effects across multiple economic sectors, while requiring little government investment or regulation in comparison to previous cultural policy frameworks (Jaaniste, 2009; Banks and Hesmondhalgh, 2009). To date, however, government efforts to implement, or extend, a creative industries policy agenda have largely used localised cluster platforms, to the exclusion of any other strategy (UNESCO, 2013). Such a one-dimensional policy approach appears to have done little to address the significant labour problems associated with creative work (such as job insecurity, under-employment and labour exploitation).

At the grassroots level creative workers still appear to be suffering from an unregulated, precarious and exploitative labour environment (De Peuter, 2011; Huws, 2006). To mitigate these effects and generate consistent work creative workers have become reliant on the collaborative networks developed with other professionals and organisations within the field (Belussi and Sedita, 2008). While traditionally such collaborations have been embedded within localised 'creative clusters', increasingly creative workers are leveraging from their local connections to generate 'non-local networks', as such arrangements appear to provide additional benefits, such as opportunities to work on larger, higher paying projects (Hill, 2007; Vang and Chaminade, 2007). Mulgan and Albury (2003) define this process as 'up-scaling', meaning the ability of creative workers to leverage resources (including networks and partnerships) from the local to larger, regional, national and global scales of operation.

For creative workers non-local networks present as the most mature, up-scaled collaborative arrangements, exhibiting benefits over and above those of clustered arrangements (Giuliani, 2013). Such benefits include access to new markets and new collaborations, and these activities may have a significant effect in improving creative labour outcomes (Boso et al, 2013), though little empirical research exists to support these claims. In contrast, there has been extensive research on the impact of localised clustered arrangements for creative workers (Cooke and Lazzeretti, 2008), showing that local network initiatives can enhance the labour security of creative workers (Belussi and Sedita, 2008), and may act as a precursor to the more mature, up-scaled arrangements sought by policy.

The lack of research concerning the impact of up-scaled and non-local networks presents as a challenge for both policy-makers and academics, as the existing research-led policy initiatives focus almost exclusively on developing localised clusters (UNESCO, 2013). To this end, policy instruments that enhance up-scaled structures may provide better economic outcomes and spill-overs from the sector, and examining this possibility is a focus of this chapter.

To provide a more solid empirical understanding concerning the benefits of up-scaled network arrangements this chapter compares the impact of local and non-local networks on the labour outcomes (exploitation and labour precarity) of creative workers. The chapter proceeds in two parts: the first outlines the theoretical assumptions regarding the conditions under which network scaling-up occurs for creative workers, while the second compares the impact of local and scaled-up arrangements on creative labour precarity and exploitation. Two research questions are addressed:

1: What are the network conditions under which up-scaling occurs for creative workers?

2: What are the impacts of scaled-up networks, and other network structures, on the labour precarity and exploitation of creative workers?

Quantitative analysis (structural equation modelling) is used to test two sets of models relating to each research question. Data were drawn from a random sample of 271 Australian cultural and creative workers.

Background

Networks, network structures and performance

Social networks exist when there is a relationship between two or more people (Borgatti and Halgin, 2011). In social networks participants seek to achieve their own goals, the goals of other people with whom they share a connection, as well as collective goals (McGuire and Arganoff, 2007; Cropanzano and Mitchell, 2005). A growing body of research has focused on the conditions under which network performance contributes to optimal outcomes (Sørensen and Torfing, 2009; Keast and Mandell, 2013). One of the areas within this field of research includes an exploration into the impact of particular *network structures* on the outcomes of actors, known as the 'structuralist perspective of networks' (Lee, 2010; Gulati et al, 2011). *Network structures* represent an actor's arrangement of relationships to other participants within a network. An actor's network structure will vary with respect to the reach, richness and receptivity of connection-types with network partners (Gulati et al, 2011), and the aggregate of these dimensions forms an actor-level resource that can have an impact on their economic performance.

The efficacy of particular network structures in improving actors' outcomes appears to be contingent on specific industries (Rowley et al, 2000). Within the wine manufacturing sector (a sector that is often included within the scope of the creative industries) Giuliani (2013) indicates that an actor's network size, structural position, cluster engagement and non-local networks have been shown to have a positive impact on the acquisition of firm knowledge. Of these, the firms that possess the strongest non-local networks were shown to possess significantly higher knowledge resources. Additionally, Hill (2007) claims festival organisations operating within the creative industries that possess non-local networks have enhanced access to resources such as funding. However, despite the claimed benefits of non-local networks less is known about the network conditions required to generate 'scaled-up' arrangement for firms and network actors.

Small worlds theory suggests that networks 'scale-up' through a complex process involving network growth, embeddedness and structural position (Watts and Strogatz, 1998). Under this theory a certain degree of local embeddedness should be a pre-requisite for the formation of non-local networks for an actor. Network actors with larger local networks or those occupying bridging positions (that is, acting as a structural hole) within a network are more likely to have contact with people from other regions, owing to their enhanced visibility and power to connect (Barabasi, 2003). Through this heightened connectivity an actor has the ability to leverage their local network relationships to connect with potentially distant links. *Time* is also expected to be a catalyst in this network amplification process, as the longer an actor participates within a network the higher the chance that they will develop larger and more complex (scaled-up) network structures (Barabasi, 2003). Accordingly, we hypothesise that 'scaled-up' networks will positively correlate with actors' *network size,* local embeddedness (*clustering*), *structural hole* and the *time* that they have spent within a network (Hypothesis 1). We test this hypothesis through a statistical investigation of the structural dimensions of creative workers' professional networks (model displayed in Figure 1).

Figure 1: Model 1 - hypothetical model

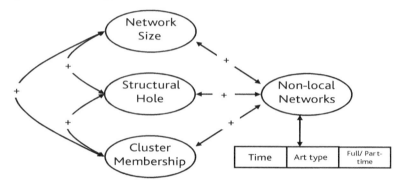

Network size

Network size comprises 'the number of direct links between a focal actor and other actors' (Hoang and Antoncic, 2003, 171). Network size is one dimension of network structure that has a theorised impact on the general performance of creative workers (Belussi and Sedita, 2008). Further, empirical research suggests that *network size* has a positive impact on the levels of innovation, survival and resource access for start-up firms in manufacturing and technology industries (Semrau and Werner, 2013; Raz and Gloor, 2007; Watson, 2007).

Structural position

Burt's (1992) structural hole theory holds that an actor who bridges the relationships between two or more groups of people will perform better than more isolated or embedded network members. Bridging actors have access to multiple sources of information and resources, and therefore occupy a position of power in deciding who receives new information and how quickly (Burt, 2000). In the creative industries Belussi and Sedita (2008) found that actors, when faced with poor permanent employment prospects, bridged multiple arts networks to enhance their access to job opportunities.

Clustering

Geographically embedded clusters of multiple creative workers and organisations appear to dominate the supply chain structures of the creative industries (Boix et al, 2011). Cluster membership is said to enhance access to resources for actors, facilitate innovation spill-overs and increase market visibility (Porter, 2000; Bagwell, 2008; De Propris et al, 2009). Clusters are used as an indication of local embeddedness in this chapter; that is, how grounded creative workers are in their local networks. Following this line, Uzzi (1996) indicates that embeddedness can have both positive and negative effects on actors. In the first instance actors benefit from having access to support through close ties; however, too much embeddedness requires significant investment and can thus be detrimental to advancement, as it takes time and effort away from building wider networks.

Non-local networks

Non-local networks are the most mature, up-scaled network configurations, encompassing the relationships that a focal actor forms with people from other regions. These contacts are generally weak ties; that is, they are based on loose connections rather than on trust. Research indicates that non-local networks can help to increase the innovation and export potential for firms (Chen, 2003; Boschma and Ter Wal, 2007) because they expose focal firms to new ways of operating and provide them with more ambitious project opportunities.

Up-scaled networks and creative working conditions

In comparison to other sectors people who work within the creative industries are subject to particularly poor labour outcomes (Banks and Hesmondhalgh, 2009; Hesmondhalgh and Baker, 2010). The treatment of creative workers within existing creative industries policy has been heavily scrutinised for encouraging employers and contracting firms to exploit creative workers by expecting that they receive an income that is not representative of the hours which they commit to a job, as such jobs can be considered as 'fun', 'interesting' and unlike the 'humdrum jobs' associated with other sectors (Banks and Hesmondhalgh, 2009). Further, the sector's promotion of freelance and subcontracted employment structures perpetuates precarious (irregular and insecure) work opportunities for creative workers, as well as poor and unregulated conditions under which work is undertaken. The subcontracting employment structures that ensue as a result of poor policies and regulation in the creative industries means that creative workers can work longer hours, without breaks and may also be responsible for their own sick leave, taxation, superannuation and equipment maintenance (Davies and Sigthorsson, 2013).

A creative worker's social network structure appears to significantly affect the number of employment opportunities afforded to them (Belussi and Sedita, 2008). However, research to date has focused exclusively on the impact of cluster membership on employment opportunities. Yet research also indicates that other network arrangements are likely to affect the work performance of creative workers (Hill, 2007). We compare the impact of network factors – network size, structural hole, clustering and non-local networks – on the labour precarity and exploitation as perceived by creative workers.

Labour precarity

Burgess and Campbell (1998, 7) define labour precarity as 'non-continuity of employment, lack of employment protections and exclusion from standard employment benefits'. Creative workers appear to be particularly prone to precarious labour conditions (De Peuter, 2011). This position of vulnerability arises because the value of creative products is very hard to predict, thus organisations within the creative industries mitigate financial risk by adopting temporary and sub-contract arrangements (Caves, 2000). Creative workers who occupy these positions have poor long-term financial prospects as they don't receive the worker benefits and leave pay aligned with more permanent roles (Hesmondhalgh and Baker, 2010). They are also at risk of being 'undercut' by other creative workers (typically those younger in age) who will often work for free to gain access to the market – termed by De Peuter (2011, 420) as the 'zero-wage internship'. Creative workers facing this situation of under-pricing are constantly seeking new work, and more work, in order to survive.

Exploitation

Related to their propensity for precarity, Hesmondhalgh and Baker (2010) suggest that creative workers also face conditions of labour exploitation. Exploitation exists when there is a 'difference between labour's marginal product and its real wage' (Perksy and Tsang, 1974, 52). Forced into taking multiple contracts and jobs, often simultaneously, creative workers can regularly find themselves in the position of working long hours without breaks, for poor pay and with little chance of accessing the usual employment benefits such as holiday or sick pay.

To further investigate the impact of network structures on the labour conditions of creative workers we test two more statistical models. The first model compares the impact of different network structures – network size, clustering, structural hole and non-local networks – on perceptions of labour precarity and exploitation by creative workers (see Figure 2).

Figure 2: Model 1: measurement model

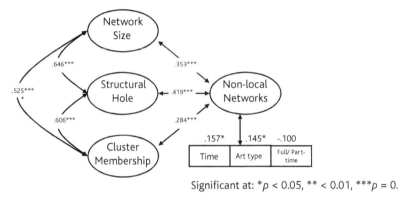

Significant at: *$p < 0.05$, ** < 0.01, ***$p = 0$.

Figure 3: Model 2: hypothetical model

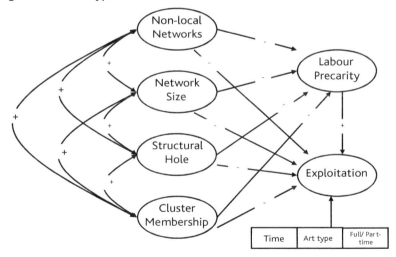

The second model aggregates the network dimensions into one higher-order 'network structure' variable (see Figure 3). While the first model has theoretical significance in showing the importance of individual structural dimensions in reality the true impact of an actor's network structure can only be shown by incorporating all dimensions simultaneously.

Noting that previous research suggests a link between cluster participation, network size and job opportunity (Belussi and Sedita, 2008) we hypothesize a significant negative relationship exists between clustering with labour precarity, and network size with labour precarity (Hypothesis 2). There is insufficient research in general to presume a statistically significant relationship between structural holes and non-local networks on labour precarity and exploitation. However, noting that structural position and non-local networks can facilitate performance outcomes we hypothesise that there may be a significant relationship that exists between these factors (Hypothesis 3). In addition, we hypothesise that network size and cluster may have an impact on exploitation (Hypothesis 4). 'Time' (years of experience in the industry) and 'art type' are used as control variables to ensure the model can be replicated in the future.

Figure 3 shows 'network structure' as the aggregated (higher-order) construct comprising network size, cluster, structural hole and non-local networks. Noting that theory suggests that networks form the market supply and demand structures for the creative sector (Potts et al, 2008) we hypothesise a significant negative relationship between network structure and exploitation, and a negative relationship between network structure and labour precarity (Hypothesis 5). We also hypothesise that labour precarity is significantly linked to exploitation (Hypothesis 6). These hypotheses are summarised in Table 1.

Table 1: Summary of hypotheses

		Summary of Hypotheses
Model 1	H1	Scaled-up networks will positively correlate with an actor's *network size*, local embeddedness (*clustering*), *structural hole* and the *time* that they have spent within a network.
Model 2	H2	A significant negative relationship exists between *clustering* and *network size* with *labour precarity*.
	H3	A statistical significant relationship exists between structural holes, and *non-local networks* on *labour precarity* and *exploitation*.
	H4	*Network size* and *cluster* may impact on *exploitation*.
Model 3	H5	*Network structure* is negatively related to *labour precarity* and *exploitation*.
	H6	*Labour precarity* is significantly linked to *exploitation*.

Method

This chapter uses structural equation modelling (SEM) to explore the hypothesised relationships listed in Table 1. Survey data were drawn from a random sample of 271 people working in the cultural and creative sectors in Australia. The response rate was 38.7 per cent. The survey used a set of developed, context-specific scales for networks size, cluster, structural hole, non-local networks, exploitation and labour precarity. Respondents were asked to respond to items on a five-point Likert scale.

Sample

The total population of creative workers in Australia is unknown, but predicted to be between 2 per cent and 4 per cent of the workforce (that is, 180,000–360,000 people) (Cunningham, 2011). Although the sample used in this analysis was random, further replication is needed to enhance the study's generalisability. Of the sample, 32.8 per cent were visual artists, 26.5 per cent were musicians, 7.3 per cent worked in the creative writing segment, 5.2 per cent worked in film and multimedia, 2.8 per cent worked in design and architecture, 0.3 per cent worked in web design and 25.1 per cent worked across multiple segments (usually across web, film and television, music and performing arts segments). Further, the majority of the sample respondents had worked in the creative industries for over 15 years (48.1 per cent), 22 per cent of respondents had between 8 and 14 years of experience in the creative industries, 29.9 per cent had between 4 and 7 years of experience, 7.7 per cent had between 1 and 3 years of experience, and 1.4 per cent had been working in the creative industries for less than 12 months. In the first model we test the degree to which the samples' 'time in industry' had an impact on the development of scaled-up arrangements.

No sampled item had more than 3.2 per cent data missing. Normality for all items was assessed using Q–Q Plot scanning, which yielded no significant deviation from expected normal distribution. Skewness and kurtosis for all items remained in acceptable ranges (between +2 and -2) (Hair et al, 2010). Common method bias was tested for, with single factor bias only explaining 21.4 per cent of the variance, indicating a low chance of common method bias.

Extensive validity testing was conducted, including exploratory and confirmatory factor analysis, to ensure scales were adequate. Items were omitted through a process of exploratory and confirmatory factor analysis, leaving all instruments as acceptable three-item scales (Hinkin, 1998). The validity and reliability scores for all scales were appropriate except for the scale 'exploitation' (see Appendix). The average variance extracted score, which is acceptable above 0.5, was 0.497 for this item. While future research should seek to improve the exploitation scale, a 0.003 differential is not likely to have a significant impact on the statistical reasoning.

Model testing

SEM requires two kinds of modelling to test relationships between factors. The first is a structure model. This is used to ensure that the tested constructs are valid and the data fits the theoretical model adequately. If the structural model has 'good model fit' a second measurement model can be executed which displays the relationships between constructs along a planned path. Good model fit is indicated by a number of measures, including a CMIN/DF score of below 5, a Goodness of Fit (GFI) score above 0.9, a comparative fit index (CFI) score above 0.9, a Tucker–Lewis coefficient (TLI) score above 0.9, and a root mean square error of approximation (RMSEA) score below 0.05 (Ping, 2004). The results for the measurement and structure model of tested models 1, 2 and 3 are displayed in Table 2. All models had particularly good model fit. The lowest 'fit' score was displayed in model 3, where the GFI measure was 0.921; however, this is still well above the acceptable level of 0.900. As good model fit is present the results presented here can be considered statistically sound.

Table 2: Model fit for structure and measurement models

	Model 1		Model 2		Model 3		
	Structure	Measure-ment	Structure	Measure-ment	Structure (lower order)	Structure (higher order)	Measure-ment
DMIN/DF	1.409	1.194	1.223	1.376	1.223	1.259	1.402
GFI	.961	.960	.919	.925	.919	.938	.921
CFI	.987	.991	.987	.969	.987	.983	.966
TLI	.983	.987	.983	.961	.983	.980	.959
RMSEA	.039	.027	.029	.037	.029	.031	.039

Results

Results for the first model are displayed in Figure 4.

Figure 4: Model 2: measurement model

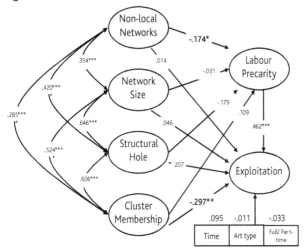

Significant at: *$p < 0.05$, ** < 0.01, ***$p = 0.001$; $n = 271$

As can be noted, 'structural hole' was most strongly correlated with 'non-local networks' (0.419***), followed by 'network size' (0.353***) and 'cluster membership' (0.284***). This finding, consistent with the hypothesis, suggests that a creative worker's structural hole position, coupled with their network size, are the most significant contributors to the development of 'scaled-up networks'. Time also appeared to be significantly related to the development of 'non-local networks' (0.157*), though to a lesser extent in comparison to other network factors.

Results for the second model are displayed in Figure 5.

Figure 5: Model 3: hypothetical model

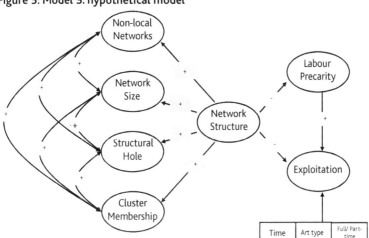

As expected, 'labour precarity' appears to be a significant antecedent for 'exploitation' (0.462***). Further, network factors in isolation do not have a very significant impact on either 'labour precarity' or 'exploitation'. The only exceptions to this are non–local networks, which have a small effect in mitigating 'labour precarity' (-0.174*) and 'clustering', which seems to decrease 'exploitation' (-0.297**). This means that creative workers' scaled–up networks have a small impact on improving their job security, and clustering actively improves the conditions under which creative work is undertaken.

Results for the third model are displayed in Figure 6.

Figure 6: Model 3: measurement model

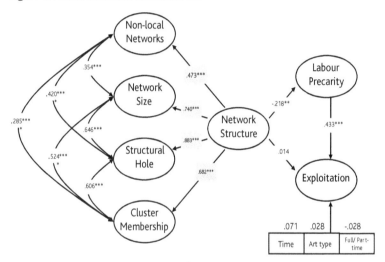

Significant at: *$p < 0.05$, ** < 0.01, ***$p = 0.001$; $n =271$

The third model indicates that when network dimensions are aggregated into the higher-order factor 'network structure', the impact on 'exploitation' becomes insignificant. This is important as it suggests that while a person's 'cluster membership' may decrease the possibility that they will be exploited this positive effect slides away when 'network structures' are aggregated. 'Network structure' has a small, but significant, positive impact on reducing 'labour precarity' (-0.218**).

Discussion and implications

A summary of results is provided in Table 3.

Table 3: Summary of results

Hypothesis	Path			Conclusion
H1	Network size	-	Non-local network	Accepted
	Cluster	-	Non-local network	Accepted
	Structural hole	-	Non-local network	Accepted
	Time	-	Non-local network	Accepted
H2	Network size	-	Labour precarity	Rejected
	Cluster	-	Labour precarity	Rejected
H3	Non-local network	-	Labour precarity	Accepted
	Structural hole	-	Labour precarity	Rejected
	Non-local network	-	Exploitation	Rejected
	Structural hole	-	Exploitation	Rejected
H4	Network size	-	Exploitation	Rejected
	Cluster	-	Exploitation	Accepted
H5	Network structure	-	Labour precarity	Accepted
	Network structure	-	Exploitation	Rejected
H6	Labour precarity	-	Exploitation	Accepted

Many of the hypothesised relationships were qualified. As the hypotheses sought to test theoretical assumptions regarding the makeup and impact of network structures this study makes a theoretical contribution. In response to the first research question (*What are the network conditions under which scaling-up occurs?*) results from the first model indicate that up-scaled networks occur predominately through interactions with an actor's network size and their structural position within a network.

In response to the second research question (*What are the impacts of up-scaled networks, and other network structures, on the labour precarity and exploitation of people working in the creative sector?*) results from model 2 indicate that non-local networks have the most significant impact in reducing labour precarity, and clustering has the most significant impact in reducing exploitation. Network size and structural position do not have an impact on the working conditions for creative workers tested in this sample. Furthermore, as an aggregate of all tested dimensions of network structure, model 3 indicates that a creative worker's network structure has only a small impact on reducing their labour precarity, but no impact on their exploitation. Finally, as predicted, labour precarity leads to exploitation for creative workers.

The significant relationship between scaled-up networks in reducing labour precarity may be explained using the theoretical assumptions underpinning the 'structuralist perspective of networks' (Gulati et al, 2011); that is, non-local networks provide creative workers with access to the types of resources, such as job opportunities, cross-region collaborations and potentially a different framework to model local operations off, delivered through tacit knowledge sharing. In effect, these resources protect creative workers from labour precarity. In this regard, O'Connor (2010) calls for a differentiation between local and global networks for creative policy aimed at economic development. Results presented in this chapter provide an empirical foundation for this claim.

Implications for policy

In recent years there has been a strong policy push to align individual creative capacity with a larger, industry model (Cunningham, 2002). In making this shift policy has been developed and enacted that transforms the traditional support and funding framework from a grant-based approach (associated with the previous cultural industries policy systems) to a market model. Such an approach has sought to ramp-up and commodify creative work, from an individual to industry endeavour, resulting in a situation whereby creative workers have had to draw on their local and non-local networks for broader economic purposes. Under this approach creative workers' networks are seen not only as private resources but rather as public assets which can be up-scaled in order to provide a functioning platform for economic development purposes. To date, however, the policy agenda has targeted local network development to the exclusion of other approaches and with little consideration of the requirements needed to leverage local networks to the next level or scale of operation. Indeed even at the local level policies appear to have largely failed creative workers, with many still struggling to obtain sustainable working environments.

Our results indicate that the policy emphasis on local network development through the frame of creative clusters is warranted, as clustering appears to decrease exploitation. However, the results also call for the need for this approach to be coupled with instruments to help establish, improve and better leverage creative workers' non-local networks. In this study it was the non-local networks that were shown to significantly decrease labour precarity, and labour precarity is a forerunner to exploitation; thus a more targeted policy approach should consider both of these network factors.

Drawing from the results of our first model we suggest that effective policy instruments targeting the development of non-local networks for creative workers should enhance opportunities for collaborations with geographically-diverse actors. Such initiatives need to target not only those creative workers who are established but also those that are emerging in their trade. In this way instigating cross-generational change through cultivating up-scaled network arrangements within the creative industries has the potential to improve significantly the poor labour conditions currently associated with the sector across the board, and generate broader, more positive spill-over for other sectors. Accordingly, the cost associated through the use of government grants that target non-local network development for creative workers may be offset by the economic gains (such as business tax and innovation) generated by a more efficient creative labour force that possesses enhanced levels of commitment and motivation and is more fairly treated.

Limitations

The research is limited by its use of a self-report survey. However, Spector (1994) argues that the self-reporting method is legitimate for gathering data about a person's perceptions as long as the instrument reflects an extensive literature review and pattern-matching is used to support interpretation of the data – as is the case in this study. A second limitation concerns the scales developed and presented. While in the main they are compliant with validity assessments the scales will benefit from further replication and maturity.

Conclusion

Effective working conditions within the market-orientated creative industries are achieved through a combination of local clustering and the development of scaled-up, network arrangements. To date research and policy has largely neglected the impact of non-local and up-scaled arrangements for creative workers, targeting instead local network development. Our results suggest that scaled-up networks within the creative sector form as a result of an actor's bridging position within a network, but are not affected significantly by the degree to which they engage in local networks. Further, while local clustering was shown to decrease exploitation, scaled-up arrangements were found to improve creative workers' job security. Thus, the development of new policy instruments that focus on both local and non-local network formation and leveraging provide an essential mix for improving the poor labour conditions that creative workers face. This in turn will enhance the ability of the creative sector to provide a sustainable model for economic development and innovation for other segments of the economy.

References

Bagwell, S, 2008, Creative clusters and city growth, *Creative Industries Journal* 1, 1, 1–46

Banks, M, Hesmondhalgh, D, 2009, Looking for work in creative industries policy, *International Journal of Cultural Policy* 15, 4, 415–30

Barabasi, A-L, 2003, *Linked: How everything is connected to everything else and what it means for business, science, and everyday life*, Cambridge: Penguin Group

Belussi, F, Sedita SR, 2008, The management of 'events' in the Veneto performing music cluster: bridging latent networks and permanent organization, in P Cooke, L Lazzeretti (eds) *Creative cities, cultural clusters and local economic development*, pp 215–35, Cheltenham: Edward Elgar Publishing Limited

Boix, R, Lazzeretti, L, Hervàs, J L, De Miguel, B, 2011, Creative clusters in Europe: A microdata approach, *European Regional Science Association: New Challenges for European Regions and Urban Areas in a Globalised World*, Barcelona, 30 August–3 September.

Borgatti, SP, Halgin, DS, 2011, On network theory, *Organization Science* 22, 5, 1168–81

Boschma, R, Ter Wal, A, 2007, Knowledge networks and innovative performance in an industrial district: The case of a footwear district in the south of Italy, *Industry and Innovation* 14, 2, 177–99

Boso, N, Story, VM, Cadogan, JW, 2013, Entrepreneurial orientation, market orientation, network ties, and performance: Study of entrepreneurial firms in a developing economy, *Journal of Business Venturing* 28, 6, 708–27

Burgess, J, Campbell, I, 1998, The nature and dimensions of precarious employment in Australia, *Labour and Industry: A Journal of the Social and Economic Relations of Work* 8, 3, 5–21

Burt, RS, 1992, *Structural holes,* Cambridge, IL: Harvard University Press

Burt, RS, 2000, The network structure of social capital, *Research in Organizational Behavior* 22, 1, 345–423

Caves, RE, 2000, *Creative industries: Contracts between art and commerce,* Cambridge, IL: Harvard University Press.

Chen, T-J, 2003, Network resources for internationalization: The case of Taiwan's electronics firms, *Journal of Management Studies* 40, 5, 1107–30

Cooke, P, Lazzeretti, L (eds), 2008, *Creative cities, cultural clusters and local economic development,* Cheltenham: Edward Elgar

Cropanzano, R, Mitchell, M, 2005, Social exchange theory: An interdisciplinary review, *Journal of Management* 31, December, 874–900

Cunningham, S, 2002, From cultural to creative industries: Theory, industry and policy implications, *Media International Australia Incorporating Culture and Policy* 102, 1, 54–65

Cunningham, S, 2011, Developments in measuring the 'creative' workforce, *Cultural Trends* 20, 1, 25–50

Davies, R, Sigthorsson, G, 2013, *Introducing the creative industries: From theory to practice,* London: Sage

De Peuter, G, 2011, Creative economy and labor precarity: A contested convergence, *Journal of Communication Inquiry* 35, 4, 417–25

De Propris, L, Chapain, C, Cooke, P, MacNeill, S, Mateos-Garcia, J, 2009, *The geography of creativity,* London: NESTA

Giuliani, E, 2013, Clusters, networks and firms' product success: An empirical study, *Management Decision* 51, 6, 1135–60

Gulati, R, Lavie, D, Madhavan, R, 2011, How do networks matter? The performance effects of interorganizational network, *Research in Organizational Behaviour* 31, 207–24

Hair, JF, Black, WC, Babin, BJ, Anderson, RE, 2010, *Multivariate data anlysis: A global perspective,* Upper Saddle River, NJ: Pearson Education

Hesmondhalgh, D, Baker, S, 2010, A very complicated version of freedom: Conditions and experiences of creative labour in three cultural industries, *Poetics* 38, 1, 4–20

Hill, S, 2007, *Making fun: New insights into the contribution of entrepreneurship around festivals and special events to the economy of Wales,* Glamorgan: Glamorgan Business School's Welsh Enterprise Institute

Hinkin, T, 1998, A brief tutorial on the development of measures for use in survey questionnaires, *Organizational Research Methods* 1, 104–20

Hoang, H, Antoncic, B, 2003, Network-based research in entrepreneurship: A critical review, *Journal of Business Venturing* 18, 2, 165–87

Huws, U, 2006, The spark in the engine: Creative workers in a global economy, *Work Organisation, Labour and Globalisation* 1, 1–12

Jaaniste, L, 2009, Placing the creative sector within innovation: The full gamut, *Innovation: Management, Policy and Practice* 11, 2, 215–29

Keast, R, Mandell, M, 2013, Network performance: A complex interplay of form and action, *International Review of Public Administration* 18, 2, 1–19

Lee, J, 2010, Heterogeneity, brokerage, and innovative performance: Endogenous formation of collaborative inventor networks, *Organizational Science* 21, 4, 804–22

McGuire, M, Arganoff, R, 2007, Answering the big questions, asking the bigger questions: Expanding the public network management empirical research agenda, *9th Public Management Research Conference*, Tucson, AZ, 25–7 October

Mulgan, G, Albury, D, 2003, *Innovation in the public sector,* London: Cabinet Office Strategy Unit

O'Connor, J, 2010, *Arts and creative industries,* Sydney, NSW: Australia Council for the Arts

Perksy, J, Tsang, H, 1974, Pigouvian exploitation of labour, *The Review of Economic and Stastics* 56, 1, 52–7

Ping, RA Jr, 2004, On assuring valid measures for theoretical models using survey data, *Journal of Business Research* 57, 125–41

Porter, M E, 2000, Location, competition, and economic development: Local clusters in a global economy, *Economic Development Quarterly* 14, 1, 15–34

Potts, J, Cunningham, S, Hartley, J, Ormerod, P, 2008, Social network markets: A new definition of the creative industries, *Journal of Cultural Economics* 32, 167–85

Raz, O, Gloor, P A, 2007, Size really matters-new insights for start-ups' survival, *Management Science* 53, 2, 169–77

Rowley, T, Behrens, D, Krackhardt, D, 2000, Redundant governance structures: An analysis of structural and relational embeddedness in the steel and semiconductor industries, *Strategic Management Journal* 21, 3, 369–86

Semrau, T, Werner, A, 2013, How exactly do network relationships pay off? The effects of network size and relationship quality on access to start-up resources, *Entrepreneurship, Theory and Practice* 38, 1, 501–25

Sørensen, E, Torfing, J, 2009, Making governance networks effective and democratic through metagovernance, *Public Administration* 87, 234–58

Spector, PE, 1994, Using self-reported questionnaires in OB research: A comment on the use of a controversial method, *Journal of Organisational Behaviour* 15, 5, 385–92

UNESCO, 2013, *Creative economy report 2013 special edition: Widening local development pathways,* Geneva: United Nations Education, Scientific and Cultural Organization

Uzzi, B, 1996, The sources and consequences of embeddedness for economic performance of organizations: The network effect, *American Sociological Review* 61, 4, 674–98

Vang, J, Chaminade C, 2007, Cultural clusters, global-local linkages and spillovers: Theoretical and empirical insights from an exploratory study of Toronto's film cluster, *Industry and Innovation* 14, 4, 401–20

Watson, J, 2007, Modeling the relationship between networking and firm performance, *Journal of Business Venturing* 22, 6, 852–74

Watts, DJ, Strogatz, SH, 1998, Collective dynamics of 'small-world' networks, *Nature* 393, 4, 440–2

Shifts in control disciplines and rescaling as a response to network governance failure: the BCJ case, Brazil

Charles Kirschbaum

Introduction

In 2003, the BCJ (Brasil Cresce Junto: Brazil Grows Together)[1] programme was created in a Brazilian state, in order to provide integrated educational, health, and social services to disadvantaged families and their children. With this aim in mind, the state government invited municipalities to join the programme. While local committees oversaw the work of sending staff to visit families' homes, the state committee supervised the local committees in order to guarantee that standards were followed. In order to promote the programme, the state's health department transferred funds directly to the municipal health department's account. The municipality, in turn, had to supplement the state's funding with its own contribution. The programme experienced a fast rate of adherence among municipalities, accompanied by an increased number of children covered until 2011 (see Figure 1). During this year, the state programme managers conducted a sharp reduction in coverage due to concerns over social impact and priorities. Moreover, the programme led to a rescaling of its governance structure: BCJ was reorganised, reinforcing the state level evaluation prerogative. This scalar shift also led to a rapid change in inter-level governance relations.

While network governance has emerged as a central topic in public administration, little is known about how governance pressures cascade into rescaling. Network governance has been identified as not only a viable, but a necessary governance mode, when either pure market or hierarchical forms of public policy governance do not suffice (Torfing et al, 2012). Furthermore, network governance has been granted the aura of an alternative to state-centric modes of control. While the phenomenon of network governance has been widely explored in the extant literature, it is only recently that scholars have specified the mechanisms explaining why some networks are able to attain long-term sustainability while others fail to even pass an initial stage (for example, Abers and Keck, 2013). There does not need to be a full disruption of operations or a complete absence of policy implementation in order for a network failure to be observed. As I shall argue in this chapter, network failure may occur whenever this mode of governance is substituted by other modes, leading to impoverished collaboration and the alienation of key stakeholders. In other words, not all failure is disruptive; failure may be more frequent, accepted and manageable, and may lead to recurrent patterns of readjustment (Jessop, 2003). Additionally, then, I shall explore how rescaling may be a response to network failure.

In order to describe a network's modes of governance, including both the interface between parts and the functioning of each part, I adapt the idea of 'disciplines of control' to network governance (White, 2008; Corona and Godart, 2009; Barkey and Godart, 2013). This framework comprises three disciplines that are ultimately related to distinct evaluation practices: 'mediating inclusiveness', which evaluates individuals and objects based on their status, 'interface communication', whose valuation practice is based on quality ranking, and 'purifying selection', whose valuation practice is related to boundary setting. I argue that rescaling efforts can imply changes across configurations based on this framework.

This framework is applied to the BCJ case summarised above, a policy aimed at pregnant women and early childhood care in a state in Brazil. The rescaling briefly described above allows a historical reconstruction of how this governance network structure occurred, and how different aspects changed accordingly. Abstracting from this particular case, I close the chapter by suggesting some general mechanisms that govern rescaling within the network governance framework.

Nuts and bolts of network governance

Throughout this chapter, I shall assume that network governance must meet the following criteria: (1) it relies on dependency between different parties; (2) it includes private actors within its deliberative sphere, while public agencies retain the decision-making prerogative; (3) it assumes formal and stable relationships among parties, while informal interaction may be a necessary (but insufficient) condition for its functioning; and, finally, (4) it deals with complex issues related to public policy formulation and implementation (Torfing, 2005; Ansell and Gash, 2008; Klijn et al, 2012). While I assume that these criteria constitute network governance, I entertain the possibility of loosening these requirements while investigating network governance dynamics. First, while most governance network proponents assume asset co-dependency as an antecedent to the network governance solution, I shall espouse a broader position. Governance networks may be deployed in order to foster dependency, where little or none is perceived in its pre-history by network actors. Second, while the literature on network governance requires full-fledged inclusion of non-governmental actors, I argue that in the course of a network history, non-governmental stakeholders might not be as participative as originally assumed, while retaining the right to participate. These two caveats converge towards the idea that the network governance design might not always be fully actualised, or may fluctuate, leading to cycles of failure and readjustments, while its legal framework remains legitimated among network actors.

In order to offer a framework that enables cross-case comparison, I suggest adapting Harrison White's control disciplines framework, developed in his book *Identity and control* (2008), as a convenient departure point. White suggests that social actors seek to secure control in order to stabilise relationships. It is worth noting that efforts aimed at control are not exerted by 'principals' over 'agents' alone (as in New Public Management) or by supervising agencies over public servants (as in the Weberian bureaucracy): it occurs among all entities and directions (bottom-up, top-down and diagonally) (Corona and Godart, 2009). Control efforts involve practices that coalesce around disciplines. These are ultimately: interface communication, mediating inclusiveness, and purifying selection.[2]

Interface communication is related to the communication between distinct deliberative bodies. In an industrial plant, for instance, this discipline is observed when suppliers and customers communicate to each other according to established standards. Within corporate governance, it is illustrated through the reports provided by directors to the board. Hence, the idea of 'quality' is central to this mode of control. If some raw material fails to meet the established requirements, 'quality control' will block its entrance into the plant. Both new public management and Weberian-style bureaucracy strongly rely on interface communication, given their report-based control and vertical differentiation. Furthermore, interfaces may operate vertically (as in hierarchies) or horizontally (as in contracts). Because deliberative bodies may be engaged in complex and conflicting stakeholder expectations, it may become a challenge to meet them all. Uncoupling (or even decoupling) interface communication and internal practices may be required to ensure systemic robustness, or to maintain autonomy (Suchman, 1995). Conversely, formal metrics can be designed in a sufficiently abstract way to accommodate local needs (Stinchcombe, 2001). This is one way in which upper levels seek embeddedness with lower levels (Torfing et al, 2012). In the network governance literature, interface communication is related to connectivity management, which allows differentiated parts to connect and communicate, while retaining the information asymmetry inherent to entity differentiation (Klijn et al, 2012).

Mediating inclusiveness is related to the degree that deliberative bodies are able to include different and numerous stakeholders in their internal decision-making processes. In contrast to 'interface communication', different actors are included in the same deliberative forum, rather than communicating through interfaces. From a control perspective, this imposes the challenge of dealing with a cacophony of voices, multiple goals and criteria, which is assumed in network governance (Torfing, 2005; Klijn et al, 2012). In the absence of an acceptable pecking order, status ambiguity leads to conflict and stalemate (Gould, 2003). For White, status asymmetry between members becomes the governing mechanism for mediation among distinct voices. In contrast, the existing literature in political science has taken a normative turn by insisting that mediation among asymmetrical and multiple stakeholders should be conducted according to fairness principles (Abers, 2003), while asymmetries should be counterbalanced (Ansell and Gash, 2008).

Control efforts related to *purifying selection* involve practices that sift through evidence in order to achieve maximum adherence to a set of criteria. This form of control includes reviewing tests and measurement devices in order to improve evidence (Callon, 1986). Selection of pure evidence becomes the dominant practice, while rejection of impure evidence as merely 'invalid', or pertaining to another forum, supports boundary protection and buffering.[3] Hence, a simple way of describing the 'purifying selection' discipline is via the activity of boundary setting throughout social systems. A university, for example, may determine that only certain employees can have access to more sensitive meetings, whereas the criteria for setting these boundaries may vary according to the committee.

It is important to show how these dimensions are both distinct and complement each other. The 'purifying selection' is different from 'interface communication' insofar as the latter involves ranking objects through a quality measure, while the former is related to establishing a boundary. Consequently, purifying selection may rely on accurate measurement, but it is not reducible to it. While ranking describes an object under several dimensions, purifying selection may elect any dimension and any arbitrary level in order to establish a selection threshold.

Along the same line, while the 'purifying selection' discipline establishes boundaries, 'mediating inclusiveness' deals with those actors and objects already included. After membership is granted, included objects and actors may differ in how they rank in terms of potentially incommensurable measures, requiring the use of prestige as a way of balancing members.

Finally, while 'interface communication' relies on quality ranking, 'mediating inclusiveness' establishes a compromise between distinct evaluation dimensions through prestige.

It can be appreciated, then, how these different control disciplines might clash or reinforce each other, depending on the concrete configuration in which they are embedded. Inclusive mediation may lead the decision-making process to espouse objective criteria closer to higher status members. In contrast, inclusion may pose challenges to establishing consensual purifying procedures. Inclusion may overcome control problems whenever interface communication becomes ceremonial. Conversely, granting autonomy to actors to make decisions enables the number of contending voices to be reduced. This occurs as follows: by separating non-convergent voices into a different forum, this new deliberative body will communicate with the original one through a regulated communicative interface. As such, the burden of convergence will be transferred to a different sphere, and if and when this new forum reaches a consensus, it will channel its demands to the original forum through regulated channels and communication standards.

An analogous idea can be applied when considering the relationship between interfaces and purifying selection. Interfaces may be established in order to buffer the forum where selection takes place and tests are purified. Consider, for instance, a committee that selects an award. This committee might prefer to keep its deliberation as opaque to the outside world as possible, communicating the criteria for selecting the winner ex-post. However, the opacity involved in the insulated tests may frustrate upper level steering (for example, Ansell et al, 2012).

I shall illustrate how these disciplines interact in a concrete situation: the daily management of a state school. 'Interface communication' takes place in several instances. A school principal at a TPA meeting might tell parents that their children are falling behind. In contrast, a principal might choose to decouple how teachers perceive their students' actual learning achievements when reporting to external stakeholders, while leading parents to believe that their children are making progress. This move could be resisted: for example, parents might inquire of the school principal why the student body had failed to attain, on average, the required levels in national tests. Consequently, internal testing and external evaluations may clash, leading to attrition in the parent–principal interface. In a discussion of the school budget with teachers and community members (mediating inclusiveness), the principal might need to reconcile incommensurate claims, such as keeping art classes or reinforcing a foreign language course. These claims might be ranked in an order that matches the pecking order underlying the relative status of the community members. Finally, we could picture a teachers' meeting in which each student's situation is evaluated in terms of her conditions to graduate to the next academic year. One teacher might claim the group should cut some slack for a specific student, who is having to cope with a difficult situation at home. In opposition to this warmhearted teacher, we might encounter a cold response from another teacher who claims that the meeting should ensure that evaluations are grounded in impersonal and objective exams. The 'purifying selection' discipline operates here at different levels: whether a piece of evidence is 'pure' and whether someone should be excluded from a classroom. I apply this vocabulary to the BCJ case in order to describe its evolution.

Network governance failure and rescaling

In this section, I extend the previous discussion by taking in account the fact that non-disruptive network governance failure is a relatively recurrent event and, like organising in general, requires adjustments. Broadly speaking, we can identify two major kinds of network governance failures: multiple objectives and spatial or temporal overextension (Jessop, 2003). These failures are, in turn, associated with deeper causes: problems of temporal synchronicity between partners (due to distinct cycles of accountability), deficient knowledge and over-simplification, and inter-temporal/systemic conflicts. Jessop (2003) suggests that network governors can take several types of action to steer networks away from failure: meta-exchange (changes in access to markets, or a new market framework), meta-organising (rescaling, shifts in deliberative autonomy), meta-heterarchy (redistribution of decision-making, while creating or collapsing autonomous agencies), and meta-governance (changes in the steering committee, changes to the governance portfolio).

Meta-organising efforts lead to changes in vertical differentiation between levels. As a result, distinct levels will be assigned to different processes, a central theme in rescaling. The rescaling effort within the potential meta-organising reactions involves redefining the nested 'hierarchisation of spaces in relation to one another' (Brenner, 2004, 9; 2009). Rescaling covers a range of phenomena, from shifting processes upstream (from nation-state to regional or global) or downstream (from nation-state to municipality), and changes in scope (for example, territorial, or jurisdictional coverage). While rescaling could be seen as a deliberated effort to cope with a particular network failure, more specifically we might interpret rescaling as a response to conflict between stakeholders who exert their voices at different points in the system. Because territories, places, scales and networks are all constitutive of one to another, rescaling implies further changes within and across deliberative bodies (Jessop et al, 2008).

Throughout this chapter, I argue that rescaling has direct implications for network governance, given that it requires changes in control-based disciplines, as reviewed in the previous section. In very broad strokes, I suggest that stakeholder pressures may lead to rescaling, which is then accompanied by changes in certain aspects of the control disciplines. Ultimately, the whole discipline configuration can change. I shall detail the mechanisms between 'rescaling' and changing 'control discipline configurations' after presenting the empirical case.

The BCJ Case

In order to develop the BCJ case, a research assistant and myself interviewed programme managers at State and local levels. In 2003, the Brasil Cresce Junto (Brazil Grows Together) programme was established in a Brazilian state.[4] Its original inspiration was taken from the 'Early Head Start'[5] and 'Educa a tu hijo'[6] programmes, based in the United States and Cuba, respectively. The original goal of the BCJ programme was to provide integrated health, educational and social services to children aged from zero to three years. Motivated by a strong belief that the most important formative years occur in early childhood, policy makers intended to prioritise this period, aiming to achieve the most impact on the later years of an individual's life.

At 'street level', members of staff visit low-income families and help them to become better integrated into the community. During these visits, members of staff play with children, help parents to learn and adopt activities, and record children's development in relation to several criteria. Furthermore, members of staff helps the family to gain access to related public services. This is done through a two-pronged strategy: by bundling early childhood services together in order to allow more efficient and integrated services; and encouraging members of staff to facilitate the access of particular families to services in the municipality or in other localities as and when needed. Given these two aspects, BCJ staff must be up to speed with the state's requirements concerning early childhood and the locality's services. In addition, while the programme is supposed to be locally customised, it has to follow the state's parameters. These strategies led to BCJ's original network design.

At the state level, the Technical State Group (TSG) performs the role of operational committee, providing training to local staff, deploying and overseeing an intranet-based database containing data on children and visits, visiting municipalities in order to assess and support local needs, and helping municipalities to develop their own customised BCJ project. The TSG is fully staffed by the Health Department and UNESCO consultants, and is accountable to the Steering Committee. The Steering Committee is coordinated by the state Health Department, but is supported by the Education, Culture, Work and Social Development Departments, UNESCO, and the State Committee for Early Childhood Integral Development, which comprises non-governmental stakeholders. This inclusive steering committee is intended to enable the participation of stakeholders from governmental and non-governmental entities, as well as diverse state departments, in order to generate state-level integrated policies that can facilitate integration at the local level.

The municipal level structure mirrors the state level in several ways. At the local level, the Technical Municipal Group (TMG) is in charge of daily activities, including the deployment of members of staff to families, training, interacting with local public services whenever needed, and overseeing correct data input in the state intranet database. The TMG is required to include representatives from multiple local departments (for example, Education, Health and Social Development). The TMG is operationally directed by a municipality's department head, usually the Health Department secretary (in a few cases, it has been accountable to the Education Department secretary instead). Subordinating the TMG to the Health Department at local level facilitates the interaction with the TSG at state level, given that the latter is under the health department's control too, while the funding required to hire visiting staff members is provided via the Health Department accounts.[7] However, the TMG is accountable not only to the department to which it is formally subordinated, but also to other departments, and to local non-governmental organisations.

Before exploring the BCJ's history further, it may be worth taking stock of its original design and contrasting it with the suggested theoretical framework. One first question is whether the BCJ fits the criteria of 'network governance' described above. Although its original design requires public and non-governmental entities to be involved, the network's pre-history of asset-dependency between actors is weak, or mild at best (compare to water management programmes, where it is much more risky to deploy decoupled initiatives). Because the relatively autonomous local departments are usually willing to function as traditional insulated services, controlling sufficient resources to carry on their activities, there is limited incentive to pull services together and integrate tasks and initiatives. Finally, while there is ample evidence that early childhood is better served through integrated approaches, policy makers do not usually embrace them. As a consequence, children's well-being is usually seen as dependent on fragmented processes.

To a certain extent, the state-level initiative to create intersectorial policies is supposed to provide an initial template for local level collaboration, counterbalancing centrifugal forces operating at the local level. Analogous to the 'shadow of hierarchy' idea, under this original design, a local tie would be nested within a state-level tie. Furthermore, local staff are also expected to informally combine programmes around a specific family's needs. In sum, the BCJ's original proponents not only faced the challenge of planning and implementing the programme, they had to convince major gatekeepers that early childhood deserved to be understood in an integrated form.

Conversely, in order to convince mayors to accept the programme, the steering committee at state level had to build in enough flexibility to allow each municipality to set their own priorities, provided that the programme's core procedures were buffered and protected. This governance design resembles a 'hierarchy of networks' in which both levels function as networks, while retaining a hierarchical relationship between them. In the interview with the coordinator of Zirma TMG, for instance, it became apparent that the top priority of this municipality was reducing child mortality. From this perspective, the educational, cultural and other dimensions (seen as non-priority) were regarded as secondary in this locality. As a result, the interaction between the Health Department and other departments in Zirma maintained an asymmetry not originally intended by the BCJ's designers. Despite this original plan, one of my interviewees reported that the TMGs fell short of full inclusion of stakeholders. Consequently, the programme's functions were frequently absorbed into the Health Department.

In tandem, while the steering committee was expected to include several departments at the state level, its efforts became more and more centralised around the Health Department initiatives. One of the interviewees, a former top executive in the state government, revealed that the attempts to include other voices (besides Health) had never really taken off, leading the BCJ programme to be quite different from the 'Educa tu Hijo' programme, which is much closer to Education.

A step further in this analysis associates the BCJ's original design with the control disciplines explained above. Two key *communication interfaces* exist: first, between the TMG and the TSG, we can observe the database containing every child history as a way of monitoring how children are developing across time, the number of visits provided, the percentage of families covered, and the ratio between staff and children. Furthermore, the TMG provides customised reports to municipal departments, which increases the programme's legitimacy to local constituents. For instance, in Despina (one of the municipalities visited), the TMG coordinator provides panel data on the school progress of those children who were covered by the programme before joining school. At the local level, the

TMG must ensure that the database is constantly updated, children will not be classified under the wrong categories, and so on. Likewise, visiting staff must make sure that activities are performed in the prescribed way, and that they can assess the children's progress objectively, and so forth.

Inclusive mediation is expected to take place at several points in the BCJ network: the state level steering committee should promote collective decision-making involving governmental and non-governmental actors; the TSG is supposed to promote integrated policies that meet multiple demands from distinct departments; and finally, at the TMG's level, local needs are expressed through different channels and multiple voices should be taken in account when designing child-centered and family-centered policies. To be sure, a fair form of inclusive mediation is not required to grant equal standing to all voices, but to provide legitimised mediation between these voices. Zirma is a case in point. Due to the prominence of health-related issues, other stakeholders acquiesced to its centrality in the TMG forum.

Purifying selection is distributed across deliberative and executive bodies. It may be observed at different levels and processes. For example, the TSG might choose to expel a municipality from the programme, while at local level a TMG might exceptionally choose to include a family under its coverage. Furthermore, at the municipal level, the TMG might exclude particular local stakeholders from core decisions. As we shall see over the course of the BCJ's history, changes in the 'purifying selection' and 'mediating inclusive mediation' disciplines at the state level triggered changes across the system.

BCJ's network governance rescaling and redesign

Within 2011, BCJ's steering committee engaged in several initiatives of programme evaluation. These initiatives comprised evaluating (1) the programme's coverage and selection criteria, (2) information quality and (3) programme impact. This set of evaluations led the TSG to rescale the programme, while adjusting its approach.

A first concern was related to the programme's coverage. While the programme was successful in covering above 70,000 children by 2011, the programme's managers were unsure what criteria was being deployed by municipalities to select them (see Figure 1). By examining the database, the TSG discovered that a visitor would typically be able to visit no more than 30 families, especially in rural areas, where distances were larger; this figure was lower than the expected ratio of 40 families per visitor. In response, the TSG deployed several of its permanent and consultant staff to visit localities and pay visits to families alongside regular local visiting staff.

These spot visits also revealed that the programme's core procedures were not always maintained, jeopardising achievement of the planned results.[8]

Figure 1: Number of children covered by the BCJ programme

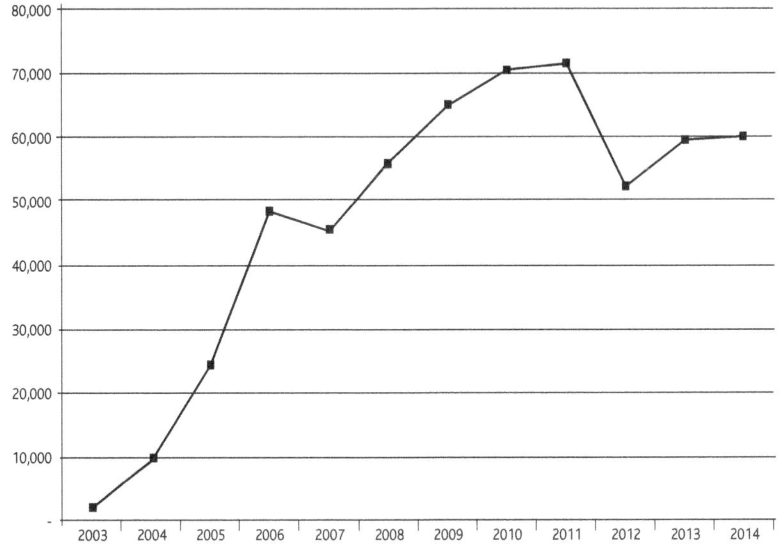

Source: Data based on the BCJ website. Numbers until 2011 are estimated.

A second concern was related to information quality. While the intranet database was constructed in order to permit vertical monitoring, the available data was not fully studied and there was little or no quality assurance on its feeding. Since the intranet database was the major communicative interface between levels, the steering committee paid special attention to whether and how it was updated. Careful due diligence revealed that the visiting staff would input data into the database in a non-standardised fashion. Furthermore, the frequency of data entry was faulty. A direct consequence of these findings was the need to review the visiting staff's efforts and their commitment to the task, the municipality–state communication interface, and the usage of the aggregated information at state level. Prior to the 2011 impact evaluation, the municipality–state communication interface allowed for sufficient loose coupling of stated higher level goals and the actual achievements at lower level. This occurred because the municipal level was primarily accountable for a simple family headcount. Now a stricter interface would mean a tighter informational coupling.

A third concern was centred on the programme's effectiveness. In 2011, the Offord Centre for Child Studies,[9] a Canadian research think tank, performed an impact evaluation of the BCJ programme, deploying the same methodology used to assess other comparable programmes in other geographic areas. It compared children from municipalities that adhered to the BCJ programme to children from control groups (that is, localities not exposed to non-observable treatments; see Angrist and Pischke, 2008). Results were positive: boys in the control group presented a 5 per cent higher risk of vulnerability than BCJ treated boys. Moreover, the parents of BCJ children presented a higher likelihood of being involved in their children's educational activities, leading to better school performance. The programme also had a higher impact among families headed by low-income mothers. In several other dimensions, however, it was not clear whether BCJ children presented better metrics than the control group children.[10]

Taken together, these concerns led the TSG to believe that visitors were stretched out to cover as many families as possible. Following the control-based discipline framework sketched above, we can observe a reflexive turn towards the 'purifying selective' discipline. A 'purifying turn' might entail elimination of the entire programme and the deployment of resources in other, higher impact programmes. This possibility was blocked as the programme did indeed present positive results, and attained local legitimacy among a large range of mayors and constituencies. To be sure, TSG wanted to make sure that the visit procedures were thoroughly followed, that the municipalities would be sensible in choosing selection criteria, and that the database would be a reliable mirror of what was taking place at the local level. As a consequence, the network governor triggered a shift among the governance components, in order to secure the achievement of better results (Jessop, 2003; Haveri, 2006).

Concretely, it meant that the programme as a whole could not afford to cover the same number of families, since it would be unable to ensure the minimum requirements (see Figure 1 for the historical evolution of children covered by the programme). Furthermore, the programme steering committee became more conscious of what selection criteria they would suggest the TMGs to apply. Taking in account federal programmes like Bolsa Família, the EDI results, and the state's caucus dedicated for policy evaluation, the TSG geared towards the following criteria: first, the most vulnerable children would be covered, next priorities defined by other state and federal policies (pregnant women under risk, indigenous and quilombola[11] populations, and rural based families), next those families where the BCJ proved to have higher impact. The lowest priority was given to families and children with lower levels of vulnerability and lower chances of impact.[12]

TMGs were swiftly instructed to supervise closely how the visiting staff updated the system data. TSG staff also started to examine random children's development tracks on a regular basis. Specifically, TSG staff would now require TMG supervisors and visiting staff to include qualitative notes in specific fields in the database, in order to provide further evidence that the metrics being reported were, in fact, a good reflection of the reality on the ground. The TSG also insisted that the municipalities adhere more strictly to the requirement to hire visitors with the proper qualifications. Unfortunately, these stricter procedures led several municipal mayors to shy away from adhering to the programme. Conversely, the steering committee at state level became stricter in terms of its approval of new memberships for municipalities that failed to present sufficient commitment to its core programme. Figure 2 shows that after 2011 the programme plateaued at around 50 per cent of municipalities.

Historically, the BCJ network revealed a much better penetration in smaller municipalities (Figure 3): larger municipalities experienced more difficulties than smaller ones in mediating conflicting voices within the TMG. In addition, larger municipalities had lower resource dependency on the state, which led them to be less committed to the programme, or

Figure 2: Percentage of municipalities that adhered to the BCJ programme

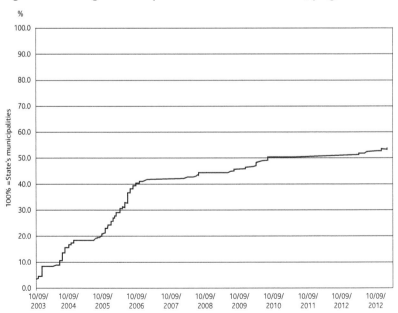

exert their autonomy in a more forcefully way. The shift in the control mechanisms might have made it even less attractive for larger municipalities to join the network.

Figure 3: Percentage of children covered by municipality size

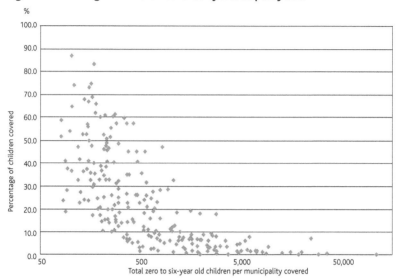

Network rescaling takes place insofar as the vertical relationship between levels changes. To be sure, the formal relationship between levels remained the same (as established by an array of different laws, including the Brazilian Constitution), which entails a high autonomy to the municipality level (that is, the TMG) to manage its local policies. Yet, I argue that the state level came closer to becoming a dominant scale, rather than a nodal scale (Collinge, 1999). In the previous configuration, knowledge was mainly used by local actors to best serve families and children. This knowledge was communicated through impoverished coding in the database, and monitored by the TSG in a piecemeal fashion, while the state failed to take maximum advantage of its position as a focal point in knowledge aggregation. By contrast, after 2011, a statistical analysis of impacts at state level was embraced, generating gains of aggregation (Jensen and Meckling, 2009). The state level consequently gained the upper hand in informing the local level about which programme achieved the highest impact.

Originally the TMG was accountable to the TSG and the municipal mayor. Both were mainly concerned to expand the programme's reach and eradicate child mortality. After 2011 the municipal mayor's relative prominence declined. This occurred for two reasons. First, at state level the steering committee was able to improve its coordination of several state policies, enhancing the intended 'blueprint' for local partnerships. Second, the TSG, as well as state secretaries, strengthened their relationships with local actors, diminishing the mayor's brokerage power. This second step was taken for the following reasons. First, the TSG relied on the broader inclusion of local actors in order to increase the alignment of local selection criteria to the new criteria cited above. Second, in order to make the state-level blueprints work, state secretaries had to be in closer contact with local counterparts. Consequently, diagonal lines of control between the local and state levels were improved. An additional outcome of this realignment was the de facto re-inclusion of local stakeholders whose participation in the TMG had been kept at a low level prior to 2011.

Efforts towards meta-heterarchy (change in institutional structures outside the network) were also emphasised as a consequence of the 2011 impact study. The state's elected deputies attempted to create an autonomous federal agency that could oversee early childhood programmes across Brazil, establishing complementary diagonal interfaces. Furthermore, deputies also proposed a new law that would recognise visitors as a regulated occupation: this would require certification, public competitions and possibly a specific undergraduate training programme.

Discussion and final remarks

The pre-2011 configuration presented low degree in all control disciplines: broad coverage was more important than selectiveness (leading to low purifying selection), database feeding was usually linked to headcount (leading to poor interface communication), and local committees (TMGs) were usually led by secretary, with strong link to mayor's interests (leading to low mediating inclusion).

By contrast. the post-2011 configuration presented a higher degree of 'purifying selection' (more formalised criteria for selecting families), higher 'interface communication' (tighter control of database input), and higher 'mediating inclusiveness' (local priorities were set after a wide-range consultation of key stakeholders). Future studies will benefit from transforming this illustrative example into measurable variables, allowing an exploration of whether the balance across dimensions changes. It would also allow us to describe the trajectory of this shift across the dimensions in a more detailed fashion, permitting further cross-case comparisons.

Substantively, the network governance debate has shifted towards the assessment of actual structures and their adherence to democratic and efficient principles (Fung and Wright, 2001; Provan and Kenis, 2008; Sørensen and Torfing, 2009). Several sympathisers of network governance claim that both democratic and efficient principles can be attained (Sørensen and Torfing, 2009). Conversely, network failures are seen as a component in the network governance dynamics and evolution. Having set a general aim here of exploring finer network governance design mechanisms, and specifically the role of rescaling, we can now step back from the concrete BCJ case and explore the extent to which the control-based disciplines help to further our knowledge of network dynamics.

Network governance brings the hope of being simultaneously less 'adversarial' and less 'insulated'. In contrast, it promises to embrace collaboration. However, network governance analysts warn us that several trade-offs may lurk within: policy makers will have to accommodate local needs and political outcomes (Torfing et al, 2012), while exerting their influence to diminish local power asymmetries (O'Toole and Meier, 2004), and promote true stakeholder participation (Abers, 2003; Ansell and Gash, 2008). Throughout the analysis of the BCJ case's original set-up, I brought no new message capable of adding to the multilevel governance narrative: upper level network governors must commit to a compromise between coupling local and global goals, and allowing a viable local convergence of interests in order to attain ownership of the programme.

The analysis of the BCJ's history brings additional insights to network meta-governance. Pressures at global level for effective impact and adherence to salient selection criteria have led network governors to shift their attention patterns (Padgett, 1981). Shifts like this may be followed by abrupt changes in policy configuration (Jones et al, 2003; Jones and Baumgartner, 2005). This was translated into a 'purifying' effort towards all tests performed in the system. Because the upper level was now accountable for certain specific metrics and impact results, it became more selective in relation to municipality inclusion, and also reinforced tight coupling through the system's communicative interfaces. One consequence, inter alia, is the difficulty in promoting the inclusion of new municipalities into the programme, since it became harder for local politicians to simply maximise the number of families reached. However, in those municipalities where the BCJ was already present, the inclusion of additional stakeholders led to an informed shift in local priorities. Rescaling seemed mandatory: because resources stem from the state level and the impact study process is associated with the aggregate level of knowledge.

The BCJ case allows us to observe that an increased focus on one dimension can lead to an increased focus across all other dimensions. In order to improve the programme's impact and reach of vulnerable families, the state level reinforced the local 'inclusive mediation' dimension. This occurred as the state level aimed to amplify the democratic feature of local decision-making by empowering local actors, while the state level fed the local actors with relevant information on vulnerability and the profile of high-impact children and families. To a certain extent, empowering the local level network's inclusiveness mirrors the state's level network increased sensibility to federal and state levels' stakeholders.

Undoubtedly, the direction taken by the BCJ programme was not the only one capable of addressing the stakeholders' concerns. Alternatively, the municipalities could have claimed that more, rather than less, decentralisation would have better fitted the network reality (Schrank and Whitford, 2009). The sudden increase in the 'purifying selection' dimension could have driven each municipality to perform its own econometric analysis, while claiming that local solutions would work better than centralised routines. In this fictional scenario, vertical communication would be constrained to econometric results; hence, we would observe a decrease in the communication interface dimension. Furthermore, it is possible that local inclusive mediation would increase even further, since local networks would be more reliant on local efforts and solutions, but with lower diagonal links to counterparts at the state level.

Alternatively, the proposal to reinforce visiting staff could be identified as an effort to reinforce the alignment of local action with global requirements, without the tight coupling of the communicative interface. This initiative refers to the meta-heterarchy effort (redistribution of decision-making) explored in the section 'network governance failure and rescaling' above.

This case also affords the insight that the same control-based discipline can be applied at different levels. The purifying selection discipline, for instance, could have been reinforced at municipal level as well as state-level in independent ways. Any municipality would then be able to claim that its own procedures were better than the state-established procedures, and consequently claim independence from the overall system. In contrast, the pressure for inclusiveness seems to be harder to uncouple across levels, as these refer to values that are embedded diffused across the governance system.

Finally, it is worth exploring how the control-based disciplines framework might help in understanding how network governors reduce uncertainty and complexity in the system, besides establishing general goals, or the 'shadow of hierarchy' (Koppenjan and Klijn, 2004; Torfing et al, 2012). For example, upper level formalised communicative interfaces and horizontal differentiation might serve as a template to be replicated at lower levels (which could be labelled 'inter-level nested ties').

Notes

[1] The programme's actual name is concealed in accordance with the programme managers' request.

[2] White called these disciplines 'interfaces', 'councils' and 'arenas', respectively. I shall not use these terms for two reasons. First, they might mislead the reader into thinking that a deliberative body is either a council or an arena, while these are analytical dimensions. Second, the very words 'council' and 'arena' may loosely refer to forums, leading to confusion on how to distinguish these concepts. Instead, I prefer to focus on the actual practices that underlie control efforts.

[3] Compare Habermas's (1996) view of the civic sphere as a 'sluice system'.

[4] I conducted 13 interviews during May 2013, at the state capital, and two municipalities, Zirma and Despina. I have attempted to cover interviewees from all levels and departments, as well as individuals who had participated in management of the BCJ programme in the past. Interviews lasted 45 minutes on average. These interviews were later transcribed and coded.

[5] https://eclkc.ohs.acf.hhs.gov/hslc/tta-system/ehsnrc

[6] http://www.ecured.cu/index.php/Educa_a_tu_Hijo

[7] This is not a rule. In several municipalities, the TMG is led by Education of Social Service secretaries.

[8] A psychologist was hired by the BCJ in order to assess the visit procedures. His evaluation revealed that several aspects of the original script were placed in jeopardy. He also pointed out that certain parts of the routine were unnecessary.

[9] www.offordcentre.com/readiness/index.html

[10] OCCS recognises that the baseline might have been affected, which would require a new study in order to achieve conclusive results.

[11] Quilombolas are the descendants of fugitive slaves who live in colonies, called quilombolos.

[12] These criteria were never formalised. Ex-post narratives reveal that these criteria were applied in an informal fashion, at several interactions between TSG and TMG personnel.

References

Abers, R, 2003, Reflections on what makes empowered participatory governance happen, in A Fung, EO Wright (eds) *Deepening democracy: Institutional innovations in empowered participatory governance*, pp 200–7, New York: Verso

Abers, RN, Keck, ME, 2013, *Practical authority: Agency and institutional change in Brazilian water politics*, Oxford: Oxford University Press

Ackerman, J, 2004, Co-governance for accountability: beyond 'exit' and 'voice', *World Development* 32, 3, 447–63

Angrist, JD, Pischke, JS, 2008, *Mostly harmless econometrics: An empiricist's companion*, Princeton, NJ: Princeton University Press

Ansell, C, Gash, A, 2008, Collaborative governance in theory and practice, *Journal of Public Administration Research and Theory* 18, 4, 543–71

Ansell, C, Sondorp, E, Stevens, RH, 2012, The promise and challenge of global network governance: The global outbreak alert and response network, *Global governance: A review of multilateralism and international organizations* 18, 3, 317–37

Barkey, K, Godart, FC, 2013, Empires, federated arrangements, and kingdoms: Using political models of governance to understand firms' creative performance, *Organization Studies* 34, 1, 79–104

Brenner, N, 2004, *New state spaces: Urban restructuring and state rescaling in Western Europe*, Oxford: Oxford University Press

Brenner, N, 2009, Restructuring, rescaling, and the urban question, *Critical Planning* 16, 4

Callon, M, 1986, Some elements of a sociology of translation: Domestication of the scallops and the fishermen of St Brieuc Bay, in J Law (ed) *Power, action and belief: A new sociology of knowledge?*, pp 196–233, Oxford: Routledge

Castells, M, 2000, *The rise of the network society: Economy, society and culture*, Malden, MA: Blackwell Publishing

Collinge, C, 1999, Self-organisation of society by scale: A spatial reworking of regulation theory, *Environment and Planning D* 17, 5, 557–74

Corona, VP, Godart, FC, 2009, Network-domains in combat and fashion organizations, *Organization* 17, 2, 283–304

Fung, A, Wright, EO, 2001, Deepening democracy: Innovations in empowered participatory governance, *Politics and Society* 29, 1, 5–42

Gould, R, 2003, *Collision of wills: How ambiguity about social rank breeds conflict*, Chicago, IL: University of Chicago Press

Habermas, J, 1996, *Between facts and norms: Contributions to a discourse theory of law and democracy*, Cambridge, MA: MIT Press

Haveri, A, 2006, Complexity in local government change: limits to rational reforming, *Public Management Review*, 8, 1, 31–46

Jensen, MC, Meckling, WH, 2009, Specific knowledge and divisional performance measurement, *Journal of Applied Corporate Finance* 21, 2, 49–57

Jessop, B, 2003, Governance and meta-governance: On reflexivity, requisite variety and requisite irony, in H Bang (ed) *Governance as social and political communication*, pp 101–16, Manchester: Manchester University Press

Jessop, B, Brenner, N, Jones, M, 2008, Theorizing sociospatial relations, *Environment and Planning D, Society and Space* 26, 3, 389

Jones, BD, Baumgartner, FR, 2005, A model of choice for public policy, *Journal of Public Administration Research and Theory* 15, 3, 325–51

Jones, BD, Sulkin, T, Larsen, HA, 2003, Policy punctuations in American political institutions, *American Political Science Review* 97, 1, 151–69

Klijn, E-H, De Rynck, F, Skelcher, C, Voets, J, 2012, The democratic character of new institutional governance arrangements: Comparing Dutch and Belgian experiences, in JM Fenger, VJJM Bekkers (eds) *Beyond fragmentation and interconnectivity: Public governance and the search for connective capacity*, Amsterdam: IOS Press, pp 142–63

Koppenjan, JFM, Klijn, E-H, 2004, *Managing uncertainties in networks: A network approach to problem solving and decision making*, Abingdon: Psychology Press

Koppenjan, JF, Klijn, E-H, 2013, Collaborative governance: Global trend or local practice? Governance as manifestation of globalization or local identity, Paper for the Global Governance Club Meeting: Nias, Wassenaar

Meuleman, L, 2008, *Public management and the metagovernance of hierarchies, networks and markets: The feasibility of designing and managing governance style combinations*, Berlin: Springer Science, Business Media

O'Toole, LJ, Meier, KJ, 2004, Desperately seeking Selznick: Cooptation and the dark side of public management in networks, *Public Administration Review* 64, 6, 681–93

Padgett, JF, 1981, Hierarchy and ecological control in federal budgetary decision making, *American Journal of Sociology* 87, 1, 75–129

Provan, KG, Kenis, P, 2008, Modes of network governance: Structure, management, and effectiveness, *Journal of Public Administration Research and Theory* 18, 2, 229–52

Schrank, A, Whitford, J, 2009, Industrial policy in the United States: A neo-Polanyian interpretation, *Politics and Society* 37, 4, 521–53

Sørensen, E, Torfing, J, 2009, Making governance networks effective and democratic through metagovernance, *Public Administration* 87, 2, 234–58

Stinchcombe, AL, 2001, *When formality works: Authority and abstraction in law and organizations*, Chicago, IL: University of Chicago Press.

Suchman, MC, 1995, Managing legitimacy: Strategic and institutional approaches, *Academy of Management Review* 20, 3, 571–610

Torfing, J, 2005, Governance network theory: Towards a second generation, *European Political Science* 4, 3, 305–15

Torfing, J, Peters, B, Sørensen, E, 2012, *Interactive governance: Advancing the paradigm*, Oxford: Oxford University Press

White, HC, 2008, *Identity and control: How social formations emerge*, Princeton, NJ: Princeton University Press

CHAPTER NINE

Institutional embeddedness and the scaling-up of collaboration and social innovation: the case of a Hong Kong-based international NGO

Eliza WY Lee and Juan Manuel Restrepo

Introduction

This chapter utilises the case of Crossroads Foundation, an international NGO (INGO) in Hong Kong, to explore how institutional embeddedness may facilitate the scaling-up of collaboration and social innovation.

For a long time in history, Hong Kong was instrumental in fostering transnational exchange of resources. Situated at the gateway of Asia, it has long played the role of a regional hub not only in trade and transportation, but also in information and cultural exchange. Such a gateway role can be traced back to the late nineteenth century when the British first took over Hong Kong as a colony. Since the 1990s with neoliberal globalisation and China's development Hong Kong has further developed itself into an important international financial centre. Through its close business partnership with South China (particularly the Guangdong region), Hong Kong has also emerged as a regional centre for providing a wide range of core producer services that drive and manage the global supply chains (Hong Kong Centre for Economic Research, 2003), covering financial, legal and management matters, innovation, development, design, administration, personnel, production technology, maintenance, transport, communications, wholesale distribution, advertising and storage, while fulfilling important gateway functions in terms of flow of financial capital, human capital, ideas and information (Sassen, 2001, 90). With the presence of these infrastructures, Hong Kong has emerged as a global city in Asia. Suffice to highlight some major indicators: it is now the world's ninth largest trading entity, sixth largest foreign exchange market and seventh largest banking centre. It has one of Asia's top three stock markets. It is home to 1,379 regional headquarters and 2,456 regional offices of MNCs and is an international logistics hub for goods moved by sea, air and land.[1]

The literature on global cities have long recognised the linkage and networking role these cities can foster among individuals, firms and organisations. Saskia Sassen (2001), for instance, argues that global cities are 'postindustrial production sites' that manage and regulate the global network of production. Thus, global cities have a networked character and are distinguished by their social connectivity. The study of INGOs in global cities is thus a valuable exploration of the strategic position that a global city can provide for international and cross-sectoral collaboration. In a way, INGOs are the nonprofit counterparts of multinational corporations (MNCs), whose characteristics of *embeddedness* in both the transnational and local space is long recognised in the international business literature (see, for example, Heidenreich, 2012)

The case of Crossroads Foundation represents the effort of a group of social entrepreneurs to actively utilise the global city status of Hong Kong to scale up a nonprofit operation from a modest informal initiative to a sizeable transnational magnitude through the scaling-up of collaboration. The case will help illustrate how institutional embeddedness shapes the opportunity for the scaling-up of collaboration. The empirical data of the case is obtained through reviewing their official documents, the relevant websites, as well as in-depth interviews of their key staff.

Forms of institutional embeddedness

Embeddedness, first proposed by the economic historian Karl Polanyi (2001), has become a key concept in various fields. Polanyi uses the concept to denote that in non-market societies, economic institutions are connected to and restrained by social institutions such as religion, morality, kinship system. On the contrary, in a market economy, the economic institutions are largely disembedded from (meaning disconnected from or unconstrained by) these social institutions and acquire their own logic of operation. Polanyi's work has laid the foundation for economic sociology as well as other disciplines, including economic geography, organisation theory, business studies and network analysis, leading to an expansion in the categories of embeddedness if not the denotation of the term.[2]

One important perspective is the emphasis on network embeddedness. Granovetter (1985) emphasises that economic actions are embedded in networks of interpersonal relations. In Granovetter (1992), he further distinguishes between relational (dyadic relations between actors) and structural embeddedness (network structure of relationships between multiple actors). Similarly, Gulati and Gargiulo (1999) argue that most organisations are embedded in a variety of interorganisational networks and that organisational decisionmakers rely on the network of past partnerships in forming new alliances. Based on this observation, he proposes three forms of embeddedness, namely, relational, structural and positional, which will determine whether two organisations will form a new alliance. Forms of embeddedness are thus antecedents of alliance formation.

In addition, economic geographers have paid much attention to territorial embeddedness. Primarily focusing on globalisation of the production process and multinational corporations (MNCs), they argue that firms can become territorially embedded in the sense that they might anchor in a place due to government policies such as tax advantages and that such anchorage in a particular location will affect their subsequent development in terms of networks, value creation and so on (Henderson et al, 2002). Hess (2004), on the other hand, critiques the 'over-territorialisation' of the concept of embeddedness in economic geography in focusing on 'local' networks and localised social relationships as the spatial logic of embeddedness' (p 174). He argues that while spatial proximity facilitates trust and relationship building, networks may transcend territorial restrictions, as shown by the transnational ethnic networks and global production networks in which 'non-local forms of embeddedness is demonstrated' (p 175).

Heidenreich's (2012) study of MNCs provides further insight on the nature of transnational and translocal networks. He argues that 'the ability to shift between different forms of embeddedness and disembeddedness is…the major advantage of MNCs' (p 551). The managers of MNCs are regarded as socially embedded actors 'whose patterns of interpretation, perception and behaviour are shaped by their experiences in their home country…as well as the transnational social space of an MNC' (p 552). Adopting a structuration approach, Heidenreich emphasises that 'the social institutions and relationships in which companies are embedded are simultaneously shaped and dynamically reproduced by skilled social actors' (p 553). Hess's (2004) framework is useful for capturing the relationship between several forms of embeddedness that are relevant to this chapter. He proposes three forms of embeddedness, namely, societal, network and territorial. Societal embeddedness refers to the societal background of the actors that influences and shapes their action and behaviour (p 176). Network embeddedness '[d]escribes the network of actors a person or organisation is involved in', which involves a process of trust building between agents leading to successful and stable relationships (p 177). Territorial embeddedness refers to the anchorage of the actors in a particular place such as a city or region (p 177). These three dimensions are seen as interlinked and dynamically influencing each other (Hughes et al, 2008): 'It is the simultaneity of societal, network and territorial embeddedness that shapes networks and the spatial-temporal structures of economic action' (p 181). Thus, forms of embeddedness can be viewed as structural determinants for explaining a variety of behaviour of organisations and their actors.

Collaboration and its scaling-up

Collaboration, especially cross-sector or inter-organisational collaboration, has been receiving a lot of attention in the management and nonprofit studies fields in the past two decades. In general, it can be regarded as a 'process of multi-organisational arrangements to solve problems that cannot be solved or easily solved by a single organisation' (O'Leary et al, 2006, 7). This implies an inter-organisational relationship that is non-hierarchical and cooperative. Thomson and Perry (2006) provide a more comprehensive definition:

> Collaboration is a process in which autonomous actors interact through formal and informal negotiation, jointly creating rules and structures governing their relationships and ways to act or decide on the issues that brought them together; it is a process involving shared norms and mutually beneficial interactions. (p 23)

Torfing et al (2012) further put forward the idea of interactive governance that emphasises the 'negotiated interaction' among actors: 'In interactive governance, agency is not directly tied to institutions. Agency takes place in contextually defined governance arenas like networks, partnerships, or quasi-markets.' In the field of public and nonprofit management, the proliferation of literature on collaboration has largely occurred under the topic of collaborative governance, with major focuses being on inter-agency and cross-sector collaboration, inter-governmental relations, public engagement, democratic participation and so on. Despite some obviously common attention toward networking and social connectivity, not much has been written to bring together the perspectives of institutional embeddedness and collaborative governance.[3]

We argue that the concept of institutional embeddedness has great potential in enriching our understanding of collaborative governance. Adapting Hess's (2004) framework, we contend that the formation and scaling of collaboration among organisations is affected by the societal, network and territorial embeddedness of the organisational actors, whose agency shapes the particular forms of collaboration and whose strategic choice makes possible the scaling-up of collaboration.

Social innovation and its scaling-up

According to OECD (2010), social innovation is a process of 'identifying and delivering new services that improve the quality of life of individuals and communities'. This involves a series of 'innovative actions, strategies, practices and processes [that] arise whenever problems of poverty, exclusion, segregation and deprivation or opportunities for improving living conditions cannot find satisfactory solutions in the "institutionalised field" of public or private action' (Moulaert et al, 2013, 2). The result is a product, service or programme that enables social change (Salamon et al, 2010; Phills et al, 2008).

Scaling-up can be understood as part of the process of social innovation.[4] According to Mulgan, scaling-up of social innovation 'comes when an idea proves itself in practice and can then be grown, replicated, adapted or franchised. Taking a good idea to scale requires skilful strategy and coherent vision, combined with the ability to marshal resources and support and identify the key points of leverage' (2012, 153). Evidence of scaling-up may be that the social innovation has attained a higher social impact (Lyon and Feranadez, 2012); it may be 'more quality benefits to more people over a wider geographical area more quickly, more equitably and more lastingly' (Carter and Currie-Alder, 2006, 126). Thus, scaling-up takes into account the number of beneficiaries, the quality of the service as well as its sustainability.

Organisations are scaling-up not only through organic growth but through different forms of collaboration (Lyon and Fernandez, 2012). Recent literature on scaling-up underscores how it could result in the loss of control and capacity from the initial social innovator (Lyon and Fernandez, 2012). Some studies have shown that partnership and outsourcing may increase the speed and impact of scaling-up (Bradach, 2010). Indeed, Bradach (2010) notes that 'finding ways to scale an organisation's impact without scaling its size is the new frontier in the field of social innovation'. Accordingly, two methods of scaling-up can be identified, namely, direct scaling-up through building capacities within the organisation and indirect scaling-up through partnership, alliance and knowledge sharing. The implication is that collaboration may constitute an important component for the scaling-up of social innovation.

International NGOs in Hong Kong: an overview

The role of Hong Kong as a gateway to China and the rest of Asia, established through its being a trading, transportation and information hub, has attracted not only international business corporations but also international NGOs. Way back in the early twentieth century, organisations such as the YMCA, YWCA and Salvation Army came to the colony to establish their local branch and provided service. In the 1950s, the influx of refugees from China brought another wave of INGOs, including Red Cross and World Vision. Many of them were here for disaster relief work. Since the 1970s, more INGOs have arrived to set up their regional headquarters. Consisting of human rights, advocacy and service-oriented organisations, these recent arrivals differ from the earlier waves in that they have not come in for direct service delivery. Instead, Hong Kong is chosen for its infrastructure and the regional linkages they can leverage for delivering service outside Hong Kong, from development programmes, humanitarian intervention, disaster relief, cultural exchange, to human rights advocacy. As well, Hong Kong has increasingly served as a regional base for fund raising, professional training, establishing connection with the business sector and so on. Thanks also to the relatively liberal political environment and an independent judiciary offering protection of civil liberties, Hong Kong stands out in Asia as an ideal base for INGOs to expand their works in the region.

Adopting the definition of Johns Hopkins Comparative Non-Profit Sector Project (CNSP), NGOs are *organised, private, non-profit-distributing, self-governing* and *voluntary* (Salamon and Anheier, 1997, 33). International NGOs frequently carry out one or more of the following activities: international exchange/friendship/cultural programmes; development assistance; international disaster relief; international human rights and peace organisations; support and service organisations, auxiliaries, councils, standard setting and governance organisations (Salamon and Anheier, 1997, 73).

According to the latest study by the Centre for Civil Society and Governance (CCSG), The University of Hong Kong on INGOs, in 2013 there were 215 INGOs in Hong Kong.[5] The sector generated an annual income of at least HK$4.67 billion. Donation and fundraising constitute the largest source of income (56.7%), followed by government funding (including local, overseas and intergovernmental organisations) (23.1%). In the same study, a survey was conducted in 2014, with findings indicating the linkage roles of these INGOs operating in Hong Kong: 36.4 per cent of the respondents regard the primary function of the Hong Kong offices as carrying out coordination and execution of operations outside Hong Kong and 23.8 per cent of them identify this as their secondary role (CCSG, 2015).[6]

It can be inferred from the overall picture here that the capacity in collaborating and networking is of crucial importance for these INGOs, whether to generate adequate income for their organisations or to fulfill their various missions. In the above study, INGOs commonly use the electronic media to maintain contact with their supporters and reach out to the wider community. They also maintain regular connection with other NGOs operating in Hong Kong, Mainland China and overseas. While they do not usually have close connection with the Hong Kong government (which can be an indicative sign that their services are mainly delivered outside Hong Kong), their relationship with the business sector is quite close. Of the INGOs surveyed, 50.9 per cent had some kind of cooperation with business companies in the past year, with fundraising, donation or sponsorship, joint projects and recruitment of volunteers being cited as the most common modes of cooperation (CCSG, 2015).

In what follows, we will discuss how Crossroads has developed from the largely informal philanthropic effort of a few individuals to an international organisation with elaborate local and transnational linkages. By so doing, we hope to explore the linkage between forms of embeddedness and the scaling-up of collaboration and social innovation.

Crossroads foundation

Operations and achievement: an overview

In 1995, a flood in northern China that affected more than 2 million people prompted Sally and Malcolm Begbie, both professionals originally from Australia and working in Hong Kong, to collect textiles in Hong Kong and send them off to the disaster area for emergency relief. What was meant as a one-off donation drive evolved into a regularised operation that finally culminated in the founding of an NGO. As the founders were well-connected with the business sector, they were able to collect from companies and manufacturers many kinds of high quality goods, from used furniture and computers that offices wish to dispose, unsold stocks of food, textiles, beddings, toys, household items, electrical appliances, to building supplies and medical equipment. They were allocated vacated premises by the Social Welfare Department as a warehouse for keeping the donated goods before they were shipped to their destination. The operation scaled up rapidly. More business companies learned about their operation and contacted them about making donations. For businesses, this was mutually beneficial as it saved them the cost of disposing massive volume of unwanted items and storing excess stocks (which makes business sense particularly considering the expensive land price in Hong Kong and thus the high cost of warehousing). Companies, seeing it as a good opportunity for fulfilling corporate social responsibility, also started to offer free delivery; shipping companies donated container space for shipping the donated goods to respective destinies. Soon Crossroads was shipping their donated goods to many parts of the world. In the process, they established connection with many NGOs and business corporations all over the world and developed a sophisticated platform that matched the supply of donors with the demand of the recipient organisations. As such, it established itself as a hub for transnational coordination of donated goods.

Crossroads has ventured into other initiatives. One innovative project is Global Hand, which is an online platform that provides brokerage facilitating public-private partnership. Business corporations, official donors, foundations and trusts from all over the world are matched with NGOs in different places based on the area of interest of the former and the need of the latter. The success of this operation prompted the United Nations to invite Crossroads's team to build a similar online platform to facilitate the partnership between United Nations and the business sector.

Another innovation is Global X-perience, which provides simulation experiences to students, NGOs and the business sector. Over 20 different types of simulation experiences on global issues related to refugees, disabilities, poverty, discrimination, etc, are offered that aim to raise the awareness of participants on these issues through experiential learning. Such programmes have been run in numerous countries outside Hong Kong, including at the latest World Economic Forum, and hundreds of multinational corporations have participated as part of their corporate social responsibility programmes. Lastly, Global Handicrafts promotes fair trade through a marketplace that operates as a retailer and distributor for fair trade goods from Asia, Africa, Europe, South America, Central Asia and the Middle East and Eastern and Central European countries. It also runs a fair trade cafe in the form of a social entreprise that helps the organisation generate revenue.

Equally important, many large business corporations offer various kinds of services that constitute substantial donations-in-kind. For instance, transport companies sponsor shipments or freight needs; accounting firms give free accounting services; many companies offer their expertise for building projects, architectural service, computer software design and other information technology support. One illustrative example of their success in engaging the business sector is having Hong Kong Disneyland to help design some of their future experiential education exhibits.

The success of Crossroads in scaling-up is evident in the following summary data which directly or indirectly indicates the increase in the number of people served:

- from the initial aid of 19 cartons in 1995, it has grown to distribute 200x20' container equivalents per year, 40 per cent of which are international distribution.
- from the initial operation of sending emergency relief materials to China, it now manages an international network of distribution covering East, Southeast and Central Asia, Europe, Africa, South and Central America and the Middle East and that straddles over 100 countries and benefits more than 580 thousand recipients.
- from the initial collection of unwanted textile goods, its donors now include manufacturers, hotels, educational institutions, hospitals, companies and individuals, totaling more than 2,800 in number.
- from having only two team members in 1995, it now has 70 full-time staff and over 10,000 volunteers per year.
- its operations has been substantially expanded to cover other operations, namely,
  - Global X-perience, which has grown from 1,200 participants in 2005 to 25,000 in 2012
  - the Global Hand Website, which was later replicated for the United Nations
  - fair trade business through Global Handicrafts and Silk Café.

In sum, Crossroads has successfully scaled up its innovation from a local and regional operation to one of global scale. The scaling-up of its innovation is inseparable from the scaling-up of collaboration, as evident in the transnational network of distribution that it has successfully developed and as well, the expansion of its collaboration with intergovernmental organisations.

Direct scaling-up of innovation: collaborative governance and capacity-building

The scaling-up of service has necessitated Crossroads to expand its capacity and gradually develop from a largely informal individual effort at disaster relief to a sizeable NGO with a more formalised governance structure. In terms of organisational management, under the co-directors is a Steering Group that oversees eight functional units and their four operations. Nonetheless, the organisational culture remains non-hierarchical and communal. In fact, despite some degree of formalisation of the management structure, its internal governance maintains much of the informal practices characteristic of small, grassroots organisations at their early stage of development. This constitutes a rather unique case in nonprofit development. From the perspective of nonprofit organisational life cycle, it is an organisation that, having gone through almost two decades of growth and development, is already at the mature stage of its development. On the other hand, it still retains a lot of features that are typical of a startup organisation, such as the exclusive use of volunteers, strong enthusiasm and emotional commitment among the staff toward their mission, a sense of 'family' and cooperation among staff, emphasis if not reliance on 'informal' communication and linkages and reliance on in-kind donation (Simon, 2001).

Volunteerism is still the only mode of staffing. The full-time staff are given one day a year to raise their own salary. The organisation relies heavily on part-time volunteers and has been very successful in recruiting them. In 2012, 9,909 volunteers representing 71 nationalities served with them and contributed 111,741 work hours (approximately 56 full-time equivalent workers) (Crossroads Annual Report, 2012). The full-time staff we have interviewed feel that the volunteer mode has served the organisation well, particularly, in ensuring that people that join their organisation are attracted to the intrinsic (rather than extrinsic) reward. Indeed, the staff we have interviewed have shown themselves to be highly dedicated to the mission of the organisation and emotionally motivated to work there. Many of their full-time staff have outstanding academic and professional qualifications and substantial experience in corporate management. Some of them retired early from their high paid corporate executive positions to join the organisation in search of a meaningful job. While they agree that the high reliance on part-time staff hinder smooth manpower planning, they have been able to attract competent and qualified people to work for them.

The current premises of Crossroads, which is an old British garrison base offered by the Social Welfare Department for its use, consists of numerous vacated buildings some of which have been turned into staff quarters. There are enough staff with family and children for them to run a communal nursery and kindergarten onsite. The organisation is thus not only a place for the staff to work; it is practically a commune for their members. The communal life shared by the members has helped foster a sense of community, hence trust, loyalty, emotional attachment and mutual understanding, all of which facilitate an internal governance model that emphasises flexibility, initiatives, engagement and consensus building, features that are essential for collaborative governance.

Indirect scaling-up of innovation: developing deep partnership with the business sector and transnational network of distribution

The key to Crossroads's success has been its ability to build strong linkages with multiple sectors, especially to leverage the potential of the dense and interlocking network of the business sector in the process. Indeed, the very mission of the organisation , as illustrated by the slogan 'where need meets resource', is to foster connectivity through bringing together different parts of the world.

Partnership with the business sector was initially built upon the co-founders' business connections. Soliciting donations in kind from different companies had the advantage of establishing deep partnerships with organisations. This was further developed through their innovative Global X-perience, which offers simulation exercises for people to experience the plight of refugees, the disabled, poor people and other disadvantaged groups. The exercises, well-received by the participants who regard them as powerful experiences, have won the long-term support of many business corporations toward Crossroads.

The deep partnership with business corporations was a process of collaborative value creation (Austin and Seitanidi, 2012). For business corporations, Crossroads offers not only good opportunities for fulfilling corporate social responsibility, but also tools for team-building as their employees participate in part-time volunteering and simulations. Through volunteering as in-kind donation, there is also a strong sense of ownership created among these corporate participants. Their linkage with the international business community subsequently connected them to the Economic World Forum and United Nations, through which they were able to further scale-up their innovation at the international level.

Scaling-up of collaboration in a global city: the dynamics of societal, network and territorial embeddedness

The successful scaling-up of collaboration is the confluence of multiple factors and can be structurally explained by the dynamics of societal, network and territorial embeddedness and the embedded agency exercised by organisational members. The initiators of the operation are corporate professionals with international experience and have long been involved in charity work. The full-time staff of the organisation are all foreign nationals of different countries of origin yet sharing some common attributes: working experience with international corporations; a higher degree in a professional area such as public policy, business or information technology; a strong sense of social mission and entrepreneurship. With such backgrounds, the leaders and managers of the organisation are united by similarity in professional experiences, values, worldview and management styles, but with very different work experiences that they have acquired overseas and which they have brought in to the organisation. In this sense, these organisational members are societally embedded but territorially-disembedded.

Crossroads's leaders have made the strategic choice to resist institutional isomorphism through preserving an informal organisational form, including adopting volunteerism as the only mode of staffing. The preservation of an 'informal' mode of governance alongside the development of a more formalised governance structure has proven to be its strength. The organisation has been able build upon the societal embeddedness of its key members to nurture a staff team that organically combines professionalism and managerial rationality with passion, shared values, mutual trust and friendship. This enables interactive governance that helps transcend its shortage in human and financial resources. All these have proven to strengthen network embeddedness among organisational members.

Another important manifestation of societal embeddedness is a shared sense of corporate social responsibility among the network partners from the business sectors cultivated through the simulation exercises and the donation of services. This shared sense of corporate social responsibility is, on the other hand, quite common among managers of MNCs. As Hughes et al (2008) argue, these corporate managers are embedded in the global production networks (GPNs), whose governance are in turn shaped by a whole range of learning spaces (virtual networks, conferences, seminars, training courses, campaigns by NGOs and advocacy groups and so on) that inculcate care ethics in their outlooks and practices. The simulation exercises developed by Crossroads are an additional contribution to this whole range of learning spaces. In this sense, the societal embeddedness of the MNC managers provides the essential glue for network embeddedness. Such societal embeddedness, on the other hand, is not bound by the physical space to the extent that the learning spaces are territorially disembedded.

Crossroads has positioned itself to be the transnational broker of need and resource through intelligently leveraging the strategic advantage of the global city, where there is a high concentration of MNCs, trading firms, hotels and so on, that ensures a high number of potential suppliers of high quality donated goods. As a trading and transportation hub, many businesses in cargoes and logistics are available with the capacity to transport donated goods to many parts of the world. The global city is also a talent hub in which many international travellers and professionals pass through, making it possible to attract talents to come and work for the organisation. Local people, including university and secondary school students are also a major source of part-time volunteers and the dense population partly ensures the relatively abundant supply of manpower. The international connection of the individual staff, in turn, strengthens the network embeddedness of the organisation through bringing in their own transnational and trans-local networks of resources, talents and know-how. This confirms Hughes et al's (2008) observation that the societal embeddedness of international corporate professionals is not 'anchored' in fixed territories. Rather, territorial disembeddedness may be the precondition for the expansion of networks and hence the scaling-up of collaboration and innovation.

Conclusion

This case study on the emergence and development of an international NGO in a global city serves to illustrate the potential usefulness of the concept of embeddedness in illustrating the conditions for collaboration to scale up. The agencies of actors are constituted by their societal, network and territorial embeddedness. These three forms of embeddedness are interlinked and dynamically affect each other through the agency of the actors, who actively utilise the resources provided by the environment in which they are embedded to scale-up their collaboration and hence their innovation. The concept of embeddedness also usefully illustrates how networks and collaboration can scale up beyond the local level (to trans-local and transnational levels) and that such scaling-up may provide the conditions for the scaling-up of social innovation.

Acknowledgement

The work described in this chapter was substantially supported by the Public Policy Research Funding administered by the Research Grants Council of the Hong Kong Special Administrative Region, China (Project No: HKU7015-PPR-12). The authors would like to express our heartfelt thanks to all the staff members of Crossroads Foundation who have shared valuable information with us. The contents of this chapter are the sole responsibility of the authors.

Notes

[1] Total outward freight movement (seaborne, river, road and air) in 2013 was 126,321,000 tonnes, while the total outward port cargo throughput in 2013 was 113,780,000 tonnes. Source of data: BrandHK, 'Facts about Hong Kong', www.brandhk.gov.hk/en/#/; Hong Kong Trade and Development Council (HKTDC) Research, http://bso.hktdc.com/bso/jsp/other_stat.

jsp; Hong Kong Port Development Council (HKPDC), Hong Kong Port Statistics Update, 25-8-2014, www.pdc.gov.hk/docs/summary_statistics.pdf.
[2] The expansion in the categorisation of embeddedness and the denotation of the term has led some scholars to criticise that embeddedness has become a fuzzy concept that lacks precision in meaning and conceptual vigor (Hess, 2004).
[3] A few such attempts include Ansell (2003); Provan et al (2009).
[4] According to Murray et al (2010), there are six steps in the process of social innovation: 1) prompts, 2) proposals, 3) prototypes, 4) sustaining, 5) scaling and 6) systematic change.
[5] Due to the historic sovereignty change in Hong Kong and its rather unique status as a highly autonomous Special Administrative Region under Chinese sovereignty, this study has included cross-border NGOs, that is, NGOs with their base in Hong Kong but whose primary missions are to carry out activities in Mainland China.
[6] Their geographical focus are mostly Mainland China and the East and Southeast Asia.

References

Agranoff, R, McGuire, M, 2004, *Collaborative public management: New strategies for local governments*, Washington, DC: Georgetown University Press

Ansell, C, 2003, Community embeddedness and collaborative governance in the San Francisco Bay Area environmental movement, in M Diani, D McAdam (eds) *Social movements and networks: Relational approaches to collective action*, pp 123–44, Oxford: Oxford University Press

Austin, JE, Seitanidi, MM, 2012, Collaborative value creation: A review of partnering between nonprofits and businesses: Part I, Value creation spectrum and collaboration stages, *Nonprofit and Voluntary Sector Quarterly* 41, 726–58

Bloom, P, Smith, B, 2010, Identifying the drivers of social entrepreneurial impact: Theoretical development and an exploratory empirical test of SCALERS, *Journal of Social Entrepreneurship* 1, 1, 126–45

Bradach, J, 2010, Foreword: From scaling organizations to scaling impact, in PN Bloom, E Skloot (eds) *Scaling social impact: New thinking* (Social Entrepreneurship Series), Basingstoke: Palgrave Macmillan

Carter, SE, Currie-Alder, B, 2006, Scaling-up natural resource management: insights from research in Latin America, *Development in Practice* 16, 2, 128–140

CCSG (Centre for Civil Society and Governance), 2015, *International and cross-border NGOs in Hong Kong*, Hong Kong: The University of Hong Kong Centre for Civil Society and Governance

Crossroads Foundation, 2012, *Annual report 2012*, Hong Kong: Crossroads Foundation, www.crossroads.org.hk/annual-reports

Granovetter, M, 1985, Economic action and social structure: The problem of embeddedness, *American Journal of Sociology* 91, 3, 481–510

Granovetter, M, 1992, Problems of explanation in economic sociology, in N Nohria, R Eccles (eds) Networks and organizations, Boston, MA: Harvard Business School Press

Gulati, R, Gargiulo, M, 1999, Where do interorganizational networks come from?, *American Journal of Sociology* 104, 5, 1439–93

Heidenreich, M, 2012, The social embeddedness of multinational companies: A literature review, *Socio-Economic Review* 10, 549–79

Henderson, J, Dicken, P, Hess, M, Coe N, Young, HWC, 2002, Global production networks and the analysis of economic development, *Review of International Political Economy* 9, 3, 436–64

Hess, M, 2004, 'Spatial' relationships? Towards a reconceptualization of embeddedness, *Progress in Human Geography* 28, 2, 165–86

Hong Kong Centre for Economic Research, 2003, *Made in PRD: the changing face of HK manufacturers*, Hong Kong: Federation of Hong Kong Industries

Hughes, A, Wrigley, N, Buttle, M, 2008, Global production networks, ethical campaigning, and the embeddedness of responsible governance, *Journal of Economic Geography* 8, 345–67

Lyon, F, Fernandez, H, 2012, Scaling up social enterprise: Strategies taken from early years providers, *Social Enterprise Journal* 8,1, 63–77

Moulaert, F, Maccallum, D, Mehmood, A, Hamdouch, A, 2013, *The international handbook on social innovation: Collective action, social learning and transdisciplinary research*, Cheltenham: Edward Elgar Publishing

Mulgan, G, 2012, The theoretical foundations of social innovation, in A Nicholls, A Murdock (eds) *Social innovation: Blurring boundaries to reconfigure markets*, Basingstoke: Palgrave Macmillan

Murray, R, Caulier-Grice, J, Mulgan, G, 2010, *The open book of social innovation*, London: NESTA and The Young Foundation

OECD, 2010, *SMEs, entrepreneurship and innovation*, Paris: OECD

O'Leary, R, Gerard, C, Bingham, B, 2006, Introduction to the symposium on collaborative public management, *Public Administration Review* 66, Supplement, 6–9

Phills, JA, Deiglmeier, K, Miller, DT, 2008, Rediscovering social innovation, *Stanford Social Innovation Review* 6, 4, 34–43

Polanyi, K, 2001, *The great transformation: The political and economic origins of our time*, Boston, MA: Beacon Press

Provan, KG, Huang, K, Milward, HB, 2009, The evolution of structural embeddedness and organizational social outcomes in a centrally governed health and human services network, *Journal of Public Administration Research and Theory* 19,4, 873–93

Salamon, LM, Anheier, HK, 1997, *Defining the nonprofit sector: A cross-national analysis*, Manchester and New York: Manchester University Press

Salamon, LM, Geller, SL, Mengel, KL, 2010, *Nonprofits, innovation, and performance measurement: Separating fact from fiction*, Baltimore, MD: Johns Hopkins University Center for Civil Society Studies

Sassen, S, 2001, *The global city: New York, London, Tokyo*, Princeton, NJ: Princeton University Press

Simon, JS, 2001, *The five life stages of nonprofit organizations: Where you are, where you're going, and what to expect when you get there*, St Paul, MN: Amherst H Wilder Foundation

Thomson, AM, Perry, JL, 2006, Collaboration processes: Inside the black box, *Public Administration Review* December, Special Issue, 20–32

Torfing, J, Peters, G, Pierre, J, Sorensen,E, 2012, *Interactive governance: Advancing the paradigm*, Oxford: Oxford University Press

Tsai, JF, 1997, Hong Kong in Chinese history: Community and social unrest in the British colony, 1842–1913, New York: Columbia University Press

Index